LIMITLESS

CHARITY BOWMAN WEBB

CONTENTS

ACKNOWLEDGMENTS

A book like this pours out a journey. This one was carved and land-marked by some of the most extraordinary people who have inspired me much and shared many adventures.

THANK YOU TO.....

Alan - my husband, full of support, kindness and humour.

My Girls - Sasha and Rhianna, for the encouragement, love and stretching! You inspire me.

Faith and Hilary, my sisters - for friendship in all the crazy journeys.

Mum - for the encouragement to always be creative and follow my heart.

Rick and Cynthia - for support and guidance, you are two of my dearest friends.

Thom and Ruth, my exceptional pastors - for so much encouragement and wisdom.

My home church, King's Fellowship in Inverness - what a releasing, pioneering, creative church.

The Blue Flame family and growing wider Creative Family - thank you for the journey together and seeing God's Kingdom advance through so much fun and presence.

Susan, Greg and Alan my fellow pioneering leaders in the restoration of the arts - it is fascinating to walk this out with you.

Lara and all my intercessors - for the hours of invaluable prayer that makes things possible.

John Paul Jackson, John Thomas and Streams Ministries International - this journey would not have looked anything like it does without your revelation and impact woven through every twist and turn.

And last but never least... to all the Burning Man team. To Lisa for opening the door to wonderland and helping me walk through it; to Robb and Daren for the wild times on strange days with the Holy Spirit that changed me forever.

ENDORSEMENTS

A few years ago there was a challenge to walk with Jesus on the "Unknown Path". This path was only accessible as we went "lower still" on our faces in humble submission and adoration of Jesus. It was a pathway that allowed for the full release of Heaven's resources to accomplish Heaven's redemptive plans. On this pathway no-one would know how to "achieve" anything, because it was all down to complete obedience to the Word of the Lord. I believe that in Limitless we have something of what this radical pathway will look and feel like. Here Charity Bowman-Webb has released something of beauty and dynamism of the creative missionary movement that starts in the heart of God and flows out through his children to a world crying out for hope, life, joy and love. Limitless is for all those who in their hearts have said "YES!" to Jesus even before they have heard His question. As you read this book it will trigger a radical shift in your heart, mind and spirit; it is a catalyst to release the waves of creative Kingdom thinking and living which will bring in the greatest harvest of souls the world has ever seen.

Alan McWilliam
Chairman of CLAN (Christians Linked Across the Nation), Scotland UK

A few years ago when I was pastoring a very prophetic church, the Lord started talking to us about the need for something different in the prayer room. He took us to the story of Moses holding up his staff while Joshua and the Israelites were fighting Amalek. His hands grew weary, and both Aaron and Hur held them up, because as long as the staff was raised the Israelites were victorious. The Lord pointed out to us that we (the church as a whole) knew a lot about the intercession represented by Aaron, but we needed to learn about the intercession represented by Hur, because both would be needed for victory in the coming season. He led us to understand that the intercession of Hur was the integration of creativity, contemplative prayer, and the prophetic. I believe that what Charity has tapped into is that very stream, the combination of the presence of God in creativity released through faithful servants of Christ.

This book is revelatory in multiple senses of the word, and it carries the prophetic edge that comes when eternal truth is revealed by the eternal God into a specific person for a specific generation. It reveals the revelation, not only in the truths communicated, but also with explanation of the ways God gave that revelation.

It is also creative in multiple ways; it not only shares the heartbeat of our Creator, but it shares it with creative language. From my personal relationship with Charity I can tell you that she is creative and understands the beautiful metaphorical language of our Father, but as you read this book you will not need me to tell you that; you will hear it for yourself. Metaphors that echo the language of the prophetic writers of Scripture pepper this book in just the right way.

If you are a creative person and do not know how to express that in the church and what your place in the kingdom is, this book will help you. If you feel you are not creative, I am sure that you know people that are; this book will help you to encourage and exhort them to step into the place that God has desired for them to fill, while it draws out your own creativity almost accidentally.

If you are a leader in the church, please read this book. Creativity has been diminished in the church, misunderstood, and even vilified by those that did not understand this gift God gave His bride. We desperately need creativity to rise to the level that God intends so that the church will dream again, dream of good works that God created for us beforehand. Come, be a part of a reformation that has already started!

John E Thomas
President of Streams Ministries International, USA

We are in the midst of an inventive cultural transformation. Limitless is a bridge called "relevant". Charity Bowman Webb is a gifted writer, plunging us into the depths of our Creator God and catapulting us upward through the roadblocks of history. In this book we are presented with insights and practical strategies. Expect your imagination to be fuelled for superluminal flight into spaces yet to be filled. A Brilliant , Must Read for All!

Susan Card
Visual Artist, Co-leader of the Advancing Art Team
MorningStar Ministries, Fort Mill SC, USA

The question before us is: shall we advance into a "limitless" future of spiritual/physical innovation and freedom, or hold fast to a complacent well-meaning status quo? In fact the future cannot be met without this choice! In this text Charity Bowman Webb provides much of the contextual information and understanding in facing this choice. Her personal experience and probing research are balanced by a distinct ability to clearly communicate without the hollow tone of self-appointed expertise or hyperbole, which is truly refreshing in the subject of arts and the church. Indeed the next reformation is knocking ......

Greg Card
Visual Strategist/artist, Co-leader of the Advancing Art Team
MorningStar Ministries, Fort Mill SC, USA

Reading this book is like listening to Charity talk, but with the benefit of having time to appreciate what she is saying. Charity sometimes uses a different vocabulary than I normally use, but it makes me think. I've watched her over the years, and she pays the price for going deeper without getting flakey.

Thom Raller, Sr Pastor of Kings Fellowship, Inverness, Scotland

I have seldom read black letters on white pages so bursting with colour! That is a characteristic of the authoress who has a masterful grasp of colour and a masterful grasp of joy. Among the aims of this book are to start many conversations about the creativity inherent in all people; to stir and encourage many of those people to overcome all their inhibitions about creative expression, their perceived limitations, whether self-imposed, culturally imposed, or ecclesiastically imposed, and to enter into the truly Limitless joy and fruitfulness of creativity available to them. It is written for followers of Jesus, present and future; it helps to break down the false concept between "your Christian life" and "your other life" – creativity belongs everywhere! I highly commend both the writer and the book to you.

Rick Hayes, Director of North Atlantic Dreams Ministry, Scotland

Charity's prophetic call and training have allowed her to be in the forefront of a shift that is taking place in the body of Christ right now and to call it once again to be reconnected with our God, who is limitless in His creativity. Charity rightly understands the role, purpose and function of creativity for this shift and how the Holy Spirit will use this to refresh and renew His people once again, transform His church and reach a lost world with His caring love. I commend her book to you. It will light a fire of passion and possibilities in you that can be limitless for the glorious days that lie ahead for the church!

Cynthia Hayes, North Atlantic Dreams Ministry, CLAN Women Leadership

Thank you Charity for this stimulating read. And thank you God for your limitless invitation to go higher and deeper in You and to search the breadth and length of Your love and riches. This book has certainly challenged me to do just that.

Ruth Raller, Pastor of Kings Fellowship, Inverness, Scotland

Influence is a weighty thing. Spiritual influence adds the weight of God and His eternal realm to the equation. Charity Bowman Webb in her book Limitless: God's Mandate for His Church climbs the wall to sound a trumpet to encourage the release of the creativity of the church and to follow the notes over the walls to take our place on the mountains of societal influence. She communicates the connection of Bezalel ("In the Shadow of God"), the wise master craftsman whom God chose to make a reality of the blueprints of His tabernacle and the Wisdom of Proverbs 8 – that combination of purity and creativity that was present at creation. Charity pursues a spiritually defined view of wisdom with creativity as so needed in these times for right influence.

This stream of creative influence flowed in the lives of Joseph, Daniel and Paul who declared himself to be a wise master builder, the apostle architect of the emerging church of the New Testament. In Genesis 49, Jacob prophesied his son Joseph's roots from the springs of God to his branches that would go over the wall for the blessing of many in a time of desperate need. In those desperate times God did a work of creative influence that transcended a time of world famine and went unto eternal mode as He arranged a craftsman to preserve His chosen people. The baseball player Yogi Berra quipped "It's like deja vu all over again". Indeed today, the spiritual vacancies on the tops of mountains and walls of arts, government, education and the marketplace are crying in the Spirit to be filled. Humpty Dumpty has fallen and all the earthy resources of "kings" cannot put it together again.

We are called to fill bigger shoes than previously thought, as we dare to grapple with our genesis design that we too are under His shadow. With dirt-under-her-nails experience as an artist, an innovative prophetic outreach leader to the counter-culture and the raw transparency of her own experience in the art and design world, Charity paints a credible vision of hope and encouragement for those with the courage to pursue our God's limitless vision for these end times.

The world is waiting for us.

Rob Mazza
Leader and Founder of Destiny Workshops, USA
Board of Elijah House Ministries, USA

FOREWORD

BONNIE CHAVDA

I have had the privilege and pleasure of getting to know Charity in her home as wife and mother, and to observe and work with her in the ministry. A trained professional designer, Charity is a vibrant, inspired woman of God and servant of the Lord and His church. Classically trained in Christian disciplines and with two decades of professional practice working as a designer, Charity carries a weight of glory and experience that she is giving away as "freely" as she has received it!

Without a doubt we live in an era of the revival of spiritual gifts and arts of every kind. The eye gate was the most respected influence early Christians considered as influential. They were ardent devotees to what they took in to their heart and life through their eyes. Second to that was devotion to what they heard. In the new epoch of global telecommunication, the whole world is literally a stage and every person with any kind of electronic digital tools is a performer. The access and possibilities are limitless. Limitless: God's Creative Mandate for His Church is a record of Charity's personal journey onto that stage.

She says "our creative DNA lies before us in God's outstretched hand" to energize our lives and influence with new solutions, strategies, and innovations. She challenges us that God's wisdom is expressed in beauty. A poem included in Limitless says:

"We are all artists
Commissioned to draw one thing –
Draw close to him.
This is the colour-filled art of the heart."

Fellowshipping, worshipping, and working together with her, I see that Charity is a Spirit renaissance woman! Her inspiration and knowledge communicated in Limitless reminds me of the landscape of her homeland, Scotland. The mandate she has accepted from her Father and Creator is one of a lover's tender kiss and of the high flung wind of the Breath of God. In striking colors, contrasts, ancient and new, sometimes in shadow and sometimes in sparkling sunlight, from rushing river to hidden glen, heather-covered heights to castle-dotted shoreline, her inspiration pours through the pages of her journal. She invites us to listen and step in to one of the most important hours of cultural shift occurring in our world.

Our Shepherd-Lover stands and knocks. Who will listen and open? Perhaps you. That's exactly what Charity did. The fruit of taking up the artisan's call to worship in expressive innovation has led her to experience what Bezalel must have when he was handed heavenly blueprints for creation of the Tabernacle where God would sit enthroned as King and join the revelry of worship. In her spirit, her work, her art, in her home, in her church, and in her ministry beyond, Charity has discovered that we are all limitless when we collaborate with the limitless Father. We can receive solutions and innovative ideas that transform our grid for evangelism and Kingdom growth, increasing significance for all roles in the Kingdom as an integral part of restoring value for people where they are already positioned.

Ask of me and I will give you the nations for an inheritance. Psalm 2:8

Culture now and future is being created every minute. As Limitless reminds us "New combinations of the arts and creativity, throughout many spheres, will become important; not only for breaking individualism, but bringing something from heaven's store house that will completely surprise us. As the world systems shake and the gospel message magnifies in the earth, the Lord is bending over His beloved as a formidable, phenomenal, creative, limitless, warrior bride".

Charity's insights, suggestions, lessons learned, and revelations received, make Limitless a handbook for every believer, layman to leader, an invitation to enter the conversation and decide to step onto the platform of creative expression of the beauty, gifts, and power of God's Spirit now.

Bonnie Chavda
Co-Founder & Senior Pastor, All Nations Church
The Watch of the Lord
Charlotte, North Carolina, USA

LOST

THE INTRODUCTON

The ledge is high above the earth beneath, hovering over the immense valley; the surrounding sky is on fire. Crimson and sulfur red, saffron and orange flame, enveloping furnace colours, and I know we are looking forward. He turns and says, 'You know things are about to change right?'. 'I know, but I do not understand this the way you do', I understate the fact. Who could know the way God does? But what are we looking at? What lies before us and how is it hidden in this depth of sulfuric beauty? My mind cannot reach; it barely knows where to start, as I leave the ledge behind me and walk into the vast empty space before, filled with the nervous unknown, lined with grace.

There is only one way to live in the glory of who He is: it is to embrace the fire. We were not meant to live barely flickering, but fully lit, vivid and brilliant in the wonder of God, a limitless source of limitless power. This is life's burning imperative, to find more of who God is, more of why He created us to walk beside Him, to find the cadence of heaven.

Sometimes it is simply about timing and redeeming what is lost, waiting for the sons and daughters of God to know who they really are (Romans 8:19). When they find out, courage is the key that opens an armory in heaven again. Yet, if you have ever walked through an armory of the Spirit, the weapons may have surprised you. Amongst the classic swords and shields, did anyone happen to see a song, a paint brush or a dancer's shoe, a surgeon's knife, a skilful spreadsheet or a business strategy?

Surely these are not weapons, some labeled 'value unknown'. From the shelves of heaven the creative mandate is being dusted off and returned to the earth. Its timing and purpose has arrived and we are about to discover roads to revelation, codes to crack enemy lines and pathways to the solutions the world so desperately seeks. I guess that takes me back to the ledge. What lies before us are heavenly road maps that beckon the journey; it is the glory of kings to seek them out.

It is the glory of God to conceal a matter; to search out a matter is the glory of kings. Proverbs 25:2

Timely defining of our creative DNA lies before us in God's outstretched hand. There are two directives: there is the general outpouring of Kingdom Creativity available to all believers to energize their lives and areas of influence producing new solution, strategy and innovation. There is also the calling of the Creative Warriors, the artisans who combine skill and anointing for specific reason. The hour strikes a wake up call for both and their intertwining purposes in the nations - strategic objectives in the times that lie ahead.

VITAL

It's a journey to address the filling of some empty spaces and intensify a fascination to probe the chambered character of God's heart.

In 2010, I had an intriguing vision. I was with Jesus on a towering cliff ledge. He wanted us to explore through a clearing in the trees behind us where an exquisite waterfall stood; an ethereal display of manifold colours falling forcefully into a pool below. Then we were running and leaping from height – we plunged the pool and submerged, swimming through luminous colours; through red, into potent blue then lucent violet. I heard the Lord say, 'This is a pool of spiritual creativity'. I came to the surface. A rainbow was now arching the waterfall, diaphanous colour and light enveloped me and the arresting beauty seemed deeply significant. I sat at the pool edge with Jesus speaking aloud my dawning thoughts of undiscovered purpose in God's beauty that lies far beyond our current realizations.

Without warning, the rocks beneath Him ruptured, yet He dangled calmly over a sheer drop, grasping the edge. I investigated to see a great chasm define below the coloured pool, and again I knew the invitation was to explore. Bracing, I joined Him in the seemingly gargantuan leap, but found myself unexpectedly floating down the many hundreds of feet where we paused on a platform. Peering over its perimeter I discovered that there were thousands of feet below, submerging into intense, white light emanating from the depths. We gazed upwards to the pool that was now overhead and Jesus started to explain that, below the rainbow pool, prodigious depths of the Spirit could be found – great understanding of the Word, wisdom and spiritual perception – if people would take the time to seek them out. Coloured rain drops descended from the pool and water was flowing down the sides of the great chasm as a large spot light illuminated upwards, highlighting the scene in its entirety. I needed to understand this significant vision– it contained answers to many questions.

The Rainbow Pool

Unpacking this vision opened new understanding. The rainbow pool is a level of spiritual beauty that others will see, a layer of creativity, a measure of the arts, but it is beneath this layer in the abyssal vaults of the Spirit that we find a substance of creativity of such gravity that it reveals the Creator far beyond our current perception. There are facets of His character and power that await discovery. This is where we can fill creative capacity and reach far beyond our current limitation. This is how to achieve longevity without the constant cycle of arduous repetition and dry depleted rainbow pools. Our mandate is to worship God and reach the world around us for Jesus and surely great keys are to be fresh, relevant, creative and powerful. It is time to open the vaults. For some, the Christian experience is that of dehydrated repetition; rainbow pools that were once a fresh measure of the Spirit are scraped dry because we have not understood that deep beneath our current experience of church creativity lie great mysteries that link us to the character of God, and they are ours to open. However, if we do not stir ourselves to go after the waterfall, we will scrape at the dry, dusty basin of earth and miss the fresh filling of new creative impact and life.

I have scraped parched ground at times, yet ironically I have many years of formal training and professional experience in art and areas of design. I must have spent the first eleven years of my Christian life acceptant. When

I came to faith I quickly realized there was little place for the arts beyond the worship band and kept most of the years of training and skill for outside of church life. This seemed the status quo and the initial Christian years were so intense with life change I did not have much capacity left to see the great void anyway. By the time I was on a stronger plateau of the faith experience, the 'normality' of accepting the void was established. Then one day God woke me up sharply but He had to take me to the backside of the desert to do it; without metaphor, I was literally in the backside of the huge Nevada desert when the epiphany happened.

BURNING

Parallel to my local church involvement ran a great love of the prophetic, the fascination of the mysterious, the enigmas and messages of God that wove through visions and dreams, and the addictive nature of time in His presence listening. Many years of training and studying the prophetic lead me into the wild west of prophetic evangelism. An inspiring lady came to Scotland from the US to teach a course and, after a brief connection, an unexpectedly random invitation landed in my inbox: would I like to join a Streams Ministries International evangelism team that went to the Burning Man festival?

Research revealed a few things that scared me toothless: top of the list was the heat, temperatures averaging 40 degrees centigrade; the thought of this alone formed a label marked 'impossible' in my mind. Second up was camping, no electricity, no showers, no hair washing! Living in a roasting tin of a dust bowl in the Nevada desert for a week seemed a very strange pastime for fifty thousand people.

However, further research revealed an extravagant and lavish arts festival with vast structures of extraordinary creativity. The untethered nature of the festival attracted the very people for whom I had a big space in my heart. I wrestled for ten days giving myself all the reasons why I could not go and I clearly felt like God was giving me a choice. There was no fail or pass test here (which actually never makes it easier). But despite the freedom to choose, the voice of the Spirit would wake me on mornings whispering, 'but what if this was going to be one of the biggest adventures of your life so far....what if..?'. Red rag to a bull, and I found myself on the backside of the desert.

There in the dust and rampant, boundless, creative mayhem was our camp where I found a team of some of the best people you could ever hope to work with. During my time with them I learned a profusion of things which would change the way I perceived as many parts of my Christian experience as I can imagine. Many silenced realizations began to rise and mix together in a heady cocktail of perfect sense. In the large tent facilitating ministry 'encounter teams', an intricately constructed set of art works composed an interior that felt like a place of sanctuary for the hundreds who poured in from the hot desert, seeking the waters of life. It was beyond the lonely vase of flowers of my church experience and it also entered a different realm from the world of interior design I worked within.

The concept of interior or space design collided with the Spirit in a way I had only glimpsed in my own spirit for years. Some past attempts to explore such creative expressions within church settings were sometimes deemed unnecessary decoration. But here it was, not purely visual but also highly esteemed by the team who fixed each piece in place painstakingly and with honor. The 'Tree of Life' in fabrics, paintings and sculpture, filled the tent and mingled with the intoxicating presence of God for the whole week.

You could argue it was merely beautiful art, but we were surrounded by voluminous beautiful art on every corner of the temporary city built for Burning Man each year and there was little sanctuary or holy awe out there. I connected missing dots; this was art made through the Spirit and with the Spirit of God, and it literally released something that I have wrestled to fathom since. I cannot find a floor or a ceiling yet, only increasing illumination.

Creative freedom continued into expressions of the Holy Spirit through ministry, making the work on encounter teams among the most fascinating I have ever taken part in. There was indeed a strict protocol and much training required for team to even be there, but the framework of cost, dedication and sacrifice were the launch pad for a multifaceted flow of the Spirit such as I had never experienced. At its most basic there was freedom to speak, sing, pray, impart, wash feet, anoint with oil. Yet, within this atmosphere there was a freedom for the Spirit to show us Himself at work in ways that made the veil grow so thin between heaven and earth that at times I could see the angelic walk right through the tent to come and assist us in ministry. It was a master class in Holy Spirit creativity, paradoxical to the lowest common denominator of religious confines, and the fruit was breathtaking.

'When the creativity of the Lord is absent it makes room for the religious spirit which wants to do things over and over again.' Larry Randolph[1]

The more freedom we allow the Spirit, the more freedom we will find for ourselves. We are suppose to be the temple for the Holy Spirit living in us (1 Corinthians 3:16), not the walls; but we can become the walls, the parameters, as we set boundaries and limitations for God. We need to allow the Spirit new levels of liberation. Sometimes we are so afraid to be free in case we get it wrong, in case we cannot control everything. Yet, if we would make our goal to listen and sync with the Spirit of God then new ideas would not scare us because this is the essence of who He is: creative and expansive (Jeremiah 29:11–13).

VISION

One day at Burning Man, we opened a prayer tunnel with a difference: we invited the seekers to enter and watched a fascinating interaction as they felt the heady presence of the Lord descend. Up till then I had never seen this dynamic outside a church setting. After the seekers, the team were up for some battery recharge in the tunnel and I made it through just one person before I crumpled, nose down in the gray desert dust, unable to rise for a long time. The people around me faded away as the vision became reality and an angel appeared holding a large sword which he extended towards me saying, 'This is for your nation'.

Eventually the world around returned with the certainty of dinner time. The vision felt strangely life-changing but I had bafflingly little clue about what it actually meant. What on earth was the sword? I asked until I heard an unexpected reply: 'Creativity'. My journey started well before the epiphany at Burning Man, but it was during this experience that the undergrowth was peeled back to disclose the faint traces of a path, initiating a surge of questions and answers and a very real sense of gold lying far below the ground.

Included

The first striking revelation for me was the awareness that we can all be creative through the Spirit in various ways. It is NOT just for the arts, it is in ideas, solutions, strategy, medical breakthroughs, mathematical formulas, teaching, relationships, families, mission, worship and more. It can affect and energize any area of our lives and churches.

Then God said, 'Let Us make man in Our image, according to Our likeness'. Genesis 1:26–28 NKJ

If we are made in the image of God then let's take a moment to look at how creative God is.

In the beginning God created the heavens and the earth. Genesis 1:1

In the very first line of the bible, we discover that the primary thing God chooses to reveal to us about His character and ability is that He is a 'Creator', in the act of creating; therefore by definition He is 'creative'. God is never meaninglessly random, so the initial line of His Word contains a crucial message to us beyond the obvious information.

Creativity is part of the nucleus of God's nature, the desire and ability to bring into being something that was not there before. Just a few verses later He says that we will be like Him, we will have His DNA. Therefore a very obvious conclusion would be that we would carry Godly creative ability in some way. We have become so removed from the understanding of what the creativity of God is within us and the possibilities of it through us, that this now bears little meaning to many Christians.

In the world immediate to us, familiarity often causes us to bypass the astonishing Creation of God surrounding us; the diversity of each leaf, the songs of birds, the rhythm of waves, the multiple shades of red in a lone petal. Sometimes the breaking dawn or a remarkable foreign landscape can reawaken awe suddenly as we are reminded of the sheer creative and stunning complexity of the world around us. Investigation into areas of science, anatomy, astronomy or the animal kingdom leave us in total wonderment of the intricacies, the systems set in place to sustain life and beauty (Psalms 96:13 NIV).

Through Creation God tries to reveal His nature to us all the time. Yet, because we so often need to translate the creative, symbolic language of a God, full of visual conversation and meaning, we can daily miss what is being said, then mistakenly believe He is not speaking to us. Many tools are accessible for His people to help us decipher the language and communications of heaven, but they can be seen as a 'specialty' rather than an integral part of church life.

As God's army we are missing a wealth and inheritance of powerful creativity banked up for us. It is hidden right in front of us, not intentionally hidden by God but hidden through lack of knowledge, lack of understanding, lost in the twists of history. We need to relearn the basics of how to access and use it. I believe there is a supernatural energy of the Spirit birthed through God's creativity; when the church moves to grasp it, there will be a release of new boldness, healing, understanding, effectiveness and power.

Definition

Dictionary definitions for create and creative expand our understanding of its attributes:

The ability to transcend traditional ideas, rules, patterns, relationships, or the like, and to create meaningful new ideas, forms, methods and interpretations; originality, progressiveness, or imagination.
To bring into existence (Genesis 1:1), to produce through imaginative skill.
To make or bring into existence something new, having the quality of something created rather than imitated.
To cause to come into being, as something unique that would not naturally evolve or that is not made by ordinary processes.
Clever, cool, deviceful, fertile, formative, gifted, ingenious, innovative, inspired, inventive, leading-edge, original, productive, prolific, stimulating, visionary, way out.

Interestingly the opposite words given are:
Uncreative, ungifted, unimaginative, unproductive, untalented.[2]

Which words do you think best describe God? Which category do you think best describes the Christians you know? Obviously none of us would like to be described as ungifted or unproductive. Yet many Christians can feel they lack the desired gifting and effectiveness to yield as much significant change as they would like, in the world around them.

Does it Matter?

ADVERTISING: It has been estimated that most children watch around 20,000 thirty-second adverts every year in the US, while your average American spends twenty times more of their time on media consumption activity than in religious activity. Many magazines are hugely funded by adverts.

FILM AND TV: In 2012, Hollywood box office sales were $10.8 billion and that was just for cinema tickets – let alone the amount of films watched at home in an age of home entertainment systems. In Britain, 97% of UK homes have digital TVs. The average number of hours spent in front of the television by adults each day is 2 hours 40 minutes.

MUSIC: By September 2012, 350 million iPods had been sold. The iTunes Store opened on 28 April 2003; it has been the biggest music vendor in the world since February 2010, and offers over 26 million songs, videos, e-books and apps for sale online. Its revenue for the first quarter of 2011 totaled nearly $1.4 billion, and by February 2013 the store had sold 25 billion songs. It is available in 119 countries. In 2012 the store had 400 million active user accounts, and served over 315 million mobile devices, including iPods, iPhones and iPads.

INTERNET/SOCIAL MEDIA: In 2013 Ofcom recorded that 21.7 million people in the UK have broadband connections and 55% of adults with home internet use social networking. Many people use the internet and facilities such as YouTube to watch and exchange video clips and website links.[3]

Many minds and imaginations are being shaped by media and creative input

THE ART BOX

Our Western society particularly has often educated us to separate creativity from other areas of education. When I was at school it was still the era when girls were not invited to take woodwork or technical drawing, but were instead offered home economics and sewing. Our choices were greatly reduced. As one progressed through school in those days and streaming increased, a clear distinction formed between all the other subjects and those labeled 'creative'; pupils better at the latter were directed towards the art class to draw apples and the like or to music lessons.

In the obsessive, blissfully naive years of art college, it was still possible to feel valuable as a creative person within the bubble of protection that championed the arts as a valid career, until you were turfed out the other end to discover a society that greatly values the activities of the left brain as reflected in salaries and opinions. A small circumference of ferociously competitive career arts survive by the skin of the bruised creative people hanging in there, but they are seen as open game for the pit bull ring of the critics. It is not a life for the faint-hearted or the gentle creative spirit so often found in the outer rings – artistic people who have to choose to live out their creativity in the turbulent financial streams so often accompanying the artists' life.

Then there is a wider group of people, the failed artisans or the many who had to leave artistic dreams behind to find a left-brain job that would pay a plausible living. But so many grieve the loss of the right-brain dynamo within them. Time allows these people the odd compartment of life to switch on the creative button now and then, but the passion wanes and with it people's dreams and identities in the humdrum of life. I have met so many who feel like this.

We were certainly not all destined to be the best fine artists in the world, but we were ALL designed by God to be creative. So what is this creativity for, and why do we feel its loss when it must be stored in the dusty attic through the pressures of life? Regardless of the arena you work in or the destiny on your life, if you have the Holy Spirit living inside you, you have God's creative power within your very being. You are supposed to be gifted, ingenious, innovative, inspired, inventive, original, productive, prolific, stimulating. We may all release this in different ways and in different fields but the point remains that these attributes are part of our Godly DNA.

LEFT AND RIGHT

According to the theory of left-brain or right-brain dominance, each side of the brain controls different types of thinking. Additionally, people are said to prefer one type of thinking over the other, thus forming skills and interests. However, this research is very much a work in progress, and although there are distinctions, using both the areas of the brain is now believed to have a much more effective outcome at times, depending on the task or ideas required. For example, recent research shows that abilities in subjects such as math are actually strongest when both halves of the brain work together. There are no absolutes in the left and right brain theory but it does give us a helpful grid in trying to understand our unique abilities and also the way that we approach and handle life.

The left side of the brain is considered to be adept at tasks involving logic, language clarity, analytical thinking, numbers, reasoning and strategic thinking, with the characteristics of being methodical, systematic and controlled.

The right side of the brain is said to be best at expressive, creative and artistic tasks, to be more intuitive, thoughtful and subjective, better at recognizing faces, expressing emotions and reading them in others; passionate, imaginative and spontaneous.

We can over-generalize but these descriptions can be helpful in our understanding of thought progression; it is also extremely rare that someone would only have the characteristics of one side of the brain, so while we may favor one side more, generally we will have characteristics from both sides, and indeed we can practice developing many areas to give a stronger balance.

In the recent decades our education systems have definitely favored the development of left-brain characteristics, particularly in high school. Thus, we have a workforce and society at the other end that is greatly lacking the volume of right-brain thinking it was intended to access. Recent changes in the education systems seem to be starting to address this dilemma and recognizing the need for both sides of the brain to develop, so they can work together with greater effect. People who consider themselves lacking creativity today may just be lacking past opportunity and education to have developed it. God made each of us different, but He did give each of us a left and right side of the brain and the creative DNA of the Creator. We can all be innovative or original, whether within the field of business or sculpture, media, teaching or whatever.

Interestingly, it is the characteristics of the right side of the brain that are a prolific aid to being able to communicate with God, as the Bible is written in very creative symbolic ways and does not lend itself purely to reason and logic; but when the right brain is in communication with the Creator, it can help us to unravel the highly creative, figurative language the Bible has been written in - it is full of enigmas, hidden mysteries and pictorial aids. Large sections of the Bible were written in the original form of the Hebrew language, and some of its earliest books were written using a pictographic script like other ancient writing systems that have been discovered.[4] So the root of the earliest language used to write scripture was symbolic and pictorial rather than letter orientated.

Mark Virkler states in his book "How to hear God's Voice":[5]
'Corresponding to the idolization of logic is the demise of creativity, which is a more right-brain function involving vision, intuition and visualization. Statistics show that almost all children rank high in creativity before they enter school at age five. By age 7, only 10% still have high creativity, and by the time we are adults, only 2% score high in creativity tests. Therefore what we are doing in the current educational system is essentially reducing the creative ability that God has placed within man. I believe it is because we are training the left side of the brain (the logical, analytical part) and stifling the right side of the brain (the intuitive imaginative side). Where in scripture do we see God suggesting we do this? I suspect God gave us two sides of our brains so we could offer both sides to Him to use.'

The enemy will try to devalue anything that could be a powerful weapon for God's Kingdom. He has sought to establish a stronghold of intellect, mind, will and reason that prevents us having a deeper connection and understanding of God. The spirit of religion motivates us to filter God primarily through the left brain characteristics, through logic and rationalization. It attempts to sift out the supernatural, the symbolic, the miraculous and creative because the outcomes cannot be premeditated and thus constricted.

SPOKEN

Around a third of the Bible refers to dreams and visions and yet this is such a small part of church teaching. In biblical times it was not thought unusual for God to speak to people in dreams and was greatly valued. God even chose a dream to reveal to Joseph that Mary's pregnancy was supernatural and he was to marry and protect her. She could have been stoned, so God needed Joseph to understand the message clearly (Matthew 1:18-24). The wise men were also warned in a dream not to return to Herod, as this would have exposed the location of the baby Jesus and endangered His life. These accounts and others indicate God deems messages through dreams as an important form of communication beyond the Old Testament. Visions abound in Revelation and throughout the Bible where people are shown the realm of the Spirit with images, places and experiences, and I will expound on this in greater detail later on.

God speaks to us in numerous different and diverse ways and many times it is not in plain speech. Even the Word of God becomes dry and arduous for people who read it through the filter of pure logic and intellect, making no room for the Holy Spirit to breathe new life on the layers of hidden wisdom and divine understanding. The Word of God is like a brain with a multitude of connective pathways across a vast volume of information that is written, but also networked, to the realm of the Holy Spirit. It requires affinity with the Spirit to illumine understanding into its pages, transposing its two-dimensional form into a multidimensional one full of interplay, history, symbolism and hidden message. It is written in such a supernaturally creative way that pouring it through the sieve of cool logic and rationale will reduce it to its lowest form, disconnecting us from a sense of close proximity to the One who created this incredible work of Spirit life.

This is the intention of the spirit of religion - not the true religion of God, but the spirit that seeks to masquerade as the character of God. It produces dry, lifeless church experience that successfully excludes much of the supernatural character of God, proffering such a limited expression of the Spirit that the relationship between God and man grows cold: growth stunted in the cracked winter greenhouse of icy religion. We can be raised to accept such a disconnection from the vibrant world of heaven, to see it as something so remote from our current Christian life that we settle for a few flowers in the garden rather than the bountiful extravaganza of different colours, smells and tastes presented to us. If we settle for less, our Christian experience crackles with the dry leaves of limitation and frustration.

It is not the destiny of God's people to live on the outskirts of the wonderland garden, to skirt around the periphery, experiencing a few good things but not even knowing there is the appealing possibility of the adventure within. Sometimes we have been taught that the entry ticket was only available to those long ago and so we try to cling to the stories of those who actually had amazing adventures and experienced the supernatural realm. Some taste intimate connection to the Spirit in a series of isolated events, spaced far apart, but feel the world at large is the far more 'real' experience. Yet we are seated in heavenly places.

And God raised us up with Christ and seated us with Him in the heavenly realms in Christ Jesus. Ephesians 2:6 NIV

Why do we get bored in church and in our relationship with God when He is the least boring person in the entire universe? Sometimes it can be because we are swimming in dried up rainbow pools. We need to mine more deeply for ourselves to find fresh source.

PERCEPTION

We frequently base the character of God on our understanding and experience of the Christian life. So as we limit Him, we assume He is the size of the container we put Him in. We can see this exampled by those uncommitted to His authority, who describe God as tedious or irrelevant. This concept is staggering to those of us who have discovered He created galaxies, yet came and spoke to us in the most intimate detail that morning. The growing awareness of His involvement with our lives is increasingly magnified through the lens of developing relationship. This lens reveals the microscopic particles of a God constantly at work in the minute, as well as the larger shifts of divine intervention. We see through spiritual eyes and live in heavenly places and it is possible for us to live vibrant, wonder filled lives as we regularly access the realm of the Spirit and live amongst His presence. Our assignment is to continuously seek after the deep places of God so that the presence and experience of God's Kingdom becomes more real to us than the world around us and a sense of the eternal is tangible.

In House

The arts and creativity of God have become lodged in a small confined space by probably the majority of the church. This is not to say that some of God's people do not see the chasmal split, but over time and history it has settled into the architecture of expectations in modern day church, much like the absence of the supernatural in certain quarters. When we proclaim a finite restriction on something, we cannot conceive, let alone activate, its potential. God as an entire concept falls into such a category for some, or for many of us it's parts of His nature that we contain and restrict. Often the prophetic also falls into this category and yet we are all called to prophesy (1 Corinthians 14:31).

In the 1980s and 1990s ministries began to rise up with a charge to bring balanced, Biblical understanding to the revelatory gifts. They created a grid for us to comprehend the purpose of the prophetic and its role within the church and our lives. They illuminated the essential development of Godly character needed to bring stability and credibility to this gift and the ministry of the prophet. Ministries such as the Elijah House, John Paul Jackson of Streams Ministries International, Graham Cooke and others have made a huge impact in educating the church in these areas, bringing liberation and new activity through prophetic ministry.

The fruit from this refinement teaching has been self evident: many people are discovering vital guidance in how to distinguish the communications of God, progressing relationship and understanding Spirit life. Like all areas of Christian teaching, it's a journey, an evolution; the prophetic gift is born in immaturity like the cycles of life God has placed as examples before us. We need to learn and practice the spiritual gifts, to embrace effort allowing maturation, not expecting an instant entitlement. Sadly the very people who proclaim to have a stunning accuracy of gift with little training or character development are usually the most deceived and the fruit appearing juicy on the outer skin, masks a worm that will eventually manifest.

In Scotland such input has brought much restoration to the prophetic and an army has risen to answer a call to stand brave, change direction and take the spiritual and revelatory gifts to the mission field with impressive impact. The point to arrive at here is simply that the arts and creativity also now stand at the junction of being very misunderstood, thus being deemed largely irrelevant as the prophetic once was. There is a fear of the uncontainable, uncontrollable nature of creativity and a perception that this must then be the basic nature of creative people; therefore it is safer in lock down. There are also church leaders who feel the void and would gladly activate something, but it's daunting knowing where to start after such an expansive absence.

THE OIL WELL

Lack of understanding for spiritual creativity, and consequently value from within the church, has led to a discouragement of its progress, so now we often see a dearth of it or ill-developed standard. Yet there is an oil well intended for our resource, waiting for the strike. This book joins with other voices who can see oil submerged. The intention is to signal that a great resource of new energy, vitality and solution lies in the depths of the Spirit if we would take the time to bore deep and investigate its potential.

Some are already beginning those investigations with dynamic effect, like Bethel church in Redding, California - churches that are full of life and power, drawing people like a magnet to the fresh resource of creativity in the Holy Spirit. It shows not only in the arts being released but in healing, in the miraculous, in the divine wisdom and new revelation of the messages and ideas, the passion for mission and confidence in a life full to bursting with God. There is most definitely a link with creativity.

But oil needs drilled and extracted with intention; it is not a one day event. A token bucket placed beside the investigative hole will not power the geyser through the earth. It requires a time of digging, drilling and then preparation to capture and harness the power released in the abundance of fresh substance. In practical terms the first steps are to pray for a unity of heart amongst the leadership and the people in a community of believers. Fractured aims are hard to focus but even if there is a small pool of genuine seekers to begin with, the Spirit will answer. God looks for the passionate and in this timely move, He will fill the hungry, the ones who have waited and asked in many unseen moments many legitimate cries from the true heart.

We must not give up just because we cannot see today what is coming tomorrow, as clearly modeled for us in the lives of those such as Daniel and Joseph. Sometimes it is not about what we have not done, but spiritual climate and timing. We live in the tests of faithfulness to hold position till army unity is ready for advance. It would be sensible to assume that God is more likely to release the new geysers where people are drilling, preparing with faith and seeking wisdom on how to build the well for longevity.

PREPARE FOR OIL

TThe challenge that comes with this potential is that we will have to make space in our current systems. Sometimes our lives and programs have become so time-tight, they are now air-tight to the breath of God and we feel discouraged that His presence seems far from our gatherings and lives, this becoming the accepted norm. He seems distant yet we continue with our air-tight existence running, filling every moment with life's necessities or super-organized church programs. Such patterns can train us to never feel at ease entering the large space of the Spirit, filled with the unknown. Once in a vision, I entered a huge room which I understood to be somewhere in heaven or the realm of the Spirit; it was like an Aladdin's cave, dimly lit on entry. As appearing light gradually illuminated places in the space, divulging all kinds of treasure, God spoke to me of their meaning and availability to me. Such experiences are deeply encouraging and directional.

THE FULL CUPBOARD

We ask God for something new over and over and nothing comes. Then He takes us to the large cupboard of our life, opens the door and it is so crammed full that items tumble out and fall on the floor; then He asks, 'If I gave you something new, where exactly would you put it?'. Abraham was asked to get up and move first before an explanation came. It's a biblical pattern that faith is often required before a more comfortable explanation of the plan arrives. This next season and release of God's Spirit is calling many of us to slow, create a space to seek, consider and listen for wisdom, revelation and strategy before expecting the geyser to simply explode conveniently amongst us and change everything by it sheer volume and exuberance. Dry, closed hearts do not tend to recognize the exuberance of God but often rise to meet it with cynical disbelief. So we must let the Spirit turn the earth of our hearts and break up the dry solid areas of soil that yield little growth and smother the seed of new life. If your God experience feels like dry crackers, I urge you to go all out to seek for the banquet waiting for you; ask God to take you there, follow the trail of the Spirit.

RISK ORDER

Another stage is to take a risk, as a well known phrase puts it; do we want the order of the graveyard or the order of the nursery? We can lean so hard on our perception of all things decent and in order, surmising its outworking to be that of controlled regimentation. It will take fortitude to release the artistic people and the creative nature of the Holy Spirit in everyone. Leaders will need courage, understanding and the willingness to yield some control, as this will more likely manifest as the order of the nursery, especially in the initial stages of reclaiming this vital resource.

With the near extinction or low level of diverse creativity in many sectors of the church, there are few mothers and fathers of this movement yet available. Such spiritual parents are not only willing to progress areas of creative skill in others but also comprehend the evolving revelation of its purpose and the pioneering nature of their calling for the road ahead. But, if we never start to commission and energize people in this area, we will never inspire any into position. And that would mean we will continue to experience dehydration in important areas of our spiritual experience or a heavy emphasis on theology and church life through left-brain filters. Such imbalance will cause us to continue isolating facets of God without embracing His complete nature. In turn this creates an unfulfilling experience of God, because we are not asked to embrace the aspects of God convenient to us and champion them alone, but to seek to discover all of who He is and allow that to change us.

Imagine a parent who only allows neat, logical activity: no to getting messy, no to pulling out everything in the craft box just to see what can be created next, no to art materials because they might leave a bit of paint on the carpet, no to games that involve volumes of mismatched toys to create Kingdoms because the outcome cannot be logically determined, no to the exploration of making gooey mixtures, no to baking because the mess is usually a bit out of control. We end up with grown-up people lacking imagination, lacking originality, and with an expectation of the mundane. If we are called the 'Children of God' in His Word, then there should be space for the passionate quest of exploration, creativity and discovery, space and freedom to play in God's presence.

In addition to the order of the nursery we must consider the order of the artisan's studio where 'decent and in order' (1 Corinthians 14:40) may be paint stains or shards of metal and wood all over the floor, works in process and drawings of new ideas. Inspiration may haphazardly line the walls; there is space to explore, to carve, to sculpt and make an essential productive mess without fear of being told it's unacceptable. We must ask ourselves truthfully if our Christian communities are places of life and adventure or places of well-intended regimental order. If we see creative life, then let's encourage more, with deeper purpose and vision. However, some quarters of the church have become so far removed from the acceptable order of creativity that we sense to don the clothes of best behavior on entering the building – formal garments and attitudes that do not allow for the spills of experimentation.

Exception can be found in the worship band, but in truth this can also become as regimented as any other area and force skills to follow tight guidelines rather than the confident encouragement to wade deeper. These questions and analogies are not intended to disparage but simply alert the need for change and action. We want to be a relevant solution for the world, but sometimes we live with such a sense of smallness, overshadowed by the looming volume of morals and standards of the world around us. Yet, a Biblical model has been laid before us many times reminding that safe, comfortable spaces, small thinking and boxes achieve very little. But faith, courage and absolute conviction that God is with us can make changes through us that generously eclipse our natural ability.

The salient point is that this encompasses a whole area of our humanity that God created within us. It is much diminished in our Christian culture from its intended portion: the ability to be creative with Him, to bring innovation to the world around us, to effervesce with new life, expressions of worship, ideas for mission, fresh solutions for discipleship and more. This is the gift already given which remains unwrapped by some, or little understood and little explored by others.

We must consider that perhaps some people lack passion for church because they see a limited role for themselves within it beyond the fundamental biblical values common for us all. Outside those requirements, which wonderfully shape and form our Godly character and faith, we all have a set of gifts and skills, things that make us more passionate about life. However, if we enter into a situation where we cannot see any space for them then even the best of characters will bore, tiring of repetition that excludes inspiration. Beyond the consideration of those already attending church are the many creative people who do not, repelled by what they perceive as irrelevant and boring religious culture. Some younger people seem to fall into this observation. With the dynamic, creative power of God unleashed, we can more fully demonstrate His nature to them and the truth that He is relevant, hugely variant and vital.

TWO BARRIERS

Two substantial barriers to releasing creativity are:

REPEATING WHAT THE WORLD HAS DONE

At times we have dismissed a volume of creativity in the church. New ideas and strategies lie unconsidered in favor of age old traditions, even if they are vastly dated, because tradition seems more spiritual than change. Media and artistry can be seen as tantamount to entertainment, thus worldly. We have encountered this type of resistance and fear of change during our experiences with outreach when we have taken the prophetic and healing gifts into New Age fairs where it is now normal to find a bulk of seekers, hungry for spiritual answers. At times we have been accused by Christians of using New Age practices. They felt the use of such gifts as dream-interpretation, using words of knowledge or discussing symbols like the rainbow were rooted firmly in the enemy camp. Indeed these were all made by God first, then counterfeited so successfully by the enemy that some Christians now believe we are stealing from him!

Surely Joseph and Daniel interpreted dreams in the Bible, and the rainbow was a sign from God to His Creation. In the same way we have for so long handed the greatest portion of the arts and the wide spectrum of creative gifting over to the world, that some now believe many are simply for worldly pursuits, without any insight that we can redeem our God-given gifts. But we can start to embrace them again so that we can develop the high level of divinely unique creativity that is intended to be our inheritance and weapon.

POOLS

Another barrier is that Christians with particular gifting can end up pooling in certain places and forming churches known for the glut of artisans, for example, or a high concentration of evangelists.

Now while there is nothing wrong with people of like gifting gathering to inspire collectively, at times this has happened with creative people and artisans more for sheer survival of faith, rather than Holy Spirit direction. People gravitate to places where they feel valued, so perhaps it has been God's protection till now that they do not fall away in discouragement. Imagine a church with predominantly evangelists or pastors: the focus becomes very limited, and excludes the balance of the five-fold ministries. The prophetic, creative people need to be distributed and acknowledged throughout the Body of Christ. The variance of other abilities in the church family can help to sharpen their gifts and character, and from that healthy place they can disciple others. Expanding their gift into the space entrusted to them, they can liberate the creative power of God, stirring the spiritual atmosphere, which in turn produces a general release of creativity within the whole church again.

I am currently watching this happen within pioneering Christian groups who have bravely acknowledged the need to restore this area. Even though they do not have a full understanding of its purpose yet, they are willing to explore. It is astonishing how the dynamic works. Inclusion of the Spirit's creativity in timely faith seems to bring the realization of a void that needs filled, a missing depth of God - then the urge to paddle, then wade, then swim. Eventually the call for God's church in this season is to plunge and sink to the depths of the Spirit, remaining there for some time. In the depths we must slow, our frenetic activities quieted; stillness has supremacy. From this place will come a profound new wisdom and creativity that will course life into the veins of the church: life that impacts people, people groups and nations. Plans and visions God has already planted in our hearts can also draw new energy from these depths.

Wisdom is needed and leaders may be called upon to take risks in allowing a greater measure of freedom for new ideas and the arts within the church, but this does not involve throwing all sanity out the window. The creative, prophetic nature of God may involve a little mess and experimentation, but not anarchy. In the chapter called 'Release' a practical and Biblical framework is offered from which creativity can be allowed to fly and the community thrive for being willing to risk. I believe obedience to this call to reposition ourselves triggers an anointing for art and general creativity that will spark prophecy, healing, restoration and supernatural activity in unpredictable and remarkable ways. There is a pioneering work to be done by some of God's people, those whom God has been developing in character and in skill for this time, the ones who will be first to advance, calling and inspiring others. It starts with the reclamation of ground stolen, God's ground, and it is time for it to be re-established in the church. It's time to look for the pioneers, the intercessors and warriors and make space for them to come forward, activating what they carry.

MISSING

A while ago I overheard something that shocked me; it was something like this: 'If you need to find a place to escape the abundance of all the art and creativity in the world around us, just find a church'. That burned as it hit. As a church-loving, artistic person I suddenly realized there was truth in the statement. Although that is certainly not the charge of every community of believers, it is generally true that we are missing much colour. So what happened? There was a time when powerful expressions of creativity and art were used constantly within the church, and it was the very place to go to see the greatest works of art and architecture that demonstrated God's glory and majesty. Such was its importance that budgets reflected the conviction that creativity and craftsmanship were an essential contribution to the dynamic of the church.

The first European renaissance emerged in the late Middle Ages, around the beginning of the 14th century, and flourished till the 17th century. A force of great revival thrived through art, literature and the learning of new concepts and theologies. It was a cultural movement that marked the transition from medieval times to the modern age swiftly spreading throughout Europe. In stark contrast, the High Middle Ages (11th-13th century) hailed Latin scholastic education for men that focused on practical and scientific studies, preparing them for professions such as doctors, lawyers or professional theologians. In the successive period of history it was fresh creativity that spurred progressive thinking in entirely new ways, part of an era that allowed the exploration of human emotion and expression, knowledge and understanding, opening the way to many advances in areas of culture. The arts played a critical role within this renaissance.

However humanism advanced emphasizing and exploring the importance of human beings becoming increasingly independent from God, gradually replacing faith as the dominant inspiration behind the arts. Later in this time frame the Protestant Christian community started to rebel against the Catholic Church's control and, although there was surely some positive impact from this movement, a gross lack of understanding for the arts was touted by the new Reformers. They rejected Catholic traditions, which for them included the development of the arts, with the exception of music. We live in the fall out: hundreds of years that have embraced the exclusion of the creative spectrum, handing it to the world with little objection, allowing the rise of this potent force outside our care. It seems that as the church, we have relegated ourselves to the fact that this vast wealth of skills and gifts, this diverse vehicle for communication is overwhelmingly under the influence of the world and not the church, with little clue how to rescue our inheritance.

MANIFOLD

But hope and faith are explosive substances for change. God is speaking to us of a new renaissance rising6, the intention to pour out His Spirit upon His people through expressions of original and revitalized creativity so that He would be evidenced to the world more completely. As a collective church, if we only reveal isolated parts of God through our limited perceptions and the grid of our cultural History, we should not be surprised if some do not respond. They are waiting for the sons of men to discover who they really are (Romans 8:19), but in order for us to do that we need to discover more fully who God really is so that we can communicate the manifold sides of His nature to the world. There are people lost and waiting for the missing aspects of God to emerge through the church; this will be testimonial to them of their Creator. This book aims to ignite a dialogue about the practical steps to change as explored in subsequent chapters, with some practical 'how to' hints given after the grasped concepts. Reclamation and education is wholly possible so that the powerful prophetic creativity of God can be restored to the Church as an end-times weapon. We need to explore and define various strands: there is the general provision of Kingdom creativity for all God's people to invigorate their lives and areas of influence producing new solution, strategy, idea and passion for God. But there is also the timely defining of the calling for the creative warriors who combine high level skill, anointing and call for specific purposes. We will begin to investigate a more panoramic view of the purpose of creativity and its potential to greatly touch the world around us in effectual ways. The sovereign timing of God moves to unearth some long-buried treasure – long-asked questions may now be answered for many who have waited patiently in the hidden places, being chiseled for the day of uncovering.

WISDOM

In these last few years of search and striving to grasp the gauntlet set before me, I have always felt the weighty persuasion that this message of coming creativity was not restricted to the artists. This curious sense of magnitude has tugged regularly, leading to many more doors than first imagined. The unfolding message is that of God's provision to increase heavenly wisdom and understanding for the church, the petition for us to mine deeply with new motivation. It is the manifestation of God's unfolding persona, the missed or barely articulated faces of His manifold character that require exploration. Within the time frame of writing this book, I encounter other voices adding weight and further explanation to aspects of this prophetic insight and the purpose for which it is sent. My personal conviction is to investigate more extensively the connection of these factors with creativity plus the specific timing of God's reason for its restoration.

As I awoke into this journey I felt initially mystified that the great void of the arts and creativity had not been recognized in the wider church. The acceptance of its near-demise has become a settled norm for most, as well as the motivation to find purpose for its existence. This was also my position, but in a 'suddenly of God', the necessity for change seemed undeniable, yet it is hard to mobilize solution without clear understanding of the objective. The hidden things are coming to light leaving no room to lash blame around the church; we must realize and accept that, for whatever sovereign reason, there is just God's timely change and restoration, there are revelations kept for this historical period and we should waste no energy looking back with bitterness that will change nothing. It is time to look squarely into the face of the future and just say 'what now Lord?'.

In the teachings of Eric Johnson, he discusses how we have often reduced God's wisdom to logic and reason.[6] The message of this book strives to illuminate that we have often reduced creativity to the art box and a few good ideas. However, the Word of God reveals that wisdom, which is a part of God's nature, is a 'master craftsman' (Proverbs 8:30) who can be combined with the creativity of the Spirit to produce astounding new life. Thus at the core of heavenly creativity resides the wisdom of God. Outside the submitted soul we see the results of their separation all around us: a world full of bewildering or dark art releasing the messages and emotions of the human soul, confusion stirring confusion and darkness; or worldly wisdom processing knowledge, often finding little original or lasting solution to problems. Or, the combination of worldly wisdom with creative skill combining the outcomes of both. Within our Christian communities, even through hearts fixed heavenward, we can still see the results of disconnection in the two areas: wisdom becomes boxed with reason, logic and factual crisp theological conclusions. We see creativity that taps a vein but releases a surface level depth compared to God's intended volcanic combination, or that simply repeats and copies someone else's fresh creativity without the depth of personal connection to the Creator.

When God's creativity and wisdom combine there are charged results: wisdom ignites new creative form, solution, invention and strategy. The first record of the combination is Creation itself, containing too great a volume of innovation and intelligence for us to wrap our heads around. Then we must consider the Word of God: if divorced from supernatural considerations and read through the lenses of knowledge and wisdom alone, this supernatural book can result in the dry experience some attest to. Its life spark is in the fusion of wisdom, understanding and knowledge with the creativity of God - the supernatural signs and communications, the symbolic language and enigmas that need God's wisdom to be understood. Much Godly wisdom is released in dreams and visions, to which we will devote greater exploration later in this book. Where people have the combination of wisdom and creativity, new excellence is evident; even in the exploratory stages of small beginnings it is energizing and powerful to onlookers. We should look out across our nations to see where this combination is taking place in society; perhaps God will ask us to be involved, to pray, to applaud.

But you, Daniel, shut up the words, and seal the book until the time of the end; many shall run to and fro, and knowledge shall increase. Daniel 12:4

In this passage the angel is speaking to Daniel of the end days and the details of a long period of time. We live in an age where there is certainly a boundless increase in knowledge since Daniel's day. The capabilities of technology have amplified our ability to access and communicate knowledge across the globe with startling speed and diversity. Knowledge is our ability to learn, assimilate and store information. It is different from wisdom which, in turn, is different from the heavenly wisdom offered to us in the Bible. We can gain a great deal of knowledge, but how we process and use that knowledge is greatly affected by whether we combine it with the wisdom of heaven or the wisdom of the world.

Wisdom is described as the ability to govern and disciple by the use of reason, insight or shrewdness in the management of affairs; skill and good judgment in the use of resources; caution or circumspection as to danger or risk. Words relating to wisdom are those such as foresight, intelligence, discrimination, comprehension, balance, savvy and prudence. Opposite words would be those such as ignorance or stupidity.[7]

The exploration of wisdom will continue throughout this book, and in the chapter called 'DNA' we will see how it becomes one of the vital components to a combination, a prototype example God has given us to access new levels for the church.

Returning to a previous point: in our limitations to represent the multiple facets of God through our constricted value systems, we have reduced His plentiful persona to less than intended. The Bible speaks of the manifold wisdom of God:

And that he would show thee the secrets of wisdom! For he is manifold in understanding. Job 11:6 American Standard Version

His intent was that now, through the church, the manifold wisdom of God should be made known to the rulers and authorities in the heavenly realms. Ephesians 3:10 NIV

John Wesley's commentary explains that the phrase 'through the church' means what is done by the church, which is to be the theater of divine wisdom.[8]

The Message Bible describes it wonderfully:

And so here I am, preaching and writing about things that are way over my head, the inexhaustible riches and generosity of Christ. My task is to bring out in the open and make plain what God, who created all this in the first place, has been doing in secret and behind the scenes all along. Through followers of Jesus like yourselves gathered in churches, this extraordinary plan of God is becoming known and talked about even among the angels! Ephesians 3:10

This described the revelation that the Gentiles could also share in the riches of what Christ achieved on the cross and it further expounds that God brings layers of His manifold wisdom to light; things that have been hidden can be excavated and expressed through His church. We are in a season where God is urging His people to search for and find the wisdom of God. We are to be an answer for widespread problems in the world by living in and demonstrating the divine, multidimensional wisdom of God that greatly surpasses the shallow, deathly wisdom of the world, so that many can be saved.

FULLNESS

Another aspect of this message that stirs us to consider its meaning is Colossians 1:15, which highlights that God has put all His fullness in Jesus; and elsewhere that we have Christ in us (Ephesians 3:19). Therefore we have this 'fullness of God' residing and breathing in each one of us.

Combining this with the prospect that some of the multifarious sides of God are yet to be divulged in the season ahead should present us with new considerations. Seek and we will find, but the key is to seek Him with all our heart (Deuteronomy 4:29). A half-hearted attempt yields only a portion of the treasure. No solution for a problem has ever escaped the Lord and so we have what we need; we just need a bigger spade and some perseverance. But, unlike the monotony of digging a large hole in the earth, effort yields a journey, an experience of God that is teeming with personal transformation. We dig, we change, we dig, we become illuminated; the by-product we discover is that of beginning to feel (as one friend described it) like a Tardis on the inside yet appearing perfectly normal on the outside. The smallness of our inner world expands as divine depths reveal their secrets.

Suddenly, our understanding of God opens up, connecting with other celestial revelations and communications, like the synapses of the brain awakening, and life's hassles grow dimmer. When we realize there is a gateway to the Almighty and His fullness living within us to explore, there are not enough days in this lifetime to come to the end of His boundaries. So let us dig until we finally understand more clearly who we really are in God, and thus what we are capable of.

In the following chapters we will continue to probe these thoughts looking at ways to tap wisdom. Not only do we require the wisdom and creativity of God but we must ascertain its use, its objective and our own objective. We will tackle concepts and considerations for reaching those who live apart from God, engaging the expansive mandate to influence nations and people groups with Kingdom message and the part creativity must play. God's Word is a store of many provisions for the believer's progression through life. This book will endeavor to examine various elements in new ways, to link with familiar and well loved truths and be a signpost to other areas of revelation being explored more fully by others, that will aid us in the times ahead. It is a journey to address the filling of some empty spaces and intensify a fascination to probe the chambered character of God's heart.

DNA - PART 1

So the people stood afar off, but Moses drew near the thick darkness where
God was. Exodus 20:21

With a spade and gold-miner's pan, I endeavored to sift through scripture.
New gold began to twinkle through the familiar and manifest a combination,
then a repeating pattern used at some of the critical places in man's
historical connections with God.

CREATION

Eric Johnson unearths a wonderful truth highlighting what happens
when God's creativity and wisdom were first combined: the astonishing
achievement of the creation of the world and man.[1]

In Proverbs 8:22–31, Wisdom, which is a part of God, speaks in the form of
a being, a persona:

The LORD possessed me at the beginning of His way, Before His works of
old. I have been established from everlasting, From the beginning, before
there was ever an earth. When there were no depths I was brought forth,
When there were no fountains abounding with water. Before the mountains

were settled, Before the hills, I was brought forth; While as yet He had not made the earth or the fields, Or the primal dust of the world. When He prepared the heavens, I was there, When He drew a circle on the face of the deep, When He established the clouds above, When He strengthened the fountains of the deep, When He assigned to the sea its limit, So that the waters would not transgress His command, When He marked out the foundations of the earth, Then I was beside Him as a master craftsman; And I was daily His delight, Rejoicing always before Him, Rejoicing in His inhabited world, And my delight was with the sons of men.

Creation is so intricate; scientists and zoologists testify to an astounding system that sustains and reproduces life with designed intention that continues to confound. We can think of creativity as random, messy and haphazard, but the Creation of God is a combined effort with wisdom to produce intentional excellence far beyond man's efforts. I want to suggest to you that God may have had a blueprint for the Creation. Blueprints are akin to architects' plans. He may have had something in mind ahead of the action of forming the Creation.

CRAFTSMAN

Proverbs 8:30 proclaims the persona of Wisdom to be a 'master craftsman', which describes someone highly skilled at their craft with a high level of excellence. The word craft is more often used to describe the forming of something in a tactile nature, a hands-on experience that seems quite adverse to our thinking of wisdom as a purely cerebral practice. Here Wisdom crafts, it forms, it is integral in the creative nature of God. Returning to the point that the primary line of our Bible spotlights the significance of God's role as the Creator (Genesis 1:1), we see that at the birth of the Creation, Wisdom was right there as the master craftsman in the process. The Creation was conceived through God's love. It is a living, changing masterpiece, in which He has concealed many mysteries for us to uncover, each evidencing more of His character. Through science and medicine, nature and astronomy, we see each facet containing astonishing ingenuity and intelligence. The Bible tirelessly urges us to seek for the wisdom of God, and in Proverbs 8 it says that wisdom can be plainly understood and found by those who pursue it. It is the key to unlocking the symbolic enigmas and mysteries of God in which answers lie hidden, and this takes us right back to the point of developing and valuing right- and left-brain characteristics so that they can work together.

Receive my instruction, and not silver, and knowledge rather than choice gold; for wisdom is better than rubies, and all the things one may desire cannot be compared with her. Proverbs 8:10-11
I am understanding, I have strength. By me kings reign, and rulers decree justice. By me princes rule, and nobles, all the judges of the earth. Proverbs 8:14-16
For whoever finds me finds life, and obtains favor from the Lord. Proverbs 8:35

If we are to make a noticeable impact for change and influence people in places of authority, we cannot do it without pursuing the deeper wisdom of God and obtaining His favor. It is time to consider that we need more than the level we presently have, to be open to new possibilities and not assume our current lot is simply to be preserved until we check out of this world. We have a system of values through which we perceive the order and manner of Kingdom ministry; what it looks like, how it should operate; often boxing the fivefold ministries into various identities in our various cultures. In some Christian communities this can exclude people who have a certain skill set, age, or are female. God is going to reorder this value system so that His Kingdom can progress through us into areas currently constrained by our boxes.

TABERNACLE

IIn Exodus we find an engaging account that I believe provides keys for the general liberation of creativity in all God's people, but also a prototype for the artisans that God is calling out to be an essential part of the army for definitive purpose. The report describes a heavenly chain reaction. After great displays of God's dramatic power, Moses leads the children of Israel out of Egyptian slavery and into the desolation of the Sinai wilderness. The Lord longs to draw close to this people so He speaks to Moses of a tabernacle, a place for His presence to abide amongst them. We find details of God's character uncovered in this story, some that seem lost to us today. Moses answers the Lord's request to meet Him in the heights of Mount Sinai, where His awesome presence would descend:

So the people stood afar off, but Moses drew near the thick darkness where God was. Exodus 20:21

At that time only Moses was permitted to access such intense visitation, but through the provision of Jesus' sacrifice there is access for all who chose to come. It is time for us to draw near the 'thick darkness where God is' (Psalms 97:2). In that place the Lord gave Moses the ten commandments; shortly after, he was called again to the cloud:

And Moses went up into the mount, and a cloud covered the mount. And the glory of the LORD abode upon mount Sinai, and the cloud covered it six days: and the seventh day He called unto Moses out of the midst of the cloud. And the sight of the glory of the LORD was like devouring fire on the top of the mount in the eyes of the children of Israel. And Moses went into the midst of the cloud, and gat him up into the mount: and Moses was in the mount forty days and forty nights. Exodus 24:15-18

In this profound, dense cloud of glory God gave Moses blueprints and very specific details for the Tabernacle. Many creative forms were to be worked in the infrastructure as well as in the holy objects it would contain. Each creative work was deeply allegorical, full of mystery, meaning, divine purpose and power that has caused studies and discussions for thousands of years.

THE MERCY SEAT

A flavor of just one such example from many possibilities is the Mercy Seat (Exodus 25:17). It was formed from pure gold and was not in fact a seat, but the lid of the Ark of the Covenant. Two molded cherubim of gold fused wing tips covering the Ark and protecting the sacred contents: the tablets of stone engraved with the law. Its symbolic implication was restitution from sin. The Ark itself was made of wood and covered with pure gold; gold refers to the divine and wood the earthly, demonstrating that vindication from sin belongs solely to God. The lid of the Ark was called the Mercy Seat because it mercifully covered the law that was inside the box.

And there I will meet with you, and I will speak with you from above the mercy seat, from between the two cherubim which are on the ark of the Testimony, about everything which I will give you in commandment to the children of Israel. Exodus 25:22

Moses would commune with God there, hearing guidance and instruction from above the lid of the Covenant Box, between the two cherubim. This is still the place where God meets with man, somewhere between the pages of His written Word and through the mercy that Christ obtained for us. The meeting point was precisely defined; the Lord wanted to meet with Moses in a place of intricate creative forms that were symbolic, beautiful and bathed in gold – a collaboration between God and Man.

GARMENTS FOR THE PRIESTHOOD

As the head priest, Aaron was to have resplendent priestly garments made for him that were embellished with important emblems and allegorical meaning.

And you shall make holy garments for Aaron your brother, for glory and for beauty. So you shall speak to all who are gifted artisans, whom I have filled with the spirit of wisdom, that they may make Aaron's garments, to consecrate him, that he may minister to Me as priest. Exodus 28:2-3

Skillfully woven garments of many colours were to be 'artistically worked' (28:6). The breastplate contained precious stones in settings of gold, each representing a tribe of Israel. Like the temple these must have been spectacular works of divine creativity on completion, deemed holy garments. Like the temple, they were only to be made by gifted artisans whom God had filled with a spirit of wisdom. The affiliation of wisdom and creativity is demonstrated once again. If the practical and logical were sufficient then it would not be reasonable to devote great lengths of time and skill to interiors and clothing, especially with all that messy sacrificing! Why apportion such energies to what we often see now as unnecessary effort? Something weighty nestles quietly in this verse yet holds dormant volcanic potential, waiting for its time again.

The garments were made 'for glory and for beauty'. Locked in some confused turns of church history is an over-glorification of beauty for beauty's sake with ungodly roots. But there is also the evidence of where divine beauty and creativity connected with mankind with wondrous results. The strong reaction of the Reformation and the sands of time have caused us to associate most art and beauty in the church with being superfluous, even worldly. With this attitude we have inadvertently aimed the firing squad at mystery and the depth of revelation that lies within the beauty of God. It is an important part of His character. Many different people would give you a range of perspectives on what they see the beauty of God to be, from nature to kindness. These are indeed most valid, but if we take the explosive and continual creativity of nature into account and then return to the fact that we are made in His image, in His likeness, why is creativity in God's people given such a low promotion?

MOSES

In this Biblical record we see that a bare tent was not sufficient. Beauty, artistic excellence and divine enigma were the interior design of this dwelling place for the Most High. Yet, there in the blazing, hot, dusty desert it would seem radically strange to demand such effort for beauty.

It is true they lived in a culture where great temples and statues to deities were common, but even so they were in transit, with hundreds of thousands of people often moving, focused on the practical – why not just put up a plain tent? I believe that the divine creativity of God releases something, it carries something; the beauty and purity of Spirit-led art is powerful and we need to understand its purpose again. Faced with such impractical requests, Moses and the people could have questioned; but their obedience to bring offerings and conclude all the work as prescribed facilitated a fusion of such magnitude between God and Man that the glory cloud resided there.

As we restore the lost gift of creativity and artistic skill to the church, we need courageous leaders who not only sense the Spirit's urge to risk but are willing to proceed with action, to allow the unexpected unfolding of God, and to honor the significance of divine beauty and not just function. There seems some timely wisdom in another example from this passage. When the children of Israel just wanted to move on into the land of milk and honey, God asked them to pause and make this a place of precise, Spirit-filled beauty. It was a place they could focus on His character and where He could change them in the thick cloud of His presence.

So Moses finished the work. Then the cloud covered the tabernacle of meeting, and the glory of the Lord filled the tabernacle. And Moses was not able to enter the tabernacle of meeting, because the cloud rested above it, and the glory of the Lord filled the tabernacle. For the cloud of the Lord was above the tabernacle by day, and fire was over it by night, in the sight of all the house of Israel, throughout all their journeys. Exodus 40:33-35 & 38

Moses was an Old Testament prophet of the Lord and he mediated for the people. The sacrifice of Jesus has purchased for us a direct relationship between us and God, so that we can go into the midst of the cloud for ourselves. What will we find there? What will be waiting for us in the Holy of Holies?

THE CREATIVE PROTOTYPE

The primary downloads were given to Moses, but it was a team of artisans, commissioned by God, who made the series of extensive plans for this voluminous project. A lead artisan was commissioned and enabled in some rather surprising ways:

Then the Lord spoke to Moses, saying "See, I have called by name Bezalel the son of Uri, the son of Hur, of the tribe of Judah. And I have filled him with the Spirit of God, in wisdom, in understanding, in knowledge, and in all manner of workmanship, to design artistic works, to work in gold, in silver, in bronze, in cutting jewels for setting, in carving wood, and to work in all manner of workmanship. And I, indeed I, have appointed with him Aholiab the son of Ahisamach, of the tribe of Dan; and I have put wisdom in the hearts of all the gifted artisans, that they may make all that I have commanded you." Exodus 31:1-6

There are several remarkable things in this chapter. This is the very first record, in the Bible, of God filling someone with His Holy Spirit. Interestingly He did not choose one of the priests or a great leader in the Old Testament, nor even Moses; He chose an artisan.

So we now see there are two parallel introductions, both of which contain foundational and acutely significant elements, and both are introduced to us with the same combination of factors. The introduction of man to the Word of God as a book for us to learn from (Genesis 1:1), and the introduction to the concept of man being filled with the Spirit of God (Exodus 31:3). First there is a blueprint or series of blueprints: God's design for Creation and the designs He gave Moses for the tabernacle where He would connect with man. The next factor is that the Holy Spirit was the dynamic through which the work was fulfilled. Next we find wisdom was present both at the making of Creation (Proverbs 8:22-31) and with Bezalel (Exodus 31:3). Finally, all those factors were combined with creativity. Both creativity and wisdom are parts of God's core nature, with wisdom even being described as a master craftsman (Proverbs 8:30). Bezalel was also a master craftsman, an artisan, working with an infilling of the Spirit of God. The results of both were divine masterpieces, places where God was desirous to visit man and build relationship with him, places where His being could connect and reside among us. Both places, the Creation and the Tabernacle, include extraordinary beauty, colour, craftsmanship, symbolism, meaning, enigma and an outpouring of creativity.

The gifted artisans, filled with wisdom, rendered every element of this intricate project, with Bezalel overseeing the work. Here we find another element combining with the factors outlined above. God asked the artisans to bring their existing skill, then He multiplied it with divine intervention. The passage indicates they had skill to carry out 'all manner of workmanship, to design artistic work' (Exodus 31:6). There would have been a capacious list of all the artistic skills required at a high level of accomplishment for such a task; no artisan can be excellent in so many areas of such diversity. There was a gracing of supernatural ability as they obediently aligned with the assignment. Moses may have acquired the original blueprints, but it is impossible for an artisan to produce artistic excellence with passion and inspiration unless they capture the vision for themselves. Even given a perfect set of drawings, there would still have been the out workings of structure and technique to figure for each unique piece. The team must have worked closely with the Spirit's leadership, doing all they felt guided to do, because it was accomplished true to the prime instructions; and God was so delighted with His new resting place that His glory abounded within the tabernacle.

We also see the importance of people having great character and perseverance in the jolly hard work it must have taken for such things as melting and casting metal in the middle of the desert to precise designs – character challenges with daily aspirations for excellence and the finest personal efforts offered for the habitation of a holy God who deserved nothing less than their best. They kept going until everything God had asked of them was finished and what they produced has been much studied and revered.

The Creative Combination

THE CREATION MADE BY GOD:
Blue prints + Spirit + Wisdom + Creativity + Skill/ability, joined with the character of God

THE TABERNACLE MADE BY GOD AND MAN IN PARTNERSHIP:
Blueprints + Spirit + Wisdom + Creativity + Skill/ability of man + More skill/ability added by God, joined with Character, Obedience and Perseverance

We should pause to evaluate why God would introduce us to this combination of factors in two of the most significant primary connections between man and God. Why would He position them so strategically if they were not crucial, if their intention was not to reveal something of His nature that would be critical for His people to grasp? I believe they are a prototype for us, showing a pattern of our potential to release the supernatural creativity of God and the power within its true form. If this is not important, then why has the enemy worked tirelessly to diminish the value of creativity within the church while it is highly esteemed in the world, working as a powerful force for his objectives? The creative combination outlined above reveals to us how we can begin to release and restore the creativity of God again in the church at the level it was intended.

There are two distinct types of people who can use this combination for great result. There is a creative DNA latent in all God's people, and when activated with the creative combination this energizes new divine solutions, plans, innovations, inventions, strategy or a level of the arts for any area of life or profession. Then there is a calling for the artisans who carry a level of anointing, skill and gifting that equips them to aim for creative excellence in the arts to ignite this combination. This may be for the church arena, but equally it could be for world culture to bring breakthrough, healing and Kingdom advance through art, craftsmanship and design. Any kind of creative skill that is not combined with the wisdom and Spirit of God is just dead works, which we can see in abundance in the secular world. However some of these works are not just silently dead, but tangibly releasing death through negative forces in play. The creative combination of the Spirit is the antidote, the life-releaser, the provider of answers.

WHAT DO YOU HAVE?

Beyond Bezalel, Jesus sacrificed Himself that we would live a life in-filled with the Holy Spirit, thus giving us access to God's 'wisdom and understanding, in knowledge and all manner of workmanship, to design artistic works' (Exodus 31:3). Our aspiration should be that of a people who spark anointed art and innovation, impacting the world around us: ground-breaking solutions in medicine and government, problem solving business strategy, financial wisdom, amazing objectives that astound people who do not know God, moving far beyond some of our current limited understanding.

Your surrendered life invites the habitation of the Holy Spirit to connect with your human spirit, providing the open relationship that can access what was given to the Exodus artisans. The divine creative DNA is installed within this connection, so a good question to ask is: what skills do you already possess that the Holy Spirit can flame with the rest of 'the combination' and add to supernaturally? As we allow God to develop our character and are prepared to be obedient to do what He asks with tenacity, like Bezalel, we could carry out stunning accomplishments for the Kingdom. Sometimes we have exactly what we need to find the solution right in front of us; motivating 'the combination' through the Spirit can reveal idea, action and provision.

Eric Johnson teaches that ministry and anointing must not be limited solely to what we can do, but it is about who we are.[1] Recognizing forgotten parts of our DNA like creativity is vital; they complete a whole picture, a weaponry. Unrecognized and uncombined they will simply continue to lie scattered and gather dust. Yet the Bible reveals the assembly of these parts enabled mighty kingdom exploits, and this is what He has in mind for us. God's people are not to be mediocre and colourless, just getting by or trying to passively fade into the background. We are called to live powerfully because we draw breath through His Spirit and advance with authority, insight and love, armed with a battery of spiritual gifts, tools and weapons.

WAITING

If we are willing to seek God, connecting in deep communion, new wisdom and instruction will come. But waiting and seeking are not an apathetic passing of time, nor are they the expending of frustrated energy. Sometimes wisdom falls in a downpour to drench; other times it seeps through your skin. In periods of seeking we may find the slow seep of wisdom leads us to develop existing skills or gain new ones. Even though the curtain remains drawn on the final vision of purpose, we can follow the sense of wise direction as we see in part.

God is looking for people of an excellent spirit for Kingdom exploits. If we make time to listen, to pursue, to prepare our capabilities, gifts and character, then He can count us trustworthy and ready for commissioning.

In the life that harmonizes with heaven, striving and comparison need find no resting place. As our feet learn to merge with the footprints of God, we find perfect timing and growth. I also believe God is willing to apportion skills and gifts we may not presently have. As a sense of purpose and positioning begins to clarify, we may find we lack vital skills for the road up ahead, and we can ask and receive skill by supernatural means. Like Bezalel, we offer to God all that we have in our hands, then ask for acceleration, a multiplication, and in some cases new skills altogether. These may be for technology, organization, administration, leadership, people skills, artistic skills and so on. Some have had entire languages downloaded in an instant; many other times it is embryonic and will require nourishment and development, which has the great advantage of learning to work increasingly with the Holy Spirit in the process. Or as Elisha asked of Elijah, we are also able to pick up the mantles of those who have gone before us. Take time to seek and ask God what you should develop in this time-frame and find out what you need to lay down so that space can be made for new training and preparation. Do not just add more – remember the overstuffed cupboard!

THE TEMPLE

When Jesus came and sacrificed His life for us, we became the temple in which the Holy Spirit of God could live enduringly – not just to visit, but to live:

Or do you not know that your body is the temple of the Holy Spirit who is in you, whom you have from God. I Corinthians 6: 19

I have heard some say that now we have the Holy Spirit we do not need any of that 'stuff'; they refer to the symbolic interiors and pieces in the temple, and consequently art and creativity in the church in general. However, by His very nature God daily originates a vast spectrum of creativity: He forms new galaxies and speaks in thousands of imaginative ways to His people continually. New discoveries are made in the fields of science and medicine that are simply the uncovering of more of His genius. Why would His people, who are made in His image, be required to be so far removed from this nature? Although Jesus came to change many things, He did not dismiss the significance of the Old Testament, but referred to it many times. It is weighty with lessons for us today.

Turning our attention to the arts for a moment, we see there was extreme beauty and excellence in the tabernacle and the gravity of this has been appreciated at stages of church history, particularly in the Catholic Church. Last October, I visited the Cathedral in Sienna, Italy; decorative embellishment seemed to cover every inch of floor, wall and ceiling. While we may no longer have the budgets or inclination for such dense, voluminous decor, these works of art were carried out by the craftsman to They inspired holy awe and brought understanding of the divine, with biblical depictions for meditation. In that era, there was no television, film or computers, so the arts and crafts were the main visual stimulant and equivalent of our entertainment. The church blazed a trail of excellence in this highly influential arena of culture, in the arts, crafts and architecture, writing and other areas.

Since the Reformation, the church has seen minute progression in this field compared to the racing evolution of creativity in culture. If God is the most intensely creative being in the whole universe, why are churches and Christians filled with so little creativity? This is not meant to just be a critical statement; it is not aimed with waggling finger, but from a love of God's church and a desire to see lost treasure and power restored to it. These are just good questions that seem far removed from the western church at present, and it is time to look for answers.

RECLAIM

As we saw in the last chapter, many art forms were rejected at some stages of the Reformation. As humanism contaminated the arts in religious circles, they were placed in the dock by reformers, judged suspicious with the risk of idolatry. The sentence of expulsion was embraced by many, with the exception of music. Is it not amazing that we still live in the agreement of this today, yet most Christians have no idea of this historical chapter? It really is time to ask ourselves why we often reject uniqueness and art in our churches, when all around us in the world, film, art, drama, dance, advertising, architecture and design release messages that people daily respond to for good or bad. With the fusion of creativity and technology, these have become immensely tapped sources.

This could be an opportunity to use creativity to communicate God to people who do not know Him. Bob Jones said that 'Creativity would be the key to the great harvest'. When I first read this quote years ago, I failed to see its possibility. However, with the advance of understanding it is no longer a stretch for me to believe.

When we grasp the initial point that the creativity of God is not confined to our current conception, we can also begin to grasp that the world stage is set to use this same resource as a megaphone for the dragons in media, the firepower of technology and the culture of the Arts to declare the enemy's agenda. Can you then imagine what is possible if God's people would connect to this creative DNA to the spark of holy wisdom to produce powerful, anointed messages and ideas that could impact not just handfuls of people, but nations. 'V-J Day in Times Square', Alfred Eisenstaedt's photo of a sailor kissing a nurse in Times Square on V-J Day is one of the most arresting and popular images in American History.[2] V-J day saw the surrender of Japan, effectively ending World War II. For many it captured the sense of great joy and relief, the end of another dreadful war full of heartache. The image inspired millions of people radiating new hope. A momentous impact from just one photo, capturing one moment. As we begin to embrace our heritage, we can also inspire and train subsequent generations to tap the divine creative flow so what may come through them can far extend what has been previously possible. However, if we never unblock the dam, the enemy will continue to draw from its resource gladly and our following generations will be as restrained as we have been.

JESUS

I was sharing my findings of the tabernacle and Bezalel with a wise friend some time ago when, he threw out a gauntlet: 'So now what you have to do is find proof in the new testament'. The glow from my excited findings began to wane as my racing mind scanned the Sunday sermons and Christian teaching of the last fifteen years. I went blank. I realised what was needed was more than a tenuous link to one or two scriptures. I panicked, then pondered, then prayed; the kind of prayer that says I have absolutely no idea where to find this and having spent all my formal training immersed in art and design and not Bible college, I was stumped. So I prayed and prayed for some weeks, asking, it must be in there somewhere. Then late one night a question dropped into my head unexpectedly, 'Why was Jesus a carpenter and not a shepherd?'. A door unlatched and answers began to emerge but so did the sense that this area will require a journey of more time and study - an unpacking of layers, many hidden enigmas that will help us understand our creative DNA and its purpose in the coming years. Others will grasp areas of this revelation more deeply and expound over time, but this felt like a start for me.

I examined the entrance of our Savior into this world. Yet even before this tangible beginning, its marvel was brought about by a very creative process – it was prophesied over time. The language of the prophetic is often allegorical in part, and does not attach to man's logic because it declares something that does not yet exist. The Holy Spirit created the child in Mary's womb through divine action, and chose the appearance of an angel to tell her this had happened. Several dreams saved the life of the baby Jesus (Matthew 1:20; 2:12; 2:13; 27:19). Dreams are deeply figurative and creative, yet God chose them as a way to communicate something as essential as saving the life of His only son for the critical purpose ahead.

This in itself should reveal the significance of symbolic language as a means of God's communication. Jesus was thirty years old before the short time frame of His public ministry. It would be rational that the period preceding this would help prepare Him for His role on earth. Jesus modeled God for us and revealed His heart and His desired connection to man. We study His life to see how we should live, how to treat others and take part in Kingdom advancement. We often study the three years of His ministry, but what about the season of groundwork leading to that point?

Jesus is often called 'The good shepherd' (John 10:11); would it not have made a lot more sense if He had actually been a shepherd, so He could more fully understand that function of ministry? Or why not a farmer – there would be much to learn about kingdom principles in that role? As I investigated other opinions, one that repeated was that of the cultural norm to follow the family business; but ultimately He did not continue this. God leaves nothing to chance, let alone the training of His only Son while on earth - His onetime deal to come in human form and teach us imperative examples and lifestyle. So, apart from being faithful to work with His dad and progress the family business for a while, there is reason past the obvious.

When we think of a carpenter today, what image materializes? I thought of a joiner, then broadened to the spectrum I learned, that this ranges from an odd jobs man to a cabinet maker making bespoke pieces of great skill. We are often taught Jesus was poor, but then some teach He was not; somewhere in the pool of opinions it is more helpful to think about the type of work He carried out and who He might have made pieces for.

The carpenter of Jesus' day would have a radically different experience to the modern day component. There were no 'off the peg' materials, no wood cut to size, no metal nails in neat plastic packets or medley of power tools. There were no warehouses for fly-by equipment stock-ups. Life and work would have been thoroughly connected to the raw materials and nature's local provision. The knowledge and use of local woods would be an essential resource, while the felling of trees and preparation of raw materials would be a fundamental part of the job. The primitive tools would yield slower progress and need more physical effort compared to using the electrically powered tools of today. The word bespoke means something made to order and unique; modern designers all know that this will be reflected in the price tag, in contrast to the magnitude of mass production. But everything in Jesus' day would have been bespoke. Every single piece would have to be designed before it was made, and then patiently crafted into an exclusive piece. This takes time and skill.

Adding to this, the Gospels use the word tekton to describe Joseph (Mark 6:3). Beyond our perception of a carpenter today, a tekton was understood to be a craftsman, an artisan, akin to a master builder.3 A carpenter would have had to understand instructions, calculate and draw up plans, and articulately present those plans to clients. It was a skilled profession, and at high level would have been much sought after. Most poorer people would have been able to make their own basic tables and chairs, and many would have no need or resource to lay cost for a carpenter. Their homes were simple and self-constructed, so they would not have hired a carpenter to build a door or patch a roof. Consequently, one school of thought places Him within the upper middle class as part of a valuable profession.

This vocation would involve much hands-on activity, working with the Creation itself – raw wood in a tactile experience. The sensation of touching and manipulating material into another form is a completely different one from reading about it in a book. There is a resultant satisfaction that cannot be generated by instruction alone. Jesus produced artistic work that required creativity and wisdom – a combination of skills to meet the diversity of producing designs, accessing needs and problems, then finding solutions. Much of His time would have been spent in these processes, while developing dialogue with the Father and constant Spirit connection so that He was ready for the most important ministry in the history of man. Nothing that Jesus did was mediocre, and He pointed us to a standard of excellence in everything He did – He never lived in the gray or the half-hearted; He modeled for us distinction. Do we think He would have done anything less while working as a carpenter?

So, 'Why a carpenter?'. It enabled Him to develop discipline in the workings of creative skill, and in some way this constant access to creativity was part of His vital preparation. It allowed Him to comprehend something, something He would have missed if this were not His training. Our perception of Jesus as an 'odd jobs man' is inaccurate; He had something to teach us in His time on earth about the creative DNA being an integral part of who God is. He demonstrated for us 'the combination' again:

Blueprints + Spirit + Wisdom + Creativity + Existing skill/ability + More skill/ability added by God, joined with Character, Obedience and Perseverance

PIVOTAL

THE CREATIVE COMBINATION AT PIVOTAL TIMES IN THE CONNECTION BETWEEN GOD AND MAN

1. THE WORD OF GOD: The introduction of the Word of God to man in the first line of the Bible.
2. THE TABERNACLE: Bezalel, the introduction of what happens when man is filled with the Holy Spirit.
3. JESUS: The bridge to reconnect God and man after the fall in Eden — an access point for the Holy Spirit to remain in man.

'The combination' was present at each of these firsts. The creativity in each example is not some vague arty gifting. It is a mix of creativity with divine wisdom, with skill and craftsmanship that can take inspired thought and channel it into practical design skills and blueprints, then administrate the project to produce an end result. It is the connecting and working together of the left- and right-side attributes of the brain. When Jesus moved into public ministry, He continued to model for us a highly creative life that lived 'the combination'. When He taught, it was often in parables instead of plain, seemingly logical speech. He chose to speak in symbolic language and stories that were full of riddle and enigma. Why not just speak in straightforward terms? As we examined before, for us to be able to unravel the mysteries of God, we must come closer; we must form relationship and seek Him for the answers and understanding, and in this process we transform. You cannot spend time in the presence of God and remain unchanged. Notably, the parables were to reveal to us the Father, His character and Kingdom; creative, symbolic, allegorical language was the chosen method of communication.

MIRACLES

The recorded methods of miracles carried no set formulas, and could even be viewed as random if we do not see the creativity of the Holy Spirit at work - a unique response for each unique situation.

He changed water into wine, laid hands on people, caused the disciples to catch so many fish the nets would tear; He divided a few fish and loaves to feed thousands of people, He calmed a stormy sea; a woman touched His cloak and was healed; He healed people without even being with them at times, He mixed saliva and mud to heal a blind man, He told Peter to go and find money in the mouth of a fish, He healed ten leapers, He raised Lazarus from the dead, He caused an ear to grow back, He cursed a fig tree, and was raised from the dead Himself.

We have struggled to organize His activities into neat logical patterns for centuries. In some quarters of church history, people just gave up and declared that only Jesus could do these things and they were not for us today. But if we take into account the creativity of God's core nature, then that's exactly what was modeled for us so that we can do the 'greater things' Jesus spoke of (John 14:12). He modeled a life that listened to and obeyed the divine creative flow that brought individual instruction for each situation. We have so many programs that teach us a set of rules and guidelines on 'how to do what Jesus did', yet few will tell us to embrace the ingenuity of God, so we learn rules rather than developing a strength of communication with Him. When we demand logic in the workings of God, we reason away His presence and ignore His longing to be among us and be free. Insistent logic grants access for the religious spirit to strangle the creative element of the Holy Spirit, and we lose the power of 'the combination' that was modeled for us, entering into a dehydrated, religious experience.

As our eyes adjust to the new levels of light, we find characters all through the Bible who model 'the combination' for us.

DAVID

King David was one of God's favorite people, a prodigious King, a man after God's own heart and a highly creative individual. There are already multiple studies that explore the concept of the restoration of David's

However, we must also consider that David embodied 'the combination' again. He was known as a victorious King of wisdom and great military strategy in war, but he was also famed in the Bible for his creative worship and intercession. He poured out his heart in the inspired language of the psalms, translating many into music – a harpist who evoked the presence of God. They contain prophecies of the Messiah's coming and are much quoted by Jesus Himself.

As a true worshiper, sold out and utterly devoted, David had the wisdom to see the essential link with creativity and the artistic gifts when inviting and hosting the presence of God, and His heart ran towards excellence in these areas. He desired to build a great temple for the Lord, a place to house the Ark of God, but permission was only granted for his son Solomon to carry out the work, because David had participated in too much war and bloodshed. In the interim, David built a tabernacle, a tent that would house the Ark on Mount Zion in Jerusalem. It was the center of a new order of joyful worship; the sacrifices offered at David's tent were those of praise, joy and thanksgiving (Psalm 95:2; 100:4; 141:2). God blessed David's tabernacle and all it represented; but, with the far greater vision before him, David faithfully gathered the finest materials for the extraordinary temple that his son Solomon would complete.

Come, let us sing for joy to the LORD; let us shout aloud to the Rock of our salvation. Let us come before him with thanksgiving and extol him with music and song. Psalm 95:2 NIV

Many believe the sacrifices of the new Church are to be of praise, joy and thanksgiving (Hebrews 13:15; 1 Peter 2:9); and also that the tabernacle of David points to the proclamation of Christ through His church and the foreshadowing of the priestly, kingly and prophetic ministries of the church (Revelation 1:6). The inference of various studies is that creativity should also play an essential part in the workings of these roles.

SOLOMON

Early in his reign Solomon had a dream...

At Gibeon the LORD appeared to Solomon in a dream by night; and God said, "Ask! What shall I give you?". 1 Kings 3:5

Now, O LORD my God, You have made Your servant king instead of my father David, but I am a little child; I do not know how to go out or come in. And Your servant is in the midst of Your people whom You have chosen, a great people, too numerous to be numbered or counted. Therefore give to Your servant an understanding heart to judge Your people, that I may discern between good and evil. For who is able to judge this great people of Yours? The speech pleased the Lord, that Solomon had asked this thing. Then God said to him: "Because you have asked this thing, and have not asked long life for yourself, nor have asked riches for yourself, nor have asked the life of your enemies, but have asked for yourself understanding to discern justice, behold, I have done according to your words; see, I have given you a wise and understanding heart, so that there has not been anyone like you before you, nor shall any like you arise after you. And I have also given you what you have not asked: both riches and honour, so that there shall not be anyone like you among the kings all your days. So if you walk in My ways, to keep My statutes and My commandments, as your father David walked, then I will lengthen your days." Then Solomon awoke; and indeed it had been a dream. 1 Kings 3:7-15

Solomon began his reign well, recognising full dependence on God to lead this mighty people and so God gave him the most extraordinary wisdom (1 Kings 3:28). His Kingdom was also remarkable and he became successful, distinguished for exceptional judgment and for building a nation of trade and influence. Many came from different lands across the earth just to hear his wisdom (1 Kings 10:23–24). As a result he acquired outstanding wealth in vast tributes from kings and queens through the development of trade with other nations.

And God gave Solomon wisdom and exceedingly great understanding, and largeness of heart like the sand on the seashore. 1 Kings 4:29

A Royal Visit

The queen of Sheba came to experience the great wisdom she had heard of and to see this Kingdom for herself, only to find its reality exceeded all her expectations:

And when the queen of Sheba had seen all the wisdom of Solomon, the house that he had built, the food on his table, the seating of his servants, the service of his waiters and their apparel, his cupbearers, and his entryway by which he went up to the house of the Lord, there was no more spirit in her. Then she said to the king: "It was a true report which I heard in my own land about your words and your wisdom". 1 Kings 10:4-5

Intriguingly, she was overcome by the evidence of his wisdom, not only from encountering his progressive methods of justice and governmental strategy, but also from the architecture, the decor of his house and even the uniforms of his staff. Solomon operated at an unprecedented level of divine wisdom which we would normally associate with the concerns of logic and reason, but the proof of this divine wisdom for others in that time was also through the exceptional levels of art, architecture and creativity he facilitated and championed.

Solomon's Temple

Solomon built the temple that had been in his father David's heart. Its magnificence was astonishing. The design and details of the temple are found in 1 Kings 6, with much of the interior being overlaid with pure gold, filling it with the movement of reflected ethereal light (1 Kings 6:22). All the walls of both the inner and the outer sanctuaries were carved with figures of cherubim, palm trees, and open flowers also covered in gold.

THE ARTISANS

Now King Solomon sent and brought Huram from Tyre. He was the son of a widow from the tribe of Naphtali, and his father was a man of Tyre, a bronze worker; he was filled with wisdom and understanding and skill in working with all kinds of bronze work. So he came to King Solomon and did all his work. 1 Kings 7:13-14

Again the head artisan commissioned for the job showed exceptional skill, also operating in divine wisdom. With his team he created wondrous works in bronze, vast pillars with beautiful artistic details of chains, lattice work and four hundred pomegranates. He made many pieces of art with metaphorical meaning, including a vast ornamented bowl or 'sea' of cast bronze standing on twelve bronze oxen and containing two thousand baths. There were highly embellished bronze carts, lavers, pots, lamp stands, basins and so many things that they were too monumental to even weigh (1 Kings 7:47). When all the highly detailed architecture, art and interiors were finished, it was time to open the doors and dedicate the temple. Fire from heaven devoured the sacrifices, and the immense, weighty glory of God's holy presence was so intense the priests could no longer stand and continue their duties, and the people were face down with holy awe (2 Chronicles 7:1-3).

And it came to pass, when the priests came out of the holy place, that the cloud filled the house of the Lord, so that the priests could not continue ministering because of the cloud; for the glory of the Lord filled the house of the Lord. 1 Kings 8:10-11

A parallel experience happened at Moses' tabernacle; like Moses, Solomon understood that with God-given wisdom comes an understanding of the importance and depth of divinely inspired creativity and works of art. They understood there was an indispensable importance contained within, and that they played an integral part of entreating and hosting the presence of a creative God. Today we would often consider the highly prized wisdom of Solomon as mainly centering on logic and intellect; we would probably consider wise people to have their minds on higher things than art and beauty, but Solomon was just as interested in those as he was in strategic and governmental affairs. That should reveal to us yet again that something is missing in our thinking: the deep relationship between the wisdom of God and creativity. We have for so long disconnected this from our perception of wisdom that we do not even think it is very relevant; but again and again at critical moments in the Bible God demonstrates for us what is available when you bring 'the combination' together.

HOUSES OF THE ARK

The Ark of God represented the immediate presence and glory of God with His people, in Israel. Where the Ark of the Covenant was housed in the tabernacle of Moses, the tabernacle of David and the temple of Solomon, there was amazing creative variety – the finest arts with multitudes of the most extraordinary details of figures, flowers and fruits. The finest gold was found, gemstones and lavish beautifully woven fabrics. There was noisy heartfelt worship poured out in praise and adoration to our magnificent God. There was creative writing, song and instruments, dance and ceremony, symbolism and beauty and more beauty; all produced through the Spirit and wisdom of God by hearts and hands submitted and obedient to what He was showing them, the joy of being utterly creative for a purpose. In these environments His presence was poured out till the people could not stand, consumed by the depth of His majestic presence. God's people are awakening with a new appetite to see His presence, and so we must look at keys from the Word to see His nature and the environments and hearts that ushered it in.

WE ARE THE TEMPLE

The temple has not gone; it did not disappear with the Old Testament, along with the creativity. We are the temple that houses the presence and splendor of God in His Spirit. The tabernacles patterned the temple of the Holy Spirit and then we became it! We, the church, are now loaded with the Spirit's creativity; we can receive God's wisdom and stimulate 'the combination' into action and become the most original, innovative people on earth, providing divine solutions. God gave the blueprints for these temples to house His glory. Then He added a kinetic brew of His wisdom, His creativity and Spirit that generated intoxicating whirlpools of His presence, with the elements mixed together. The creative DNA of God's people must be stirred again. His artisans need to be filled with wisdom, to see their purpose. I believe there are specific artisans called for the purpose of helping to open and sustain deep wells in the church in this time – places where we can find this holy wisdom and more creativity expressed through a multitude of people in a multitude of different ways.

I must add at this point that if you are indeed with a group of people who already understand and operate in all this within the church, then hopefully these words will bring further encouragement and affirm what you are doing. There are always pioneers for every move of God, and they often begin as small groups forging a way forward faithfully.

POURING OUT NEW WINE

God said of the last days:

I will pour out my Spirit on all people. Your sons and daughters will prophesy, your young men will see visions, your old men will dream dreams. Acts 2:17

This relates to Ephesians 5:17-19:

Therefore do not be unwise, but understand what the will of the Lord is. And do not be drunk with wine, in which is dissipation; but be filled with the Spirit, speaking to one another in psalms and hymns and spiritual songs, singing and making melody in your heart to the Lord.

In the same place the Lord tells us to be intoxicated with the Spirit that He is pouring out; He tells us to have wisdom, and divulges that the result of being full of the Holy Spirit is that you get creative! Psalms are creative writing; many hymns are like poetry – we are to sing with spiritual songs (meaning 'songs with divine wisdom' in Strong's Concordance).[4] Singing and making melody in your heart to the Lord does not just speak of singing someone else's words and songs alone, but to sing our own, to go off the page and follow the trail of the Spirit. The point is He wants us to be filled with the Spirit, completely drunk. In that place of presence we are altered and new possibilities and solutions kindle; healing and breakthrough are frequently found. The presence of divine light allows us to progress to new space where we are no longer bound by what we have formerly perceived, but learn to tap a spiritual dimension that illuminates different outcomes. That is Godly creativity.

So as we begin to seek these things, what will we expect? We must be prepared for the unforeseen that may even seek to shake the debilitating excessive reason and logic out from amongst us, confounding our brain so our spirit can triumph. The very point is that something new, fresh and innovative will come, and it may look exactly like that – new!

WALLS

When Joshua and the children of Israel were facing a problem, God activated 'the combination' to do something which seemed illogical. Joshua 6 tells the story of a rising challenge as they were claiming the promised inheritance. Jericho was an imposing walled city that they were to claim for their own, but they needed the tactics of great military force; that is certainly how we would have approached it today: the more logical strategy the better.

However, the plan that God gave Joshua, the blueprint that would deliver the city into their hands was surprisingly not to storm the city with the vast number of fighting men among them. Instead, priests were to carry the Ark of God around the walls, blowing rams' horns and trumpets, with the fighting men of Israel following behind. On the seventh day they were to do this seven times; the wall collapsed and it was theirs for the taking. Instead of a rational solution, God gave them a plan they could never have come up with themselves: it involved musical noise (a highly inventive method), wisdom and the presence of the Spirit. It also involved great faith for the unusual, and obedience to carry out what they were told. As we look at the indomitable walls around the cities of world culture with little idea how to break in, the creative DNA of God is a powerful weapon that will not yield to our logic and control; it will require ears to hear and hearts to obey the seemingly radical answers that will come.

MICHELANGELO

Michelangelo is a historical example of a remarkable outpouring of creativity. During the Renaissance of the 15th century, Pope Julius II urged him to take on the gigantic project of painting the Sistine Chapel. But painting was not Michelangelo's passion: he was a sculptor who favored marble. Julius was resolute of the artist's involvement and drew him with the tempting carrot of a substantial sculpture commission on completion of the ceiling. He painted over 5000m^2 of biblical scenes, taking four years of painstaking work, with some team assistance. Frescoes were painted by plastering one area at a time then swiftly painting the space while still wet. The overt subject matter of the ceiling is the doctrine of humanity's need for salvation as offered by God through Jesus. The now iconic 'Hand of God' image is a beautiful and simple depiction of God reaching to man in relationship. It is now over five hundred years old and is still one of the most astonishing and famous works of art in the world, seen by many thousands of people in situ and millions through media and books.

So, here is the most incredible thing: Michelangelo was not a brilliant painter before the ceiling project. The only painting he had done was during his brief stint as a student on work placement with a famous artist. It is said that he made many mistakes at the beginning of the process – he had to persevere. If you look at the remarkable images and messages, the layout and the astonishing practicalities that he had to overcome, the achievement is superhuman in nature. God gave him wisdom, understanding, and all the 'manner of workmanship' required to carry out the supernatural commission; a platform to convey God's message of redemption and love to millions of people over a five hundred year period. How incredible that he could be used to produce this awesome work of art with barely the skills for the job.

Four Horns and Four Craftsmen

Then I raised my eyes and looked, and there were four horns. And I said to the angel who talked with me, "What are these?" So he answered me, "These are the horns that have scattered Judah, Israel, and Jerusalem." Then the Lord showed me four craftsmen. And I said, "What are these coming to do?" So he said, "These are the horns that scattered Judah, so that no one could lift up his head; but the craftsmen are coming to terrify them, to cast out the horns of the nations that lifted up their horn against the land of Judah to scatter it." Zechariah 1:18-21

Zechariah the prophet had a series of visions during the reign of Darius, who ruled in the same time frame as Daniel was alive. In this vision the horn represented demonic strongholds that have oppressed the nations, crushing them till people are left depressed and hopeless and can no longer lift up their heads. Who does God send to save them? Craftsmen. Not quite what we would expect, if we go by our current conception of craftsmen. In his teaching, Eric Johnson expounds on this passage by saying that craftsmen in the Bible are characterized as people who carried a level of excellence in their craft.[7] So this is the type of character that is sent to break the strongholds over entire nations and restore life again. This would speak of a high level of competence for problem-solving and strategy in the mountains of society, to break the negative spiritual citadels affecting government and many areas of culture.

Many nations are certainly crestfallen and lacking hope in these times. The craftsmen were able to 'terrify' these strongholds that no one else was able to destroy. Divine creativity, in its true form, links with the other factors in 'the combination', becoming a limitless weapon against oppression. It sparks answer because the Creator is limitless, and there is no problem too large or multifarious. After the work of the craftsmen, the people are able to start the work of restoration, to rebuild cities (Zachariah 2:1). So the craftsmen come with creativity, wisdom and the Spirit of God to tear down national strongholds, and then the devastation can be restored. This is a noteworthy account, if we can grasp what we have and see what our tabernacles were meant to contain and release through the Holy Spirit that dwells in them.

END GAME

The second last chapter of the Bible describes where we are going: we return full circle. In the Garden of Eden man began his journey with God in amongst the most potent beauty of unspoiled nature in all its glory. We end the story to begin a new chapter of eternity in the City of God. (Revelation 21:14-21) Far from a departure of beauty we find, true to God's nature, symbolism and confounding artistry: a city with walls of pure jasper, full of colour hues and pattern, with the foundations of the wall embellished with a blaze of gemstones. The city is made of such pure gold that it is clear like glass – imagine the profusion of light bouncing from each surface. There are gates carved from a single pearl to entrance the city of the King in its lavish and dazzling beauty. If this does not reflect an important part of the nature of God, then I'm not sure what does. I used to be so dim-sighted that I had to pray for weeks just to 'see' the value of creativity and the arts in the Bible; but when answered prayer reached across and flicked on the light switch, I not only began to understand what the emerging truth is behind God's creative nature, but also its constant continuum of evidence and explanation for us through His Word. I am shocked at how blinded I have been and at how much needs to be restored to God's people.

DNA - PART 2

Very truly I tell you, whoever believes in me will do the works I have been doing, and they will do even greater things than these, because I am going to the Father. John 14:12

Obedience will be the key to a continuing stream of innovative downloads for believers. If we seek for wisdom and new strategy but refuse to carry it out when we are granted answer, it will not encourage God to give us more. The Bible shows us we are a trusted friend of God when we obey, and divine communications will carry increasing clarity. We submit to Him – it is not the other way round. God knows what is the very best thing for the situation and for us, way beyond our comprehension – in every case. He knows that journeying through a process will not only address a problem but change us for the better, so He requests a work of connectivity and partnership. We do not face anything alone when we let God be Lord of our lives.

CROSSING OVER

Something rather astonishing happened as I began to 'cross over' and absorb the germinating revelation. I began to tap a different blood flow of the Spirit inviting new adventure in a 'suddenly of God'. Compelled to test the theory, I started to ask God for blueprints; the stream began to flow and I saw an art form in a vision, the like of which I had never seen before. A large circular, silver sculpture was suspended before me as an interplay of light fizzled from a labyrinth of strands. It seemed powerfully beautiful and impossible to capture in anything I could render. I asked the Lord how on earth I would make such a sculpture? Metal wire and glass began to define its structure. But what was this art form and what of its purpose? I heard it was a 'portal' and it would help to open thin places of the Spirit, helping others to experience the presence of God. I stretched to assimilate, stunned by the request to make the piece from the vision. This was not what I had bargained for - I did not train in sculpture! I had general art training and qualifications in fashion, textiles and interior design, but not sculpture or metalwork. More menacing thoughts contributed to my argument: if I made this sculpture called 'Portal', everyone would think I was nuts! I knew obedience was going to be the motivator to begin.

Then I had to cross the next hurdle: where on earth would I get the materials and what were they? My current location in the Highlands of Scotland is not exactly the art material capital of the world, unlike the glut of outlets I had known during London life. I felt directed to the local DIY warehouse and subsequently to various building materials. Over the weeks and months I practiced following the instruction of the Spirit to hammer and mold a frame, then sculpt with hundreds of meters of wire and pieces of glass. As friends visited the house over those months, reactions ranged from marvel to bemusement as this strange apparition took shape.

A white wooden portal followed as inspiration consumed all my spare moments to make and form with the Holy Spirit in a torrent of new creative vitality and a sense of artistic purpose such as I had not experienced in my own art for many years. It was the resolve of exploration, of blind faith. I had no idea if these sculptures would even see the light of day outside my house, but obedience to build felt like the most important component.

Shortly after having completed the second sculpture, I was driving to teach a course and listening to the recording of a creative workshop on route. The workshop was coaching artists to paint from a place of divine connection, and as they moved into an extended time to practice the theory, live music continued to run. The building presence of God in the car was so delicious I felt cheated at not being able to ditch the steering wheel for an easel. So I let the music roll on in worship and asked for a blueprint for the next sculpture; after all, I had actually managed to make the last two somehow.

An intense vision filled the windscreen and the presence thickened to a gluey syrup that was making it really hard to drive straight. I saw these dream-like wings radiating a furious white light and I understood they would represent an angel of creativity that God was sending to help me. Again they were metal in frame, but intricate panels held a network of silver and glass that twisted in perfect spontaneity of much greater complexity than the previous sculptures. They were wildly beautiful, powerful and big! Lost in the divine moment and gluey presence, I was busy marveling at their ethereal beauty when the pop of the bubble sounded and earth returned with an alarming realization - I was supposed to make these? 'But Lord', I said, 'how on earth would I ever make these, and where would I store them?!', taking an inventory of the walls in my house.

I have never felt the presence of God leave my prayer space so fast - it was drained from the car like the immediacy of a crash. What did I just do? Would 'sorry' work round about now? I tried, and I clearly heard Him say, 'I didn't ask you to make them for you, I asked you to make them for Me'. I repented, a lot, and said I would never argue with Him again when He asked me to make something. It was time for another trip to the DIY store. I have tried to stick to that declaration as the requests have become increasingly challenging, but then there was the day He asked me to write this book! We see the challenge, but He sees the outcome that completely changes us and helps others, and the Kingdom gathers ground.

Time passed and the wings were completed inch by inch as I listened, guided in joyful creative union with the Spirit. A rendering of the vision was attempted, so that made three. They were to make a debut appearance at an event where I had taken on the leading of a new creative team; we would tentatively experiment with our new art forms as part of the atmosphere design in the prayer space and see what happened - it was expectantly nerve wracking. At the last minute there was an oversight by the venue: with a fully booked conference, they had under-calculated fire exits in the main hall. Delegates would now all have to go in the room intended for prayer, the room with all the art; there was no choice!

Our small pioneering creative team watched in awe as God maneuvered the arts right into the core of His purpose in diverse ways throughout the weekend. The silver 'portal' sculpture hung suspended above the front area before the stage, and as the main speaker opened a significant prayer line one day, something supernatural took place. I had left the room to prepare for teaching a seminar but was hastily dragged back in time to catch the fading phenomenon. There were no windows in the room except some curtained skylights, but a sharp beam of sunlight had seemingly appeared from nowhere and lit up the sculpture - and only the sculpture - like a thousand watt bulb. One friend saw it, yet right beside her one of my sisters did not. Cameras captured the minutes as it radiated and then it was gone; we were stunned. How was that possible? And quietly I knew it was my sign - keep going.

Although I am mainly referring to artistic works in these paragraphs, the illustrations are to offer personal experience of the new concepts being explored in this book. Any one of us could receive Godly input into our areas of creativity, whether a spreadsheet or groundbreaking new business plan. The Angel Wings have turned out to be one of the most inspiringly personal things I have ever made. To my sheer astonishment they have graced missions and hung in front of thousands of people. Always hung with faith and not presumption, they seem to contribute a spiritual dynamic to environments that detonates hunger for new creative spiritual life in people and whole groups. I marvel. And God did give me somewhere to hang them when they are home, a place that has become sacred for me, on the wall in my prayer and work room that also hosts vibrant church meetings. They are a gift to me in a way I did not think possible.

Technically I am learning to build large metal and glass sculptures; technically we should always try to improve. However, before I knew the Lord and fully gave my creativity to Him, I always worked in the dark shadow of 'it is not good enough, not perfect, someone else could do better, I must do better next time' - a love-hate striving relationship with my own art and a sense of impending failure that comes from a world where the goals are all placed in the wrong direction.

When I began to make these sculptures, I have never felt so at peace with my own creative heart. It is as if striving and time-frustration cannot find a resting place; they must leave. I must strive only to weave peace, joy and the presence of the Spirit into these works of art so they can release what God wants them to release: His holiness, His presence, His healing. From the simple beginning of asking for blueprints, a dam burst – more sculptures have followed, but also the immeasurable joy of being commissioned to be one of the gate-openers, calling the artisans and the creative DNA of God's people back to life and value. Even in these early days, the army is rising and the gatekeepers must open the gates in faith, building atmosphere, making seemingly crazy pieces of art, experimenting with new business strategy, trying new divinely inspired ideas or whatever it is that we are asked to do.

We must encourage others to do the same where we see the Spirit at work, until we understand it is not at all crazy – it is supernatural and divinely creative. In the journey so far, the restoration of Holy Spirit creativity in my own personal life has been like walking through a dream. My gift was buried in the box marked 'little worth, only for your spare time'. But with two children and a full-time job, I had little spare time, and what is the point in using it or something of little worth anyway? When worth was returned to me, it exploded all over my spare time, my work time and my family with such glorious new life and joy I knew it could not compare to its shallow counterpart: the artistic passion I had grieved from art college days, the last place I allowed to indulge such passion.

But we are given much because the objective changes; these blueprints are not to give me a personal stage, an accolade to flaunt, or an impressive career path. They are to release prophetic message in faith so someone else can be touched and draw more deeply into God's presence; someone else can get free and become impassioned. That's the kind of creativity He wants for each one of us. The countless rewards for us are just part of the deal when they are not our main objective.

PERFORMANCE TO PRESENCE

We are schooled by the world for a personal stage. The end goal of artistic and ingenious prowess, the highest accolade, is that we are given great fame and credit for our work. I trained in fashion and textiles at an esteemed college in London that has produced many famous fashion designers like Alexander McQueen and Stella McCartney. If you have ever seen the 90s comedy 'Absolutely Fabulous', I do not remember it being so far away from that environment. But beneath the extraordinary level of talent and glossy exterior of fame was a brutal environment, and the message for us young designers seemed clear from the outset: you must either reach fame or become a loser. Mediocre was tantamount to failure - unspoken, but between the lines. Fame was the focus and you were to work as hard as humanly possible to get there and stay there. I did not know God at that time, and during those four years it seemed that any innocence I may have entered with was chewed in the mashing system.

Damien Hirst is deemed the richest artist in the world; he is much hailed for projects like those involving chopping animals in half and storing them in formaldehyde. While researching I found some interesting things; a film showing that some extolled original ideas were in fact done by others before. His art provokes shock and questions. One absorbing piece is called 'I Am Become Death, Shatterer of Worlds'. Its form is similar to that of a three-pane stained glass window, but made from thousands of butterfly wings. Once you get over the thought of someone pulling thousands of butterflies apart, the symbolism is very telling.[5] Butterflies speak of transformation, windows of revelation - Jesus was the shatterer of worlds. Damien Hirst has done much art with a religious theme, yet does not profess strong Christian views; he is seeking, exploring. He once said, 'You just want someone to tell you, you are great'.

We are schooled in many ways to be competitive, and while there is nothing wrong with a little healthy competition to spur us on to higher standards, it rules the world of the creative. We seek to become better than another, to be seen as more talented, more gifted and therefore more valuable. Our self-worth becomes completely wrapped up in our gift, and many live their life constantly striving for empty success or with the dark cloud of failure and rejection hanging overhead. That was what I experienced in the world of creativity; it was all about obtaining the value and favor of man, not of God, because we have made it all about performance and not presence. Even within areas of the church, we have not seen its true form or understood its true purpose.

At some level we have all been told this message from the world, and without realizing it we have often developed our thinking and goals accordingly, seeing success as how man responds, how man rewards. But God's Spirit does not share the stage, and Jesus did not teach us to aim for personal stages - we are to give up our own life to serve others. To truly change direction and begin to release creativity and art that has the power of God on it and can change atmospheres, we must aim to move in the completely opposite spirit from the world: to be completely free from misguided competition, not to aim to be seen as better than someone else but to work in unity, lifting one another up.

If you are super-gifted in some creative area, then look to see how you can be a blessing to other people or find someone to teach and raise up. If we channel all our energy into selfish ambition we will be a slave to the values of the world, and we will be rewarded by its values with feelings of failure, constantly self critical, striving for success and recognition. Whatever we bow to has power over us. Many creative Christian people who have trained in or learned from this world system have this ingrained within them, and it is at war with the other parts of our Christ-like nature. But so often we have not been shown or told that this value system still remains within us, controlling our creativity; and so we bring that into the church and try to make it about performance, looking for a stage instead of seeking to make blueprints from heaven that have a specific purpose.

The other struggle has been that frequently there is nowhere for the creative outlet to go at this stage in the church. Creativity is still seen as irrelevant and lacking purpose in many quarters, and so people become frustrated and sometimes disappointed. However, I believe God is restoring its purpose with understanding and revelation; it's not just about an increase of art. There is a restoring of its wider message, so it becomes embraced by the whole church, where it can bless and serve, bringing strength.

In seven years of college and thirteen years in the field as a professional designer, I have never felt so in harmony with my creativity and what I am producing. Not because it is perfect - we should always have the goal of improving our skills and aiming for God's best - but it is because I have been delivered from the prison of worldly expectation and perfectionism. The goal of my creative works is not to give me rave acclaim but to point to the Creator Himself.

I have shared part of my new journey to explain how different it is from my previous training. I do not come up with all the ideas myself and then try and make it happen as I was taught to do in Art and Design College. I try to plumb the deep wells and ask God what He wants me to do, to reveal, to form, to discharge into an atmosphere. What does He want me to make in partnership with Him to the best of my ability? When pieces or projects are finished, whether sculptures, or atmosphere designs, teaching or writing a book, it is not all about my capabilities. I cannot claim the originality all for myself because the ideas and outworking came from a collaboration with the Holy Spirit to champion Kingdom.

Kingdom always seeks to bring others healing, grace, the embrace of the Spirit and the liberation of their own creative DNA. An excellent spirit does not seek a personal stage, strive for riches or strive to be known. It offers freely back to God all He has given, and that's when He can use us in ways that are beyond our own summation of ourselves or our gifts. We are to aim for a superlative spirit, the quest being presence, not performance.

WELLS AND SOURCES

It was another of those epiphany moments, but this one was way back, my first year as a Christian. I had just left another life-changer of a conference and, as I sank into the seat on a London train, my heart was full and the Spirit was chatting with energetic excitement as we revisited the weekend's events. Then we hit the subject of my art, my most precious focus in the years of young adulthood before I had collided with God.

I saw a well open, but not a good one, and a revelation proceeded to blast me off the mountain of my art education with a stick of Spirit dynamite. I had been plunging the wrong wells as vision for my artistry, educated and encouraged to find inspiration from any source imaginable, without an ounce of Kingdom wisdom or boundary. My art works appeared before my eyes, inspired by seemingly harmless sources during their conception. Now I saw the foreboding darkness disguised among the Egyptology, the decorative forms of native Indian spirit guides, the energy obtained from personal pain and striving, the years of work hard then play hard in places designed for the lusts of the soul. All of it had been channeled into creative works, along with the aims of self promotion, acknowledgment and triumph, and I saw the deathly outcome of it all. I never realized until that moment that the bucket in my hand was black, as I drew from these sources. I was stunned. Yet, the self-disgust was replaced by the promise that God would now teach me to drink from the wells of the Spirit and to produce art and creativity from that source. It was as if I had just left a dimly lit room and walked smack bang into full sun, remaining dazzled for hours.

Inspiration must come from somewhere to propel action. All sorts of creative skill is trained to draw from wells, be it in business or media, fashion or science. There is the well of the soul producing a commentary on emotions, perceptions, ideals, life's experiences and so on, but its parameters are found in the soul of its creator. So, even if the outcome is technically of a high standard, its result is limited, sometimes shallow and often repetitive in theme. There is also the dark well of the enemy inspiring creatives to produce work through which his characteristics are disseminated. We do not have to look too far to find a great volume of this, especially in film and television. If we are trying to grasp the fact that the Holy Spirit can rest upon and radiate light through an art form or type of creativity, then we must also see that a wrong spirit can rest upon creativity that is darkly inspired. It is a mistake to think that, because a creative work is only a TV program, a painting or a fashion line, it is therefore harmless. If what it produces lies outside Kingdom principles, then it affects people, their perceptions of the world around them and, in turn, how they respond. For example, women respond to fashion that dictates wafer thin body shape as beauty, and the response is that many women in our culture feel they are not beautiful or lovable enough because they do not look like models or fit tiny sizes.

I was in an art gallery last year with my family on a visit to Aberdeen. There among the beautiful architecture of the building, we stood in the lobby surrounded by some of the gallery's most prized works: a Tracy Emin, a Damien Hirst. I turned to see a large, imposing painting of someone's portrait, but it carried such a darkness that both my children were instantly afraid and we quickly left the room. I was not afraid of what rested on that painting, but I recognized how quickly they were affected and I realized there was an atmosphere of seeping evil being released by several paintings in that area, and confusion from others. Some were just shallow commentaries on the world with expensive price tags. It struck me how the girls and I felt the weight on that painting. As we all daily practice listening and being sensitive to the Holy Spirit, the flip side is that discernment sharpens to what is also dark. A spiritual presence rested on that canvas, a foreboding that extended beyond its mere image – much like the fear instilled by a horror film, even though you know it is actors and fake blood, it seeks to leave the mark of fear if unchallenged.

So, if that is possible and currently all around us in the world, let us consider what would happen if God's people reclaimed their DNA for this area and started to produce all sorts of solutions and artistic works that carried the Spirit of God upon them; works that can alter atmospheres. I have seen God speak to people through paintings while they simply looked, as they felt the magnetic pulse of the Spirit reaching their heart. Testimonies tell of people being radically healed through Spirit-inspired art and innovation.

For years I had been drawing from the wrong wells in ignorance, and my gifts needed cleaning up. Repentance is the most amazing scrubbing brush we will ever be given; it purifies what we have, then God restores a much greater volume because our vessels can now contain increased heavenly glory. We become trustworthy to minister more revelation. First we must lay down all that we have and ask to be cleaned. After my early bombshell, I actually destroyed volumes of art that were darkly inspired; although this was costly at the time, what has been returned to me in the journey outshines the greatest of worldly acclaim, because I get to walk in light and not darkness

CLEAN THE PIPES

We must all allow God to clean us up. We are vessels through which the Spirit can flow, but He does not want to meet lots of undesirable grunge in your spiritual ducts. It limits the process and the outcome to less than intended, and frustration bites. We must examine what wells have been our source, not only the artisans, but all of us. It is time to ask the Lord where have we gone for inspiration, energy, solutions, ideas and gifts?

We need to repent of where we held the black bucket in our hand and drew from the wells of the soul, the world and the enemy to fuel the gifts that He gave us. Next, where have we used our gifts for the wrong reasons, looking for recognition, success and personal accolades; striving to achieve these things as slaves to the world system? There may be a season of disappearance, of reduction, as our gifts are buried for a while in the refining of motive to prepare us for destiny. We must not fear a season of gift-hospitalization, a time of surgery to extract the cancer - the great healer knows His work well and, once restored, it will be the journey of a lifetime.

Spiritual Gifts and Ministries

Gifts could be described as a special ability, something freely given. We have all been given spiritual gifts from God to live a life full of meaning and Kingdom objective. As well as spiritual gifts, we will have abilities and skills, things we seem to have aptitude for. We normally develop these so they become part of the line of work we follow or things we like to do in our spare time. But how much do we distinguish and progress the spiritual gifts God has given us? So often the principles in the natural world mirror the spiritual world to help us understand the methods at work. Spiritual gifts are also bestowed to us rather than earned but, just like other gifts, they are embryonic and need maturation.

The Church Box

Sometimes the use of many of our spiritual gifts (listed in 1 Corinthians 12:8-11) are kept for church settings alone and remain locked in this reservoir, but they are potently effective in the world. A pastor's heart can be the very thing that's needed in an office or a youth program full of hurt, wandering individuals seeking navigation and compassion. As we immerse in deeper waters to fulfill the mandate of the great commission, let us consider a broader scope. If the only place a pastoral gift can serve is from the front of a church, then that limits the options of those appropriately gifted and does not address the many hurting people out there as well as caring for the existing flock. Spiritual gifts can either be limply lying on an abandoned dusty shelf or full of invigorated life, coursing with the breath of the Spirit. We have a choice.

And he gave some, apostles; and some, prophets; and some, evangelists; and some, pastors and teachers; For the perfecting of the saints, for the work of the ministry, for the edifying of the body of Christ: till we all come in the unity of the faith, and of the knowledge of the Son of God, unto a perfect man, unto the measure of the stature of the fullness of Christ: That we henceforth be no more children, tossed to and fro, and carried about with every wind of doctrine, by the sleight of men, and cunning craftiness, whereby they lie in wait to deceive. Ephesians 4:11-14

The main purpose of the five-fold ministry roles is actually to make the body effectual. It is not just to personally accomplish Kingdom work but to multiply ourselves, as it were, mobilizing the gifts in others. Growing maturity should lead us to prepare a spiritual environment that eases the way for others to fulfill Kingdom ventures. However, we often define what each role looks like and regularly assign them to church meetings, then categorize an age range and whether male or female in some areas of the church. But God is starting to wire in a little TNT around those perceptions as He assembles His people in these ministry roles in ways that will not fit our current perception. We will need to consider such things as an apostle to the business world or the mountain of the arts, an office pastor or a prophet to the mountain of media, and begin to increasingly understand these roles to support the people within them.

1 Corinthians 12:8-11 also lists the spiritual gifts given to empower the body of Christ. It lists words of wisdom, words of knowledge, faith, healing, miracle working, discerning of spirits, tongues, and tongues with interpretation. Romans 12 also lists the gifts of administration, encouraging, giving, serving, showing mercy and prophecy.

1 Corinthians 14:1 tells us to eagerly desire the spiritual gifts, especially prophecy. We mainly assume prophecy is spoken with words, with perhaps the odd 'prophetic act', but with this mind set we limit God.

But he who prophesies speaks edification and exhortation and comfort to men. 1 Corinthians 14:3

If we consider prophecy to be mainly spoken, then let's think about what 'spoken' looks like. We probably picture our own communications, speaking to each other in person or on the phone, but when we envision God speaking to us, we would never consign it to such small territory. We know of the still small voice, dreams, visions, pictures, scriptures, sermons, nudges, knowings; He speaks to us through other people, through the actions of our children, through nature, even through film and dance, through music and so much more. 'Speaking' can be conveyed in innumerable ways to impart spiritual message and effective power, but again stone-cold logic tries to limit and box the ways this can manifest. We need to uncover the depth of Kingdom communication again. Prophecy declares, it changes the atmosphere, it releases something in the heavenlies. Why do we think it is mainly limited to the human voice when God has given us so many creative gifts, so many ways to express His messages?

The gifting of God needs the connection of Spirit blood-flow to bring forth life. Equally, people can take their God-bestowed gifts and tap the soul or pernicious darkness with detrimental effect. For example a clairvoyant may have a revelatory gift from God, but they plug the source of darkness and work through soul not Spirit, producing known information and guesswork for future events.6 Or instead of being apostles in the Kingdom, prideful, controlling leaders and managers arise that dictate, coercing people to fulfill their vision. Teachers can become lost in head knowledge, teaching independently from the life-giving wisdom of God breeding confusion or empty knowledge. There is some excellent teaching already written on the spiritual gifts, and so this subject is worth further investigation outside this book (see recommended resources[7]).

We need to consider what happens when we connect these spiritual gifts with the skills and abilities developing in our lives such as business acumen, a medical career, engineering, working with children, etc. Our spiritual gifts should interface with and empower our natural abilities, so they can also become vehicles for the spiritual gifts. We can presume that a prophetic gift looks like someone giving a 'word' at the front of church on Sunday, but we endanger a narrow passage for the administration of the spiritual gifts, and the spacious intention of their effect. From my early years as a Christian, my passion for the prophetic has lead me to seek further training and understanding from ministries who specialize in teaching about this area of scripture. It is not the remit of local church to be able to specialize to the nth degree on every gift and area of service, and so we can seek more in-depth input while learning and participating fully with a local church family.

After years of training and practicing the revelatory gifts, I was catapulted into an entirely new consideration when someone put two words together for me: 'prophetic evangelism'. The connection had never even crossed my mind; the words collided to form a commission and ripped an internal space that could only be sated with its fulfillment. Several years of leading outreach teams and joining others like the Burning Man Team, has led me to be utterly convinced that God can energize natural abilities and learned skills, firing them with spiritual gifting that takes us galaxies beyond personal qualifications. If we answer the unconventional call and consider new blends and paradigms, we can find ourselves up to things we thought only adventurous Bible characters got to do. There are many new recipes to come – the mixing of spiritual gifts and natural abilities for use in unexpected ways that are hard for us to preconceive, much like trying to imagine new colours we have never seen before. There are combinations to deepen our worship, and others that will enable us to break into areas of culture where it has not been previously possible.

SPIRITUAL INTELLIGENCE
While digging with a large spade and becoming more convicted of the importance to signpost a new and more expansive wisdom coming to God's

people, I came across a message that is being developed by Kris Vallotton of Bethel Church on spiritual intelligence.[8] He shares further foresight concerning our consistency of body, soul and spirit. Latterly only intelligence quotient or IQ was recognized, which has to do with the area of body, or more specifically brain, competency to process information. In more recent years it has also been recognized that people have an emotional intelligence or EQ. This is a competency to identify, assess and control the emotions of oneself and of others, or the processing of information through the soul.

He now defines a third category called spiritual intelligence, which describes the ability of our spirit to process information; it is a degree of capability to discern and understand things in the spiritual dimension of our world and not just the natural dimension of the five senses. He goes on to outline how some spiritual gifts fall into the category of spiritual IQ. There is the gift of discernment, which allows us to identify spiritual entities that influence people, groups and geographical areas; it also helps to determine where people are in their levels of spiritual maturation. The gift of knowledge qualifies us to fathom things about our natural world through communication with the realm of the Spirit. The gift of wisdom gives us the competency to rightly apply knowledge in a way that builds for the future. The gift of prophecy is the capacity for foresight, to see the future before it happens and the ability to understand a person, organization or geographic location's divine purpose.

Then Vallotton highlights that through the mind of God we have the ability to process all aspects of life from an eternal and multidimensional perspective through the supernatural connection to the Spirit. Life becomes poured through a filter that does not limit, but sees Heaven's resources and infinite probabilities that transcend the laws of physics and the restrictions of physical realities. As we combine our potential spiritual intelligence with new heavenly wisdom, there will be profound results.

However, we speak wisdom among those who are mature, yet not the wisdom of this age, nor of the rulers of this age, who are coming to nothing.

But we speak the wisdom of God in a mystery, the hidden wisdom which God ordained before the ages for our glory, which none of the rulers of this age knew; for had they known, they would not have crucified the Lord of glory. But as it is written: "Eye has not seen, nor ear heard, nor have entered into the heart of man the things which God has prepared for those who love Him." But God has revealed them to us through His Spirit. For the Spirit searches all things, yes, the deep things of God. For what man knows the things of a man except the spirit of the man which is in him? Even so no one knows the things of God except the Spirit of God. Now we have received, not the spirit of the world, but the Spirit who is from God, that we might know the things that have been freely given to us by God. These things we also speak, not in words which man's wisdom teaches but which the Holy Spirit teaches, comparing spiritual things with spiritual. But the natural man does not receive the things of the Spirit of God, for they are foolishness to him; nor can he know them, because they are spiritually discerned. But he who is spiritual judges all things, yet he himself is rightly judged by no one. For "who has known the mind of the Lord that he may instruct Him?" But we have the mind of Christ. 1 Corinthians 2:6-16

Paul showed us in this passage that we have access to wisdom that transcends the wisdom of the world. Only the spirit can comprehend the things of God's Spirit, and so we need to develop spiritual IQ, intentionally maturing our ability to hear from God clearly and regularly, so that we can mine the wisdom available. He has given us the 'mind of Christ' at great expense and cost to Himself. It is claimed by scientists that people only use a fraction of the brain potential they actually have.

The same could be said of our spiritual potential; with all these gifts, the mind of Christ and the provision of the Holy Spirit to teach and train us, how much of our spiritual capacity do we actually use? How much more could we activate? Jesus said we would do greater things than He did on the earth (John 14:12). It is very timely for us to consider this area so that we can provide answers in the failing world around us, truly representing God, rather than operating at a low level of potential. In the New Testament it says that God would give us things we have not thought of because we have the mind of Christ (1 Corinthians 2:9); this is the gold waiting for us to quarry. We can tap the wisdom from another age that's hidden in a mystery.

CLOSE

After salvation, the master key is close relationship with God, one of intimacy and integrity, fatherhood and friendship. Jesus said to his disciples:

Greater love has no one than this, than to lay down one's life for his friends. You are My friends if you do whatever I command you. No longer do I call you servants, for a servant does not know what his master is doing; but I have called you friends, for all things that I heard from My Father I have made known to you. John 15:13-15

We can enter all the wisdom and ingenuity we need but the key to Heaven's warehouse is a relationship with God. As we live in increasing obedience and intimacy, we transform from servants to friends and a closer collaboration is formed. In my twenties, shortly after the completion of my honors degree, I fell ill with chronic fatigue syndrome (also known as ME). I had reached the place of obvious mess that so many reach while living a life that excludes God. I ran fast and far to escape childhood pain, first to another country then headlong into an environment of training that only applauded workaholic perfectionists. Eventually my body revolted and packed up for two long years; from super-frenetic to enforced stillness, and in the hollows of utter frustration I finally stayed still long enough to hear God's entreatment and I began to listen. Before any public declarations of herculean life change, I had a series of supernatural experiences during prayer. With no one around to explain or reduce them, they were what they were - precious and unidentified.

In an early conversation of genuine pursuit, I was trying to chat with God as best I knew how, when the room around me disappeared. I was standing on a beautiful tropical beach with a lush forest backdrop. The sun suspended before me, an immense ball of fire dipping the water of the ocean, resplendent on horizon's throne. A man appeared beside me, incandescent in white, and I understood this was Jesus. We talked, oscillating with delighted laughter, and I could not remember the last time I had laughed with such lightness. I could run, dance and cartwheel, things that had now eluded my natural body, and as I exclaimed the wonder of those returned abilities in that moment, I also professed the sadness that they were no longer mine in reality. His reply was unexpected: 'You will be healed'.

We sat together on the beach for a long time facing the flaming beauty of the sun, embraced by the warm reaching rays; then it connected, this was the Father. Enveloped in their collective presence, the infinitely powerful Creator and the compassionate man that sat patiently beside me, there was the sense of complete acceptance that I had never encountered let alone thought possible, and it broke my rigid, injured heart. Finally we stood as Jesus extended his cupped hands towards me containing something alight with fire; I looked to see a red orchid flower, which He then placed in my hands. 'This is my heart', He said, 'and I am giving it to you'.

I jolted as the world around me returned with the abrupt normality of a human being, a real one, home from work; and it was a real room and I had been there all along, but not there. I had barely encountered church at that stage, and had not made a commitment to follow Christ or even heard there was such a thing as a vision. I had earned no special merit and my life was a decomposed mess, but one thing I had been doing was seeking His presence - in the still and the tears I had waited and asked for His presence.

That was fifteen years ago and my experience of God's desire to connect, to speak with us and to show us things has never diminished. It is not that we have some unique one time salvation experience because that's a bit like someone wooing us into marriage then chatting to us once a month if we are lucky. That is not the passionate lover of our souls described in the Bible. A few months after the vision, I attended a healing conference and was healed of ME, making a public affirmation of faith. I can still remember traveling home on a London tube in the most mystifying bubble of peace, the strangest non-chemical high I had ever experienced, which made the natural world seem surreal and my new-found eternal home feel like a dramatic reality.

So many of us know these verses:
I am the Good Shepherd; and I know and recognize My own, and My own know and recognize Me - the sheep that are My own hear and are listening to My voice; and I know them, and they follow Me. John 10:14, 27 (Amplified Version)

Behold, I stand at the door and knock; if anyone hears and listens to and heeds My voice and opens the door, I will come in to him and will eat with him, and he will eat with Me. Revelation 3:20 (Amplified Version)

These passages may be familiar, but have we grasped that it is about so much more than presenting our lists to God at prayer time, or expecting to only hear an eternal message through the sermon on Sunday? There is a multicoloured world of extraordinary ways He can speak to us, as outlined before, and He wants us to explore His supernatural world with Him. God can and will speak to us through anything He chooses; frequently it is through everyday events and objects around us, signs in nature, people we know and those we do not. World events and shifting seasons speak His message for those who have ears to hear. One friend of mine receives fascinating directive through movies; I am discovering God can certainly speak through the arts in extraordinary ways. There is nothing God cannot communicate through, if He chooses, but the pivotal question is: do we hear Him?

In the elementary stage of my Christian faith, I had started to hear from God and began to presume that many of the rumblings inside my head might be from this divine source, especially when praying for another person or situation. Thankfully, this stage coincided with John Paul Jackson's arrival to Scotland, to teach his foundational course, 'The Art of Hearing God'. Compulsion booked my place and I devoured the material with astonished awe, but it was also like a year's supply of groceries in one weekend - it would need to be ruminated and considered in smaller meals. I spent the following year searching the Word to better understand the communications of God, weaving through Corinthians into the wonders of Daniel, until I realized that what I had begun to bud was potential revelatory gifting, not a fully mature oak in microwave timing. There was no effortless turning of a tap that afforded me perfect discernment and exactitude, with no room for blunder. Instead I understood the door agape before me was the invitation to enter an otherworldly journey of gradual maturation, with a thousand possibilities. My relationship with God and the road ahead now looked completely differently.

Many of us have heard the analogy about the bride and groom on their wedding day, lovingly taking their vows, after which the groom hands the bride a book and says 'there you are darling, if you ever want to ask me anything or talk to me ever again, all you need to know is in this book; so we will not talk again from this point onwards!' That may sound ludicrous, indeed callous, but you may be surprised how many of God's bride live with the belief that such are the expected ethics of God; perhaps the odd platitude will be extended if we are in a desperate dilemma or on very well-behaved days. However, an open heart can be greatly guided by good teaching from people who have plumbed this subject, helping us to take the cold mystery and turn it into a profound, intimate connection that does not recede. We can have the most delectable ingredients lying all around the kitchen, but without bringing them together, the wedding cake stands as raw ingredients. Flour is dry to taste, moments of clarity like a few raisins, a little milk like one-way prayer; and a finger dipped in the icing mix is so momentous in this disconnected cake that it is remembered for years as the day God reached down and spoke. Yet God's intention is for us to be passionate bakers in the kitchen with Him; blending, whipping, laughing, chatting, asking, seeking, and growing in understanding in a developing thriving relationship that brings together the ingredients until the most extraordinary wedding cake is complete.

We make it so complex, but we are repeatedly-modeled heavenly paradigms through the natural world. If you want a vibrant relationship with another person, you make regular time to get to know them and let them know you; it is not consigned to the annual Christmas visit. You are with them when it is hard and when there are amazing things to share. This is the lowest common denominator for our relationship with God, because He far exceeds the human framework; there are no limitations on His time and patience for us as we earnestly seek. Unlike us, He spans time and space, the present and infinitude, the definable and the indefinable, a never-ending source of creative intrigue, and He has all the time in the world for you. The more we dig, the more we find. Increasing, affectionate communion releases the peace that passes understanding on days when there should be none.

The 1970s and 1980s saw the arrival of new breakthrough materials to teach further perception in this area, such as Streams Ministries International with John Paul Jackson, and Graham Cooke and The Elijah House. These materials are as potent today, and have the benefit of time-added accumulating libraries of resources to help us unpack this arena more fully. The ship to deeper waters can be boarded at any time by any of us with the ticket we all possess, Jesus. An impassioned relationship with God is the greatest key to revelation and perspective for God's Word, as well as divine communications for us and through us to others. It is an access point to walking in Godly authority, healing and the supernatural power of God. It readily begins with time spent learning and practicing to hear what He is saying till we can hear frequently in a quiet room or a busy street. If that sounds frustratingly impossible right now, then the starting place is to pray and ask for this.

Having taught prophetic courses for some years, I have had many conversations with students and I understand there are frustrations and hurdles to overcome. A few will say they tried to talk to God for a while and could not hear much; so do it again, pursue with vigor, run after, chase down, do not give up, because God promises He will absolutely answer. Perhaps there are road blocks that praying and seeking will reveal; work with God to clear them, find help from others to deal with them, do what it takes and do not sit for twenty years behind the blocks feeling demoralized. Life awaits on the other side.

So I say to you: Ask and it will be given to you; seek and you will find; knock and the door will be opened to you. For everyone who asks receives; the one who seeks finds; and to the one who knocks, the door will be opened. Which of you fathers, if your son asks for a fish, will give him a snake instead? Or if he asks for an egg, will give him a scorpion? If you then, though you are evil, know how to give good gifts to your children, how much more will your Father in heaven give the Holy Spirit to those who ask him! Luke 11: 9-11

TThis is the verse God gave me when I started to ask repeatedly for more ability to hear His voice; as more came, I asked for more and more came, more understanding, more revelation. Our journey is to never stop asking, because we will never run out of new delights to discover with the Father.

SERIOUS?

If you deeply desire to spend time with someone and you phone them once but they do not answer, do you just give up? We can give up so easily and then blame it on God. He has been pursuing us for years; just because we do not know how to hear His voice does not mean He has not been speaking to us all the time in a million different ways. Now it is your turn – how serious are you? We want the impressively powerful and profound things of God, but sometimes it is on our terms. As long as we get to keep our comfy slippers on and it all happens within our programmed schedules and life plan, it is fine; but then we wonder why nothing deepens, why the taste of flour is dry in our mouth. We must ask and learn to listen, developing a two-way exchange, respond and begin the cycle again. When we hear answers and fail to respond, to cherish, to bother, we must not be surprised that God would not want to share the weighty and fascinating secrets of His heart with us.

Often He must test our hearts to see if they are willing for the process of purity, for His revelation and presence are of immeasurable value. He speaks in His grace, but there comes a point when He desires us to grow up, to appraise the true price of knowing the kaleidoscope of His conversation and sweet taste of friendship. He tests to see how deep our dedication runs in pursuing 'The lover of our souls', to see if we will just take some gems and run back to a life that exists in the parallel train track with God and not intentionally, inextricably interwoven. Out of intimacy flows the power and love of the Spirit that brings comfort, clarity, strength and ultimate rest.

Moses loved to be in the presence of God.

The Lord would speak to Moses face to face, as one speaks to a friend. Exodus 33:11

His face was so luminous with glory after time in the presence of God that the people were alarmed (Exodus 34:29). He actualized relationship; they talked together as friends regularly, He listened to God and learned that the thick glorious presence of the Lord is the most unprecedented place to be.

When the people saw the thunder and lightning and heard the trumpet and saw the mountain in smoke, they trembled with fear. They stayed at a distance and said to Moses, "Speak to us yourself and we will listen"....The people remained at a distance, while Moses approached the thick darkness where God was. Exodus 20:18-19,21

God's people need to be the very ones to draw near 'the thick darkness where God is' and find Him, not to be the ones to stand afar off watching, afraid of what might happen if we get too close. We live in a time of immense opportunity, revival and reformation; in the Kingdom cloud we will find all we need to be transformers. People are drawn to the majestic presence of God way before they even know what it is, so if we intentionally fill with, then distribute the glory into an environment, we can trigger spiritual change and response in the most evident ways.

BUILDING YOUR HOUSE ON THE ROCK

He is like a man who built a house, and dug deep, and laid the foundation on a rock: and when the flood arose, the stream beat vehemently upon that house, and could not shake it: for it was founded upon a rock. Luke 6:48

There is much quaking of world systems to come, and the building tsunami wave of the Spirit that is on its way will strike with force. It will be a magnificent time for the people of God to be about their Father's business, those who are sure-footed with a solid house of relationship and certainty in God. It is time to submerge and sink, allowing the Spirit a connection that will keep our lives solid in stance, not sucked into the whirling vortex of fear and instability in the world around us. As tremors increase in frequency and ferocity, it is the role of God's people to provide some firm confident answers for the world. If your life is fixed to 'the Rock', while others are swamped in the sinking sand, you can extend the life-giving hand of shelter and wisdom; you can offer real solution and hope and not just another fearful voice proclaiming the frightening instability of the stock market.

We are in a time of digging deep pools of the Spirit and repositioning ourselves in anticipation. Bill Johnson said that 'Revelation shows us our inheritance and faith enables us to do something with it'.9 We can ask God to reveal our unique inheritance for our time on earth – where is He asking us to serve? Then let's ask for the faith to impact it. As we progress in the ability to hear from God, we find He so often speaks in riddles and symbols. Remember the answers lie in His inner courts, in the addictive pursuit of unfolding mysteries and messages. The independent nature of man would have us live distantly, distracted by daily life and grabbing urgencies. We would take seemingly obvious answers, moving on hastily to our next activity. To find real life-changing solutions we must drench and float for a while. In that place we build on rock and receive the fortitude we need to live the principles of the Christian life. Without this, we seek man's approval, the ideas of others, answers from friends, affirmation from people, direction from the newspapers. We scrape at the bottom of dried up rainbow pools eating dust, and life seems rocky, tossed to and fro in the current climate. The presence of God illuminates all the riches He has given us, like going to a vast megastore; it is all there, everything you need. We can be guided through the shelves so we resource exactly what is required for each changing day.

He is so willing to break things down for us, to give us great ideas and starting points. God is not limited by our thinking. This book is written to passionately implore the Church to identify unique gifts and roles for the great commission and develop profound relationship with God. It is time to explode the lid of limitation and ask God to divulge new and creative ways to use the skills we have in our hands already, so that He can multiply, like the widow's oil (2 Kings 4:1-7). I believe some of us will be totally shocked at what we will hear from God, liberated from a hundred misconceptions about what it looks like to demonstrate the King and His Kingdom to those in the world around us. Jesus commissioned us to go and love people - there are tens of thousands of ways or more to do that.

PROTOTYPES

*Who will interpret the dreams of Kings? Who will move in divine wisdom
at a high level to direct their paths again?*

Woven through the compelling stories of the Bible are entrance points to
wisdom and mystical understanding that help us navigate the passage of
life with all its twists and turns. Within the stories of Daniel and Joseph lie
many parallels with our current age, and their lives model prototypes that
carry critical enlightenment for present reality. They illumine facets of the
character of God.

The following information demonstrates that there are many strong
similarities in their lives. What is astounding is that both of these biblical
characters were enslaved in polytheistic cultures with opposing moral
codes and different language to their indigenous nations. Through the many
trials of their faith was the ultimate test to stay faithful to the true God
amongst the saturation of idolatry and hedonism. The emphasis was not
on their gift, but their life stories modeled for us a long season of character
refinement aligned with education and the development of practical skill.
They exampled submission to the leadership they were positioned to serve,

despite its tyrannical nature. Both stories illustrate for us the cultivation of Kingdom character that releases spiritual gifting on a formidable level.

Daniel and Joseph both rose from obscurity, from the lowest positions within these foreign cultures to governmental posts that were second only to the most powerful Kings on the earth in their times. We often look at all the problems in the world and the prime influences atop political and governmental chains, wondering when and how Christians will make a serious difference; but God has given us the tools in our hands to rise – we just need to understand what these tools are and allow ourselves to be formed for their use at a high level. The following information is designed to help underline the parallel features in both stories; we will then examine the elements and characteristics that combined in both men to be used so eminently for God's purposes.

HISTORICAL SETTING

DANIEL: Old Testament. The story is set in the courts of the Babylonian Empire during the life of Nebuchadnezzar II (634-562BC) who ruled the Neo-Babylonian Empire from 605 to 562BC.

JOSEPH: Old Testament. The story runs through the beginning of Joseph's life with his family in Canaan to his slavery in Egypt and his involvement in the courts of the Pharaoh of Egypt. The most likely period for Joseph is the period of the Hyksos Pharaohs c.1570-720BC.

FAMILY BACKGROUND & EDUCATION

DANIEL: He lived in Jerusalem, came from a noble family, and was well educated (Daniel 1:3). After an eighteen-month siege, Jerusalem was captured in 587BC, and by 572BC Nebuchadnezzar was in full control of Babylonia, Assyria, Phoenicia, Israel, Philistinia, Northern Arabia and parts of Asia Minor.

JOSEPH: He lived in Canaan; one of Jacob's twelve sons and Rachel's firstborn. Schooled by his father to help manage the family estate, and given a coat of many colours as his Father's favorite son. He had two dreams about his future (Genesis 30:22-23; 37:1–10).

Captivity in a Foreign Land

DANIEL: He was taken away from his own family into captivity when Jerusalem was ransacked and Solomon's temple was razed to the ground. Thousands of Jews were taken into exile in Babylon by Nebuchadnezzar around 587BC (Daniel 1:1-3).

JOSEPH: He was taken away from his own family and sold into slavery by his jealous brothers, then taken to Egypt (Genesis 37:19-36).

The Captor Culture

DANIEL: BABYLON: It was the largest city in the Neo-Babylonian Empire and the main seat of power for the known world from 608 to 539BC, making it the most powerful nation on earth in Daniel's time. It was seen as the hotbed of vice, and its remains lie in Iraq.

JOSEPH: EGYPT: It was one of the most powerful nations on earth and dominated many other cultures. The River Nile was its main source of life for fish and growing crops. The Pharaohs ruled Egypt in succession, believed to be embodiments of the hawk-headed God Horus, the ruler of sky and heaven. There were twenty-nine dynasties over three millennia.

The Creative Culture

DANIEL: Babylon was a highly creative culture in this time frame, known for its wealth, architecture and gods, with many elaborate temples and artworks made in their honor. Temples dominated urban social structure –

a person's social status and political rights were determined by where they stood in the religious hierarchy. Nebuchadnezzar was a spectacular builder, rebuilding all of Babylonia's major cities on a lavish scale; Babylon became immense, a beautiful city of legend. It covered more than three square miles and was surrounded by moats and ringed by a double circuit of walls, with the river Euphrates flowing through the center. A giant ziggurat 'House of the Frontier Between Heaven and Earth' was built along with the Tower of Babel. The Hanging Gardens of Babylon were one of the Seven Wonders of the Ancient World. Craftsmen enjoyed high status, and a guild system came into existence that gave them collective bargaining power.

JOSEPH: Ancient Egyptian art attained a high level in painting and sculpture. It was notably symbolic, with a complex combination of realistic forms with stylized design. There was much emphasis on deity and life after death. Ancient Egyptian architecture was so astounding and skilled that it has become among the most famous in the history of civilizations. A capricious array of buildings and monuments were built, with many remains still evidencing this extensive empire thousands of years later. Temples to the many idols were constructed, and had decorative columns covered in highly coloured frescos of hieroglyphics and ornamentation that speak of their gods, wars fought and the details of their culture. Temples were aligned with astronomically significant events, such as solstices and equinoxes. The vast pyramids were built as tombs for the Pharaohs, and many that remain today testify to their lavish scale and architectural achievement.

LIVING IN AN UNGODLY CULTURE

DANIEL: Babylon means 'Gateway of Gods'. Daniel was surrounded by a culture where the worship of multiple gods and idols was an integral part of daily life. He had to take a risky and firm stand to continue to worship God and adhere to Hebrew customs (Daniel 1:5-16; 2).

JOSEPH: Joseph was also immersed in a culture where the worship of Egyptian gods dominated. The pyramids were spectacular burial sites for the Pharaohs because they believed their Kings were gods incarnate. Egyptians regarded life to be controlled by a force called Mahat. Joseph also had to take an exceptional stance to continue in his devotion to God (Genesis 39:2; 39:6-11).

TRAINING

DANIEL: He was trained in the language, literature and culture of Babylon for service in the royal palace (Daniel 1:4). He had to obey his leaders and teachers and had little freedom as a captive.

JOSEPH: He was trained on the job in the service of Potiphar, Pharaoh's captain of the guard, who put him in charge of his entire household to administrate and manage his estate and staff (Genesis 39:4). He had to obey his master and had little freedom as a slave. He would also have had to learn about and abide by Egyptian culture and customs.

WISDOM

DANIEL: Daniel possessed extraordinary wisdom, even at a young age. 'God gave them knowledge and skill in all literature and wisdom; and Daniel had understanding in all visions and dreams' (Daniel 1:17, also see 1:14; 1:20; 2:14; 2:23).

JOSEPH: He must have shown exceptional administrative skills and wisdom to be placed in charge of the estate and staff of one of Pharaoh's high ranking employees (Genesis 39:2–6). He demonstrated great wisdom when he ran from Potiphar's wife (Genesis 38:6–11).

CHARACTER

DANIEL: Daniel's Godly character developed while he was captive in a foreign and oppressive culture that did not honor God. He had to learn to walk in a deeper level of faith and trust, emptied of all pride. There was no avenue for self-promotion or even choice in the earlier part of his training, but instead he had to learn submission to leadership, faithfulness and intimacy with God no matter the environment. This level of character enabled him to be entrusted with revelation and wisdom to influence the greatest nation on earth in his day, at the highest level. He had to resist the temptation of pride and the indulgences of the culture available to him when elevated in status. He risked death to interpret the writing on the wall (Daniel 5) and in the story of the lion's den (Daniel 6), to show his obedience to God.

JOSEPH: Joseph was also trained into a high character. He endured the heartbreaking and brutal rejection of his brothers and was taken away from the land of the Hebrews. He stayed obedient to God and his masters even through the injustice of slavery, false accusation and imprisonment (Genesis 40:15). After he interpreted the dream of the chief cupbearer, confirming that man's restoration to Pharaoh's court, the cupbearer forgot to bring his case to Pharaoh, and Joseph spent two more years in prison, denied comfort and freedom in some grim conditions (Genesis 40:23; 41:1). He had to learn to be faithful with the gifts God gave him and, like Daniel, he had to retain his high character and relationship with God once promoted to Vizier and given more freedom and resources.

PROMOTED & DEMOTED

DANIEL: He was promoted as the son of a noble family in Jerusalem (Daniel 1:3), then demoted into exile and taken away from his family by the Babylonian captivity (Daniel 1:1). After promotion to the King's service (Daniel 1:19), he was further promoted to ruler over the entire province of Babylon and the wise men of the King's court when he interpreted the King's dreams (Daniel 2:48). He was demoted with exclusion from the wise men during the reign of Nebuchadnezzar's son Belshazzar (Daniel 5:8, 10-12), but then promoted to the third highest ruler in the Kingdom when he interpreted the writing on the wall (Daniel 5:29). He was later promoted by King Darius to one of the three administrators, over the one hundred and twenty ruling satraps, who governed the Kingdom (Daniel 6:1-2); but then

then he was demoted and falsely accused by his fellow administrators and satraps and thrown into the lion's den. Lastly, he was promoted back into position, and his accusers removed from power (Daniel 6).

JOSEPH: He was promoted by his father and gifted a coloured coat that distinguished him from amongst his brothers (Genesis 37:3). However, he was then demoted by the brothers to slavery and exile from his family (Genesis 37:28). Promotion came in the role of master and administrator of Potiphar's household (Genesis 39:4); then demotion followed through the false accusation of Potiphar's wife and the punishment of prison (Genesis 39:20). He was promoted again and placed in charge of the prison (Genesis 39:22-23). He was then promoted to Vizier (the highest official in Ancient Egypt) by Pharaoh after interpreting his dreams (Genesis 41:40–41).

DESPISED & REJECTED

DANIEL: He would have been looked down on by the indigenous people of Babylon as the rank of a foreign captive. He was despised and rejected by the other administrators and satraps he worked with, who tried to have him killed (Daniel 6).

JOSEPH: He was despised and rejected by his brothers and sold into slavery because of his father's favoritism and the implications of his dreams that his family would bow down to him (Genesis 37:1-11). He would have been constantly despised by the Egyptians as a slave and treated accordingly. He was betrayed by Potiphar's wife because he would not do what she wanted (Genesis 39:6-17), and then by Potiphar who believed her accusation and threw him into prison (Genesis 39:20).

DREAMS INTERPRETED

DANIEL: Daniel interpreted Nebuchadnezzar's dream of the great statue, revealing the reign of four empires yet to come in the future (Daniel 2:27-45). He also interpreted Nebuchadnezzar's dream of a tree (Daniel 4:19-

27). Daniel himself had a series of dreams and visions regarding the future (Daniel chapters 7-12).

JOSEPH: Joseph interpreted the dreams of Pharaoh's baker and cupbearer (Genesis 40) and was remembered by the cupbearer two years later and recommended to Pharaoh (Genesis 41:9-13). He interpreted Pharaoh's dream about the years of famine and offered a remedy (Genesis 41:25-32).

A Sudden Rise to the Top

DANIEL: Daniel interpreted Nebuchadnezzar's dream of the great statue (Daniel 2:27-45) and was made ruler over the whole province of Babylon, rising to become the second most powerful man in the Neo-Babylonian empire next to King Nebuchadnezzar.

JOSEPH: Joseph interpreted Pharaoh's dream about the coming years of plenty and years of famine, and was made Vizier (highest official in Ancient Egypt), rising to become the second most powerful man in Egypt next to Pharaoh. He was renamed Zaphnath-Paaneah meaning 'the man to whom mysteries are revealed' (Genesis 41:39-40).

Kings Reconize the Power of God

DANIEL: After Daniel interpreted the dream of the great statue, King Nebuchadnezzar proclaimed that no one could speak against God throughout the whole Babylonian Empire (Daniel 3:30). After further humbling he declared that God was the highest God to 'all peoples, nations, and languages that dwell in all the earth' (Daniel 4). Daniel worked with and greatly influenced the Persian King Darius. After Daniel was rescued from the lion's den, Darius also wrote to all the nations saying that in every part of his extensive kingdom people must fear and reverence God and extol His virtues (Daniel 6:25-28).

JOSEPH: After Joseph interpreted Pharaoh's dreams about years of plenty followed by years of famine, Pharaoh declared the Spirit of God to be superior by appointing a Hebrew slave to become the second most powerful man in Egypt, with his primary qualification being that he had the Spirit of God strongly present in his life (Genesis 41:39-40).

INFLUENCE ON CULTURE

DANIEL: He would have been able to bring vast influence in the high governmental positions, with the latitude to demonstrate Kingdom values and culture. He held fast to his devotion to God, which in itself was a powerful demonstration in a culture rife with idols.

JOSEPH: Joseph would also have been able to model Kingdom principles through his life and through the way he handled the extensive task of gathering the abundance in the years of plenty, then stewarding it in the years of famine so that many people lived. He gave the glory to God for this world-saving solution.

References for this section: 1-3

From the comparable journeys and elements of their lives, it is important to look at the factors present to learn what enabled them to be such powerhouses of Kingdom effect. Both Daniel and Joseph lived in cultures similar to the world that surrounds us today, a world that barely recognizes God in many nations, a world desperately needing solutions and breakthroughs yet unable to save itself no matter how hard it tries. God's people have been given the DNA and a composite of factors that can lead us, like Daniel and Joseph, to have some of the very answers the world needs right now, so that many people can come to know a saving God.

WISDOM

The Word tells us that Daniel had unprecedented wisdom, a wisdom that was beyond his years, even from when he was quite young. He was not just intelligent and well educated, but he accessed the divine intelligence of God that furnishes us with the advantage of heaven. From that access point we can find conclusions that we could not come up with ourselves, no matter how adept and educated we are. If it were only about wisdom as we currently see it, why are there still so many problems in the world, when there are lots of well educated people around trying to solve them?

Young men in whom there was no blemish, but good-looking, gifted in all wisdom, possessing knowledge and quick to understand, who had ability to serve in the king's palace, and whom they might teach the language and literature of the Chaldeans. Daniel 1:14 (also Daniel 2:14; 5:10-11; 5:14)

Daniel and friends were being trained for the King's service, and when it was time to present them to the King:

The king talked with them, and he found none equal to Daniel, Hananiah, Mishael and Azariah; so they entered the king's service. In every matter of wisdom and understanding about which the king questioned them, he found them ten times better than all the magicians and enchanters in his whole kingdom. Daniel 1: 19 New American Standard

Both Joseph and Daniel were noted for the unique acumen they displayed, and thus both were promoted to highly influential posts. Let us now take a look at some of the skills they possessed and how these equipped them for the call of God.

SKILLS

They both demonstrated perseverance and spent perspiration developing a level of excellence in certain skills. Blending these skills with heavenly wisdom caused a striking distinction, noted by their leadership. Nebuchadnezzar found no equal to Daniel, and Potiphar was so impressed with Joseph, a mere slave in his household, that he set him in charge of everything he owned. These are testimonies of exception. To be found preeminent in wisdom by kings and powerful people means they carried something above their own ingenuity. If we are faithful to develop what God has given us, we will be given more (Mathew 25:14–28).

He who is faithful in what is least is faithful also in much; and he who is unjust in what is least is unjust also in much. Luke 16:10

God has often reminded me of this scripture as a form of encouragement and direction. When we feel as though things look small and uphill, if we are faithful to give our very best to God no matter how small our portion seems, He will trust us increasingly. The plan is that we would end up experiencing Kingdom adventures exceeding all expectation. He is just looking for us to be faithful, hungry, humble and teachable. These were the characteristics Daniel and Joseph both demonstrated.

CREATIVE

The superlative wisdom of God is a 'Master craftsman' (Proverbs 8:29b-30), so if both Joseph and Daniel possessed this wisdom, then they could utilize the creative DNA of God. They did not merely display IQ but emphatic evidence that they were operating in the otherworldly ingenuity of the Spirit. The level at which they interpreted dreams requires a fine capacity to understand heavenly metaphorical language. They exhibited capability to bring solutions on a national scale.

THE COAT OF MANY COLOURS

It is interesting that God has used colour as an essential part of Creation itself. Can you imagine a world without colour? Colour contributes a beauty and depth that black and white completely lack in comparison. The Bible clearly uses colour to symbolize things, such as gold for the glory of God (as in the tabernacle of Moses and temple of Solomon). Colours are so important to God (Revelation 4:3; 21:19), and I think we have yet to discover increasing meaning for their existence. In his course 'Understanding Dreams and Visions' John Paul Jackson has begun to unfold greater truths in this area, discussing complex links and balances in God's divine order that involve colour.

Joseph was given a coat of many colours. This could speak of the aptitude God gives us for a variety of different abilities, but it also expresses God's artistry. When we look at Creation, its colour and order display a supreme beauty, far beyond that of man's making – it amplifies the glory of God. The colourful Creation voices its Creator, but it also broadcasts the character of a God of variation, beauty and ultimate creativity. If Joseph is a prototype for us today, then a multicoloured mantle would indicate these things are also to become entwined with our assorted gifts. It is powerful to form something that did not previously exist, like a structure or an idea. Joseph proposed new solutions that saved the world from starvation in his time. Thus this creative DNA spanned across and defined his calling – it was his destiny to use this DNA to access the strength of heaven.

Wisdom + Creativity + Spirit + Skills = divine solutions and strategies.

These elements were seen in his administration, his leadership, his ability to interpret the dreams of the king and his governance. The tabernacles of Moses and Solomon taught us what these elements could do in the church and how that can impress outwards on the surrounding nations. Joseph and Daniel are examples to us of what happens when you take 'the combination' into world culture in mission.

DREAMS

Although there is occasion when God granted understanding for a specific dream (Judges 7:13-14), Daniel and Joseph were the only two dream-interpreters mentioned in the Bible who were consistent in this skill and sought this spiritual ability. This is striking if you consider all the other similarities they carried and the comparable outcomes of their lives.

As for these four young men, God gave them knowledge and skill in all literature and wisdom; and Daniel had understanding in all visions and dreams..... And in all matters of wisdom and understanding about which the king examined them, he found them ten times better than all the magicians and astrologers who were in all his realm. Daniel 1: 17 & 20

Interestingly, wisdom, knowledge and skill are all mentioned right alongside dream-interpretation. If these are the only dream-interpreters named in the Bible and they both exhibit very similar qualities, then there is much to be learned from the coalition of factors in their lives. Dream-interpretation is often deemed as no longer available to the church and given over to the New Age, but it is a Biblical tool and is simply the ability to understand night parables, enigmas and the symbolic language that God loves to express Himself in. Its very nature is revelatory. It cannot be done through rationalization or fit neatly within an academic framework because it cannot work divorced from the interaction of the Spirit. But, to become a good dream-interpreter takes application and much effort, allowing God to shape and mold the other parts of our character in parallel education.

God loves to converse with us. However, it really is up to us to learn about His chosen methods of message, then catch and grasp them. There is nothing more wonderful than to walk with God and hear His voice, as it connects us with the bliss of heaven's Kingdom that provides comfort and direction, wisdom and acceptance, so we can then live through those lenses. Without this correlation and growing spiritual sensitivity, we can live in a very narrow corridor of the faith experience, compared to the multicoloured panoramic portion God intended.

Dreams are extremely important to God, but we have almost lost this precious form of communication and, like creativity, given it away. The New Age has readily embraced this medium, connecting it to the translations of the enemy to bind and bring erroneous message. God is broadcasting many dreams to His people, but more often than not we do not understand they are from God or what they mean. They can be a plentiful source of exclusive help and information waiting to be tapped. It is normal to spend around a third of your life sleeping; that's a lot of time to receive dreams containing directive. Although not all of them will come from God, we may be shocked at how many dreams He does send us in an effort to catch our attention. Our first Biblical example is found in the story of Abraham (Genesis 15:12-17), and we also find other Old Testament records such as: to Jacob (Genesis 31:10), Joseph's dreams of his future rule (Genesis 37:5-9), Pharaoh's dreams (Genesis 41:1–7), Nebuchadnezzar's dreams (Daniel 2:1-3).

Dreams were considered such an important form of communication that several were given to protect the life of the infant Jesus (Mathew 1:20-21; 2:12-13; 2:19-20; 2:22-23). God has used dreams at many a principal juncture in history to say something crucial, yet we now tend to think of dreams as vague and irrelevant. If God values them as important enough to use as His chosen method of communication to protect the life of His son during His time on the earth, He does not estimate them insignificant.

When Solomon took over the Kingship from his father David, God visited him in a dream and told him he could ask what he wanted. He asked for wisdom to rule Israel well and was given wisdom of such prominence it was famed throughout the world. Can you imagine if Solomon had decided it was 'just a dream' and therefore not of much consequence, as we do today? He would have missed this illustrious gifting and the capabilities it brought him (1 Kings 3:4-6). In the stories of Joseph and Daniel, God chose dreams to unbolt the door for an Israelite to rise to second in command, to greatly imprint the culture of nations and the hearts of two kings, bringing about public declaration from both as to God's supremacy above all other gods. God still uses dreams to converse with those who are listening, and many inventions, keys and strategies have been downloaded in the night watches through dreams.

Otto Loewi, a German physiologist, received breakthrough information for his work on the chemical transmission of nerve impulses in a dream. His work was awarded the Nobel prize for medicine in 1936.[4]

Friedricht Kekule von Stradonitz had two astounding dreams that led him to major discoveries in the field of organic chemistry. He told his colleagues, 'Let us learn to dream!'. [4]

Madam C.J. Walker (1867–1919) prayed for a cure from a scalp infection that caused much of her hair to fall out. She had a dream showing her to mix specific ingredients; when she tried it, her hair grew back with astonishing rapidity, so she began to manufacture and sell the product and became the first female multimillionaire through her business. [4]

Ellias Howe invented the sewing machine in 1845; while struggling to nail the mechanisms of his concept, he had a dream that gave him the answers.[4]

Dreams bring us information and inspiration for our life and walk with God. Our soul does not resist the voice of God when we are asleep, it does not dismiss the message before the download is complete. We cannot filter God's voice through our own biases, fears, hang-ups and experiences. There are no distractions when we are asleep. If we only learned to tune in and try to understand the language of God, what could He be saying to us that we constantly miss? God loves to forewarn or give a 'heads up' to prevent mistakes or so that we are better equipped for situations (Job 33:14–18). Sometimes there will be a series of dreams with a similar or repeating theme to impress an important message until we understand its meaning. But we can miss all of this by thinking God does not speak to us through dreams and visions, through the supernatural and the mysterious, even though the Bible is full of examples that this is His divine nature (Hosea 4:6). Dreams may seem full of seemingly small and even trivial things to many on first glance, but as we draw closer we can decipher mysteries that change our lives. God is the God of the big and the small; the seemingly worthless can be disclosed as most precious.

We live in the times of a phenomenal outpouring (Joel 2:28), and a voracious spiritual hunger is the clear result. The world is more open now to the supernatural than ever before, and if God's people can bring answers to supernatural mysteries, we can rise to meet this new spiritual appetite. We will explore this in more detail in the chapter on 'Purpose'. There are now a large number of testimonies recorded of Muslims having dreams and visions of Jesus that lead them to pursue an understanding of the gospel. After encountering Jesus in her dream one night, a Muslim lady asked Jesus what she should do, so He showed her a Christian man and told her to "ask this man tomorrow when you see him". The next day she saw the man in the street and declared "You are the one!".[5] Even though it is dangerous to preach the gospel openly in many parts of the middle East, God is breaking through into the lives and hearts of Muslims by supernatural means with dreams and visions – what an opportunity for Christian dream-interpreters to be able to help explain their experiences and bring more understanding about the one who has visited them. Scripture strongly suggests that Joseph and Daniel didn't just wake up with the perfect gift of dream-interpretation, but it highlights a process of life and gift training. The breathtaking results enabled them to rise above the plethora of counterfeit spiritual sources in that day.

Therefore I issued a decree to bring in all the wise men of Babylon before me, that they might make known to me the interpretation of the dream. Then the magicians, the astrologers, the Chaldeans, and the soothsayers came in, and I told them the dream; but they did not make known to me its interpretation. But at last Daniel came before me..in him is the Spirit of the Holy God, and I told him the dream. Daniel 4:6-8

Like Daniel, we stand in an age where people consult a crowd of spiritual sources, often oblivious to their dark taproot. But we have the 'Spirit of the Holy God' too: He is the Holy Spirit. As God's people we need to grapple with His chosen methods of interchange and work to translate them for a world that is looking for answers in all the wrong places. The grappling develops gravity, which in turn brings the kind of authority and ability that God can entrust, resulting in commissions of great caliber. We may not all feel the call to pursue dream-interpretation at the level of Joseph and Daniel, but we are ALL called to understand the communications of God to us, as His children; otherwise we will live as disconnected orphans, believing we have a distant God and missing a rich depth of relationship available.

God is seeking for those who are eager to chase after the excellence of His Spirit, to move into positions of prominence and influence in the societies of the world so they can bring answers and demonstrate Kingdom. These positions do not always have to look like the managing director of a company; it could be on the parents group of your children's school, in the office you work in or any kind of group in which you are able to have influence. We normally start in smaller arenas to help us grow in skill, confidence and the readiness to lean on God in that position. Joseph did not start as Vizier; initially he helped with his father's estate and affairs, then proceeded to a managerial position in Potiphar's house. Next he was placed in charge of the palace prison activities, before rising to the second in command of the nation of Egypt as Vizier. Where has God placed us? What do we have in our hand already that God can motivate in a new way? How can He kindle our creative DNA to fuse with wisdom for the place in which we stand? God wants to use us in prodigious ways exactly where we are everyday and not only as part of an organized outreach from church. It can look like impacting one person, yet it takes extreme courage to be obedient to the nudge to pray for a neighbor or to stand for something just; these are the things that grow us from soldiers to warriors.

'Who will interpret the dreams of kings?' It came at me from left field unexpectedly one day as I was musing on some teaching about the 'Seven Mountains' and reaching culture. Immediately apprehensions rumbled through my head: 'But how, Lord?'. What a thought! Going back a decade, I remember deciding to train in dream-interpretation. After taking several courses to train in the prophetic, I decided to undertake a program to learn to be a master certified dream-interpreter. It seemed like a good plan and felt like this was what I was supposed to do – 'how hard could it be, right?'.

I had been practicing prophetic gifting and I felt like I had traveled the road for a little while and heard from God regularly; all those sorts of boxes were ticked. The goal of the course was to complete many hundreds of correct dream-interpretations progressing in various stages of difficulty, so I jumped in and got going. With a job and two tiny kiddies, I had to pray for the time and the mental energy. Suddenly, it was hard.

As the months turned into years I felt like I knew less and less, not more and more. I had walked into a colossal cave with a little lamp and a little smug presumption that I knew what might be lurking in there, only to discover it had no borders or edges and the finest treasure was to be found thousands of feet beneath me. As the cave grew, so did the sense of humility and awe. One day, in the earlier part of the program, I was snatching an hour from frenetic family life with toddlers to nail some more dreams on the ladder, racing to solve as many as possible in the constant crunch of time, counting dreams like tests passed, and growing frustrated that they always seemed to take so long. The seeping presence of God filled the room, as holy conviction froze the clock and my misdirected zeal. 'Each dream represents a part of someone's life; they are precious and it is a great privilege to be allowed to interpret them', He said. My repentant heart was gifted the new lenses of heaven's high value of dreams that day. When God messages us through dreams and we are faithful to try and discover what He is saying, prayer and pursuit will cultivate clarity.

I found something else in the abyssal cave of dream-interpretation training: unanticipated and sometimes rather excruciating character carving. Perhaps if I had read Daniel and Joseph more closely at the time, I may have understood this was an essential part of the journey, not an annoying addendum to life's other activities. I pushed through many a weary session trying to interpret dream after dream, trying to understand riddles and enigmas until my eyes crossed. The deeper I dug the more I learned to cry out to the Holy Spirit who was not going to let me get off this train by jumping on the next platform in indignation. The final phase of training was an extended assault course. The frustrations of many unexpected and nonsensical situations outside my control dealt pride the final blows that produced the wafer-thin steak of surrender.

Graduation did not mark the end of training, as our journey to mature in God is lifelong, but it did switch the journey's direction significantly. God chose this intense training to change me. I had not recognized the work of this multifarious honing process until near the end. Beyond the skill of dream-interpretation, it had been nailing character, growing humility and spiritual wisdom, and increasing my ability to understand the communications of God in many areas, not just dreams. For God to grow us into the type of maturity needed to be Daniels and Josephs, we have to allow God to train us in many areas of our lives. The journey will be different for each one of us, with unique twists and changes along the way as we respond increasingly to God's metamorphosis. The outcome is increasing access to a limitless God who can work through us to bring groundbreaking change and teach following generations what we discover. There is a restricted time on this earth, but one that affects our eternity. We are living in times when people everywhere need understanding, wisdom and celestial help.

For behold, darkness shall cover the earth, and thick darkness the peoples; but the Lord will arise upon you, and his glory will be seen upon you. Isaiah 60:2 English Standard Version

Although it is true to say that we do live in times when there is much darkness around us, God has promised that, as His people, we will shine – we just need to allow His light to radiate through us. We have nothing to fear; in fact we live in uncommonly opportune times, ripe for us to plunge holy resource to reshape the world around us. Let us ask and pray to enter the repository of heaven in faith, to gather what we need (Mathew 7:7-10). The opportunities we seek can be granted through prayer, but as they open before us, an obedient response is central to obtaining increasing future provision.

In the last days, the times we live in now, God said that He would pour out His Spirit upon all people (Joel 2:28), not just Christians but all people, and the evidence is all around us. The 'kings', those people of influence and power, are dreaming again. I have met people who are having supernatural experiences from God and investigating interpretation from nebulous and even diabolical places. Pursuing instruction and practice in the ability to interpret dreams and sharpen our revelatory and spiritual gifting is certainly one way for God's church to rise and meet the blatant hunger, leading people to the true God and demonstrating His power as Jesus did.

An outpouring of dreams is part of the Joel prophecy, but what the church still lacks is a number of people skilled and mature in the ability to fathom and translate the supernatural language of dreams and other methods of correspondence. Although some are progressing in this area, they will be run off their feet as appetite increases, unable to meet the demand. We are already experiencing this in Scotland, seeing so much possibility in so many arenas, yet we still lack the volume of laborers needed who will invest to prepare. The times implore us to seize opportunity and willingly pay the cost to advance to a more profound level than we currently occupy.

Who will interpret the dreams of kings? Who will move in divine wisdom at a high level to direct their paths again? Daniel and Joseph evidence the combination for the mission field of world culture, but they also demonstrate that God is giving significant messages to people of notoriety, through dreams, enigmas and mystical experiences, and He intends to pour out much more. We are surrounded by signs in a world dominated by an interest in the metaphysical. We must remember that God speaks to the world and His children in parables and mysteries so they find clarity at close proximity to the source.

Affectionate relationship for eternal destiny is His ultimate goal for us - a life with love and power, not just access to a divine calculator. If we can interpret the messages of God, men and women of authority in our culture will come to us for answers, above the soothsayers and diviners of our day; then we can be used to bring Kingdom ascendancy, connecting them with their Creator. It is a commission worth pursuing.

Reference 6 for recommended dream interpretation training

RELATIONSHIP

The pivotal element for both Daniel and Joseph was their relationship with God (Daniel 6:10). Tested beyond where many of us would have quit, they stood fast, uncompromising in the hedonistic and often crushing culture around them. Such resolve is found in one place alone: in a depth of bond with their Creator that knows complete acceptance, worth and love. It comes through grasping His character, His heart for His people and the exceptional history of His infallible faithfulness. We can become so distracted by the negative things occurring in the world around us; but the world around Daniel and Joseph was far from easy, and they had no choice but to live immersed in its center, as many of us have no choice in modern times. However, if we would pour ourselves into a devoted affinity with God, the negatives would not get our attention and the daily struggles would not be the first thing to rise to the surface. Earnest gratitude bubbles from the spring of daily wonder by His side. Memories of breathtaking adventures on the fields of battle and victory help us to find a Kingdom vantage point when the grunge of life feels far from glorious.

Although Joseph's experiences sound ghastly, the presence of God must have intertwined so closely through his life, that he had the resolve to love God and keep going. The Lord bestowed his life with remarkable favor, ingraining him with the evidence that God was with him so he could hold fast through the harder times. Potiphar couldn't help but notice that God gave Joseph success in everything he did. The blessing that pursued Joseph flowed into Potiphar's estate, and so he entrusted him with his entire household (Genesis 39:2-6). This same presence and favor of God followed Joseph to prison:

Then Joseph's master took him and put him into the prison But the Lord was with Joseph and showed him mercy, and He gave him favor in the sight of the keeper of the prison. And the keeper of the prison committed to Joseph's hand all the prisoners who were in the prison; whatever they did there, it was his doing. The keeper of the prison did not look into anything that was under Joseph's authority, because the Lord was with him; and whatever he did, the Lord made it prosper. Genesis 39:20b-23

When the favor and blessing of God are like a palpable presence in our lives, we just keep running into His goodness and it spills onto others. No matter what situations we may encounter, if we develop this kind of presence and relationship with God, we live in the divine strength of knowing we are loved and guided – the strength of plan and purpose, even though we see in part.

CLEARER

At one time an onerous situation wove through my life involving people I had known well. Their choices had resulted in a messy fall-out on some of us who were close to them. Sometimes the situation would ebb more comfortably into the backdrop of busy life, but at other times it would surge to the forefront, presenting another round of hostile emotions. One day I unexpectedly ran into them in a church meeting; my sadness at the situation began to rise yet again, and during worship I wished for the umpteenth time they would move to Outer Mongolia and take the painful reminders with them – my heart was weary of the situation. Yet instead of being allowed to hide in the toilets, I felt I needed to worship all the more fervently, to kneel in a more public place than would be comfortable. I had been around God long enough to know that, either you answer that request, or you come right back round the mountain another day to sit the test again; so I moved, kneeled and worshiped.

I entered a vision of flying higher and higher above the earth. I could see the people involved on the ground, in the middle of a mess, playing in it.

I was so high by now the scene was miniature and I heard the Lord say 'Don't play down there in the mud with them'. The vision left me with such a sense of power to choose emotional distance from the situation, yet release a new level of supernatural compassion that I had struggled to access. I saw the situation with a new clarity, which was just as well, as the greatest test occurred at the end of the meeting when I was to stand silent before more venting of opinions from a narrow viewpoint. But silence was the obedience that released wisdom to see there was no access point for balance yet, so I just prayed for compassion and to feel the height of heavenly perspective. Cultivating a deeper level of relationship with God gives us stability, strength and spiritual intelligence far beyond our natural ability - it carries us higher, above the mud and the struggle.

A pattern forms as we look at some of the heroes God examples for us in the Bible: people like Moses, David, Solomon, Elijah, Esther, Deborah, Jonah and others, who faced more than many of us would today. However, they were capacitated to live powerful lives to impact kings, queens and people of influence and governance in the world. The vital ingredient for us is to develop a close relationship with God, the source of all knowledge and power (Daniel 2:20).

Oh, the depth of the riches of the wisdom and knowledge of God! How unsearchable his judgments, and his paths beyond tracing out! Romans 11:33

THE CREATIVE COMBINATION

Both Daniel and Joseph walked in the combination of factors that we looked at in a previous chapter. It is the same combination present at Creation and found in the craftsman Bezalel. He demonstrated what 'the combination' looked like as God partnered with man to demonstrate it in His church for worship, glory, power and wisdom. Daniel and Joseph demonstrated what 'the combination' looked like when it is taken into the culture of the world.

THE COMBINATION
Blueprints (ideas from Heaven) + Wisdom + Creativity + Spirit + Existing skill/ability + More skill/ability added by God, joined with Character, Obedience and Perseverance

In areas of the church some of these elements are well taught. But the concept that the creativity of God incorporates His metaphorical message and conversation is still less well taught, and the wider scope of creativity that God longs to reveal through man is still operating at a minimum in many places. We should take heart that there is more firepower available, and God can show each of us how to activate and live out this combination. As we seek for illumination of purpose, present and future, we may see skills we are going to need but do not currently have. We can pray for new skills or the increase of existing ones, and I believe that, as we seek to rise with faith for more expansive commissions, He is willing to equip the church in all sorts of new skills and tools. Instead of looking at limitations and what we cannot do, we can operate new faith for heaven's downloads to increase competence, capacity and spiritual intelligence for the roles that need to be fulfilled.

Over the last seven years I have found myself thoroughly surprised that God has had me developing mission teams and events. The one thing I never saw myself as was an evangelist! When I began to develop in my role, I swiftly realized I was going to need to be able to do a lot more than type in a Word document. When my generation was still in high school, computers had not yet taken over the world, and there was no option to learn the workings we now use for everything from work to shopping. Mine is the generation that received a sudden shove into the deep end of scary technology as it rapidly took over our society like an alien invasion. We were assured that all we needed was a manual, but when I discovered the manual was ten inches thick and written in a very strange alien language, I despaired. My co-leader Mark would be asked to do the simplest things, like create a table for me!

One day I tried to 'fix' something, but this seemed to have the opposite effect and left my computer barely breathing on the desk. I went in search of medical attention from my techy husband, who diagnosed that I had 'chopped the tree down and all the branches had fallen off'. It took serious prayer to redeem a hard drive that should have been lost forever. In my frustration one day, a thought popped into my head: instead of living with the fear of technology and praying in panic to save my computer from my various tree-chopping activities, I should pray for the ability to understand the technology I needed for work. Over the last few years I have not only learned to do just about everything needed for my job, but I recently realized that I have also lost the fear and dread of technology. I have learned to pray and find resolution to problems, and even cultivated lots of new tricks through following the leading of the Spirit. Trees no longer quiver when I enter a room and press the on switch. With new confidence I persist in asking for more, because I need it – technology never sleeps in its advancement.

My faith has increased to ask for more in all sorts of areas of skill and gifting, not just for myself but also to encourage others in this. We can do things we have never had the knowledge or aptitude to do before, and we can receive divine information and understanding, like many biblical characters. Joseph and Daniel took 'the combination' right into the heart of the most powerful empires in the world in their day, and God used them to ignite an explosive reaction. He didn't show us these examples so we could have great bedtime stories – He wanted to show us we have the same combination, the same DNA, the same relationship with God available to us. However, 'the combination' needs the right soil to grow, and that soil is character.

CHARACTER

The formation of Godly character secures a tough bedrock for gifting and anointing. It is hard to walk in close proximity to the heart of God and behave badly, because the Spirit convicts without condemnation; the motivation of love and God's faith in us helps us change, aiming upward. We must allow God to train our character; if we resist, He will not be able to trust us with weighty revelations, with positions of power and great impact, because He knows that we can harm ourselves and others around us. Character is the long-term stabilizer. People who focus on building their gifts but neglect their character do not sustain, and often leave a tide of debris behind them. If we want to be continual as Joseph and Daniel, a maturing Godly character and tightly woven relationship with the Lord are the factors that sustain; they will draw us to the Word, to wisdom, to humility.

Joseph and Daniel confronted many tests; the promotions and demotions worked maturation that could hold more gift and responsibility. It is God's purpose through testing to prepare for promotion - it is not to toy with us. A cocktail of unattended hooks such as performance, pride or wounding, shaken together with much gifting and anointing, can produce a destructive force in our own lives and for others connecting with that cocktail. The humility test will emerge regularly and if we stay close and stay low, we will identify the test with increasing speed and can respond appropriately.

We often have the option to pass tests more quickly than we think. If our channels are accustomed to open frequently with God, we are able to hear the reasons for the test and the response that's required more easily. Many times we can make tests a long slog, blaming the lack of clarity on the crackling, jumpy reception from heaven. But if we practice crystallizing our reception daily, it is so much easier to understand what's going on when the waves rise and roll (James 4:6). It would be nice to assure that all tests will be quick and painless, but as we keep in step with the rhythm of Heaven we find great comfort in the understanding of what God is doing. He can reveal so much to us in such times through our dreams and His whispers.

If we do not understand what God is doing we can become discouraged. It is easy to feel we must have done something wrong or think the enemy is attacking, sinking into a defeatist mire. Sometimes silence has purpose, but mostly God seeks to share with us what He is doing in our lives so we can pray, stand, and be encouraged that He is with us. He does not want us ignorant. Jesus taught us that the outcome of a close walk with Him would transform us from servants to friends, and He tells His friends what's going on (John 15:15). Part of character training for Joseph and Daniel was learning to serve the people God placed in authority over them. Remarkably, they received much favor, even though their leaders were not Godly or just, but actually dangerous and severely scary. Heads were regularly chopped off and the lion's den was not a pet parlor. As we follow God's lead with humility into the situations we live in, we can pray and expect that God will give us favor and opportunity with those in authority over us.

Joseph demonstrated the out-workings of exceptional character when he was presented to Pharaoh after more than two years as an innocent in prison. When Pharaoh asked Joseph if he could interpret his dream, Joseph immediately pointed to God as the source of revelation and not his own gift (Genesis 41:16). There is no record of revenge on the cupbearer for forgetting to petition for his freedom two years earlier, and he shows complete respect for Pharaoh and serves under his leadership, leaving the past behind and stepping forwards into destiny. His developed character is sorely tested when his brothers appear unexpectedly in Egypt, but he is able to extend extraordinary forgiveness and see the providence of a loving God in his journey (Genesis 42).

SIGN OF THE TIMES

Ezekiel was a young man amongst the three thousand upper-class Jews who were exiled to Babylon in Daniel's day. He was considered a prophet and visited by various Jews for his wisdom and insights. Jeremiah lived in Jerusalem in the same time frame, and they both prophesied to warn the Jews of God's judgment for their behavior, even though the Jews would not listen. These were very tough times, when Israel did terrible things and turned against the Lord with idols. The Word says that their behavior was even worse than Sodom, which is hard to contemplate (Ezekiel 16:16, 30,

48-50), and God came down heavily on them (Ezekiel 6:11-14). If we look at the world's behaviors today it would fit this description - idols everywhere, nations turning their back on God's ways in their governing and educational systems, and the appalling injustice in many countries, particularly against women and children in terrifying numbers.

O Pharaoh king of Egypt, O great monster who lies in the midst of his rivers. Ezekiel 29:3

Both Daniel and Joseph lived during very troublesome times, with tyrants as rulers. The Jews were in such disobedience to God that Daniel and his three friends (Shadrach, Meshach, Abednego) stayed in the faithful minority along with Ezekiel. All these men were asked by God to do some very challenging things without the support of a big thriving church behind them. Yet it is because of their faith and fortitude that God did so many exploits through them that emphatically impacted a nation.

WORKING WITH THE SUPERNATURAL

From so many accounts in Scripture it is made plain to us that there is a heavenly host on hand to help us, yet we are often scared to explore connection or kinship in the fight, so we keep this apparent enigma at a distorted distance. But we need to embrace the supernatural host and not be afraid to work with them. If we live a Christian life that does not acknowledge the supernatural ways of God in current times, we will miss opportunities to work with the heavenly help God sends us. In the following record it is abundantly clear that God sent angelic help to save his servants. They refused to bow to the idols of King Nebuchadnezzar, who was in the action of carrying out his threat to make toast from anyone who disobeyed.

Therefore, because the king's command was urgent, and the furnace exceedingly hot, the flame of the fire killed those men who took up Shadrach, Meshach, and Abednego. And these three men, Shadrach, Meshach, and Abednego, fell down bound into the midst of the burning fiery furnace. Then King Nebuchadnezzar was astonished; and he rose in haste and spoke, saying to his counsellors, "Did we not cast three men bound into the midst of the fire?" They answered and said to the king, "True, O king." "Look!" he answered, "I see four men loose, walking in the midst of the fire; and they are not hurt, and the form of the fourth is like the Son of God." Daniel 3: 22-25

We read of so many Biblical accounts like this where the supernatural realm entered our natural world and connected to work with God's people. So why does a large portion of the church still shy from acknowledging and working with heavenly forces? The enemy has successfully fueled a school of thought that biblical components such as angels, dreams and other supernatural experiences are dominated by the New Age. However, these things originated from God and have become counterfeited within the New Age - they need to be returned to the cache of the Kingdom, not resigned to the storehouse of the sinister.

RECOGNIZING DIVINE HELP

Acts 12 also tells a story of angelic help sent to rescue Peter from prison, but there is another twist in this amazing event. Once free, Peter went to the house of some believers and knocked on the door; without getting up to look, they assumed it was just his angel and couldn't possibly be him, so they stayed put. This tells us they must have been most familiar with angelic presence, and the concept of working with it – it was commonplace (Acts 12:15). In the Bible, at least four types or ranks of angels are mentioned: Archangels, Angels, Cherubim and Seraphim. God may give a revelation or instructions through the medium of these heavenly messengers, or God may Himself give a revelation, as is shown in the Revelation of John through the person of Jesus Christ. Daniel, Ezekiel and Jeremiah all saw visions and future insights; they had supernatural encounters with the angelic which carried with them responsibility.

The divine activity of the Kingdom is sent to message, strengthen and enlighten us bringing courage for the fight. The Bible teems with accounts of the activities of the spiritual realm. If we are to be God's effectual people of influence and power in the nations then we will need to learn interconnection with the assigned help God sends us. Working with the realm of the Spirit is not for Christian entertainment and not to be taken lightly or idly. The angelic is sent to help where the Kingdom is being progressed; maturity and holy reverence is required to collaborate with heaven's help, as we learn to partner with integrity, God trusts us to handle commissions of increasing influence.

In the times we live in now and for those up ahead, this is an area that needs to progress as we see the plans of God unfold, we will need to coordinate with heaven's armies. We can begin to understand more about this area by studying these things in the Bible, reading the accounts of angelic encounters and the purpose for which they were sent. We can pray for understanding to be able to work with the realm of God's Spirit with growing sensitivity. I find this area fascinating and as I have prayed over the years for illumination I have been increasingly aware of angelic assignments for specific commissions and also what is available for me and others in the spiritual atmosphere of a place or time. I am still asking and praying for sensitivity and revelation in this area, there is so much more for us to access.

I have a friend who paints in the most extraordinary way. She positions herself in the presence of God, then she attempts to capture what the Holy Spirit is saying and showing her on canvas. The ethereal quality of her work is very tangible. She often incorporates a figure in her paintings and while moving into a season of new imagery, she began to paint a beautiful dancer leaping forwards with explosive supernatural activity around her. Over many weeks she painted various versions to get the figure just right and paint her within differing spiritual atmospheres. She began sensing this image like the reality of a person with a character, a presence, a heartbeat.

While we were praying together one day and asking God to reveal the angelic presence around her ministry, I saw the lady she had been painting, but as an angelic form. As I shared this, a surge of pent-up emotion from the experiences she had encountered while painting this figure broke loose, in the sudden reality that she had been painting her angelic helper all along. The sweet syrup of God's presence filled the room.

I have often seen angelic help moving into battle position while our teams are doing an outreach or event, and at times my co-leader Mark and I have been aware of the same angels at the same time. The enemy has attempted to contort this area, making God's people afraid to acknowledge the supernatural, in case they border New-Age philosophies. Yet our Bible reveals God's help, and answer is sometimes sent to us through visions, dreams and the angelic activity of His kingdom. If we seek to keep a correct focus with Jesus as the central point, and not the pursuit of supernatural activity itself, it will serve to aid us in the great commission while revealing to us more of the fascinating character of God.

My journey in this whole area was given a superb foundation by taking the Streams Ministries course 'Understanding Dreams and Visions'. Investing time in this training or similar is a gateway to the exploratory grasp of this area of God's Kingdom. Its compelling and wondrous attributes lead to much adventure and the encouragement that we do not labor alone. Like Elijah, we can lift our vision to see there is more with us than with our adversary (2 Kings 6:15-17). If we live mainly within the experience of our five senses as Christians, passionate fire and faith diminish, life seems so ordinary and limited, and in all honesty we become dull and limited as our light burns low. He never ever intended for our experience of Him to be dry and devoid of the creative, colourful, extraordinary Kingdom of His Spirit, or to live beside it but not able to see or sense it. God never meant us to walk apart from the supernatural because He is supernatural - how can we understand more about this area of His character if we exclude it from our experience of faith?

A couple of years ago I was with a team on outreach. We were in the initial stages of an encounter appointment, and the young lady before us was explaining her current life path that focused on high-level training in various New-Age therapies. I stood to place my hands on her shoulders behind her, asking God what He wanted to do, and began to pray silently. In the Spirit I saw a pythonic snake rise from her mind; facing me, it hissed violently in defiant confrontation. My spirit engaged the fierce combat with an unexpected tactic: an inward, involuntary giggle ascended with the confidence that this spirit was about to collide with the power of God, and I knew who would come off worse. A thought resurfaced from the files of my mind, something I had heard from a fearless mission leader in recent months. He had shared that, when a demon appeared, he would simply ask his angel to take care of it. By then I had grown familiar with the presence of a formidable warrior angel assigned to me when I began to lead mission teams and events, so I asked him to deal with this demon, and watched as he snapped the head off the corpulent reptile with ease.

The spiritual atmosphere electrified as I turned to watch two more angels walk through the walls of the tent on either side and come towards me. Their strikingly vivid presence left me undone, caught in a strange paradox of trying to retain my composure for the person I was ministering to and the team I was leading, yet surrounded by other-worldly assistance. A silent conversation ensued; I asked who they were and why they were there, but before the answer came I recognized the female angel on my left as my daughter's guardian angel, who had started to appear after a spell of bullying at school. The sense of my daughter's presence enveloped (she was only seven years old then and I was thousands of miles away from home), and the tangible emotions of her absence joined this increasingly crowded paradox. 'Shouldn't you be back protecting Sasha while I'm away?' I asked, shocked at her arrival. She explained that they were not constricted to time and space as we are – she could return to Sasha like slipping back through the curtain of time to the same point of exit. She had come to help me understand I had an impartation to deliver, something connected to my calling as a spiritual mother, which this lady needed. I felt I would see the young lady again one day, probably many years later, but in that time she would find God and be transformed. Trust comes next.

Throughout the encounter the lady was submerged in the presence of God for an hour, barely moving, eyes closed, sinking. The other angel present brought further reinforcement and her gracious presence loosed a steadying strength through the strangest of days. When the encounter finished, I watched them slip back through the tent walls and vanish from view. That was one of a series of extraordinary experiences that began to change the way I understood the partnership with the angelic. I had not stumbled upon a new formula, but a realization. Setting the stage for the Holy Spirit to have expansive, creative expression allows a flow of activity that powers through formula and into surprising new creative freedoms. In balance, we must be equally aware of the responsibility such activity brings and that it needs to be handled with honor and increasing maturity. Angels respectfully come to help us and carry out Kingdom commission. We are to treat God's creations with dignity, asking the Father to teach us the protocol and mechanics of such an alliance so that the breakthrough effectiveness of the Kingdom can be dispensed.

In the summer of 2012, I led the Creative Team at CLAN Gathering[7], a Christian event that took place in St Andrews, Scotland. It was the pioneering year for this team, and a large and strong group quickly answered the call to come and serve in various areas of ministry, using their artistic gifts. In the main worship sessions, our 'movement in worship team' used a marvelous assortment of coloured banners and flags to dance and sculpt stunning formations. Live painters connected with the dance and music to produce stirring works of palpable presence. In my role as team leader, I had unhampered visual access to these areas in full swing during worship, and I felt the Lord telling me to photograph the action. I considered that my camera was fairly rudimentary and struggled with the dim lighting and moving parts, but the request was strong and daily, so I clicked. Between my photos and those of other creative team members we were flabbergasted to find extraordinary images containing supernatural and otherworldly activity. The evidence was so abundant and blatant in some, that we could not help but hear the voice of God and His loud encouragement in those tender steps of pioneering. 'I am with you, keep going!'

IN THE GRIP OF THE WORLD

If we can be encouraged that the book of Daniel holds an essential and prototypical message for us today, then there is further wisdom in Daniel Chapter 3. King Nebuchadnezzar had a monumental statue formed to represent his deity and power. He published a command that all must bow to this effigy when directed, to show utter submission to his rule (Daniel 3:1-6). This equates starkly to the present world system, as we see nations departing from God, Kingdom values (once stalwart at their core) now being squeezed of juice till barely the pith remains and base standards seep in to replace it. Nebuchadnezzar wanted everyone to bow to gold and idolatry. In the West, particularly, we have seen many years of self accomplishment and finance as the focus, and the building of personal empires and own goals, with the ensuing loss of community and 'love your neighbor as yourself'. The vacuous promise that wealth held many solutions and provided safety, security and happiness was believed by the masses. In those same years, idolatry has been rampant across many nations, encouraging the pursuit of any deity or desire; but now God is addressing those who have bowed to the gold statue (Psalms 96:5 & 13; Psalms 97:7 & 9). In this biblical account it was those in power and government that bowed, modeling the example; but then godly men in positions of influence and government took a vigorous stand, changing the heart of a king and a nation. Such was Nebuchadnezzar's domination that this did not just affect Babylon – his decrees were far-reaching throughout the world.

CREATIVITY USED AS THE GATEWAY TO IDOLATRY

Then a herald cried aloud: "To you it is commanded, O peoples, nations, and languages, that at the time you hear the sound of the horn, flute, harp, lyre, and psaltery, in symphony with all kinds of music, you shall fall down and worship the gold image that King Nebuchadnezzar has set up; and whoever does not fall down and worship shall be cast immediately into the midst of a burning fiery furnace." So at that time, when all the people heard the sound of the horn, flute, harp, and lyre, in symphony with all kinds of music, all the people, nations, and languages fell down and worshiped the gold image which King Nebuchadnezzar had set up. Daniel 3:4-7

The influences that set moral standards in the arts and entertainment industry cause the innocence of just twenty years ago to seem like nursery school. The idolatrous, pleasure-seeking themes amplify throughout fashion, film, TV, art, dance and music. There seem few boundaries to many topics, most of which offer little biblical grid or message of hope or redemption – just the themes of lust, greed, threat, violence, perversion, darkness, fear and confusion. Some creativity is now a compelling force in the hands of the world, sucking in the masses with hypnotic repetition, dulling the senses and heart to a holy benchmark and binding the soul in shadow. The gift of creativity has been developing in the world, with little substantial competition from Christian sources for many years now, and so the missives of menace have matured at vigorous pace. Some creativity remains a prevailing open passage for idolatry, a mechanism for people to worship at the altar of whatever allows them the fix of the flesh, the next sedation for the soul, undiscerning of the darkened path that is forming beneath their feet.

But answers lie in the lines of this biblical story. Even though Shadrach, Meshach and Abednego were high officials of the kingdom, they refused to bow to the prodigious idols in the surrounding culture, taking a valiant stand, even to the death. Their uncompromising submission to God protected them from the principalities and powers over that region where they served. If we refuse to compromise and blend with society, if we decline to feed on the filth the world deems permissible and popular, if we pray in faith where God requests and do not completely detach from the cultures we live in, we can help to open new entrance points into areas of culture, gateways that distribute the character of Kingdom influence right to the heart of the power. We need not be restrained by the old wineskins of evangelism, but take our paradigm from Daniel and friends who did not use religious lecture to rail against the wrongs of others – they simply modeled Kingdom principles without budging.

Shadrach, Meshach, and Abednego answered and said to the king, "O Nebuchadnezzar, we have no need to answer you in this matter. If that is the case, our God whom we serve is able to deliver us from the burning fiery furnace, and He will deliver us from your hand, O king. But if not, let it be known to you, O king, that we do not serve your gods, nor will we worship the gold image which you have set up." Daniel 3:16-18

Perhaps we may find ourselves in the feverous furnace of pressure and extreme challenge, but take heart: it was in that moment that God released the supernatural potency of heaven to do something so sensational that it influenced the most powerful nation in the world in that day.

"Look!" he answered, "I see four men loose, walking in the midst of the fire; and they are not hurt, and the form of the fourth is like the Son of God." Daniel 3:25

THE DECLARATIONS OF KINGS

Nebuchadnezzar made a lavish declaration throughout all the Kingdoms under his rule, that no one was allowed to speak a word against God (Daniel 3:28-29). Then he promoted the three godly men to positions of increased influence (Daniel 3:30). He is further chastened by God in chapter 4 with several years of exile, but on restoration he extols God throughout the whole earth as the most high God.

When Joseph interpreted Pharaoh's dreams of the coming famine and provided a strategy of victorious response, Pharaoh also found himself proclaiming:

And Pharaoh said to his servants, "Can we find such a one as this, a man in whom is the Spirit of God?" Genesis 41:38

Instantaneously he appointed this Hebrew slave with power over all Egypt, second only to himself. Egypt was the greatest world nation of that time. That is a declaration that the God of Joseph was the most omnipotent and wise God over a culture saturated with false deity. Egyptians believed themselves far superior to Hebrews, so this was indeed an extreme proclamation.

In his teaching on the 'Seven Mountain Mandate', Lance Wallnau makes a startling point: as Christians, we have been so focused on the poor we have stopped going after kings (people of influence and power). While we are called to aid the poor, equipping believers to progress Kingdom in places of cultural influence and igniting metamorphosis in the minds and hearts of powerful people could bring about considerable change for the poor and for justice on a broader scale. We need to pray for strategy to take nations, as well as the people in our neighborhood. Reaching out to individuals will always be part of our mandate as God's people, but we were also told to disciple and influence nations (Mathew 28:19) as Joseph and Daniel did. God is searching for such people who are prepared to operate throughout areas of culture and places of power.

Does not wisdom cry out, And understanding lift up her voice? She takes her stand on the top of the high hill, Beside the way, where the paths meet. She cries out by the gates, at the entry of the city. Proverbs 8:1-3

Divine wisdom awaits us in the higher provinces of God, if we lift our eyes and pursue new levels of the Spirit. It is available for us at the gates of the city, the cultures of the world, for us to reach people who do not know God and to communicate His incredible Kingdom and love for them.

PURPOSE

Divine wisdom is not intentioned for church circles alone, its turbine was also destined to collide with world culture. The key is to direct the lava flow out the door.

It seemed like it was what we were supposed to do, like that 'next step' people always talk about – such an easy thing to say from the land of sofas and coffee. Surely the gifts were also meant for outside the church? I'd heard of a a story or two of people doing this in comfortably faraway places like the USA. I remember the phone call from Trevor. He was the first of our team to go into the land of the unknown at a local musical festival, bravely setting up our station in its blissful simplicity that year. The gazebo merely popped up and the sign was held together with the wonders of string and tape. Our assigned position in the 'Healing Fields' was not quite as expected; in fact it was not expected at all in among the clairvoyants, reiki and animal healers – a mini village of New-Age remedies and the unexplained. His shrilled voice revealed the unanticipated nature of our predicament that became all too clear when I arrived, ready for some kind of undefined action. Rows of tents led to the great, foreboding Druid Temple at the far end, looming like a mother-ship over the proceedings; and there we were, a little pop-up nestled between the New Age and the free condom tent. 'If only the church could see us now!', I said. But what did we know then? What did we know of these people except what we had been taught: that they were somehow dangerous; they believed 'bad' things and therefore they must be avoided, deemed darkly suspicious.

PIONEERING

We turned into a discreet huddle to have communion and pray in a mix of fear and disbelief that we could have possibly ended up in this predicament. But what rose higher was a dormant excitement and an unfamiliar love for these fascinating people surrounding us. What could we do now?! We had no tricks hiding up our quivering sleeves. We had no idea what we were doing except for a couple of prophetic courses; no fancy ninja inner healing moves to impress the hoards of people that were about to pour through the gates of the Belladrum music festival and find their way down here to the Healing Fields. It became all too clear that God absolutely must show up or we were done for, and none of the three of us had come to embrace failure - just naive adventure.

'Free spiritual readings and dream interpretation' was all our sign said. We finished communion, relishing the moments of quiet prayer in the safe huddle at the back of the small tent - the last remnants of the cozy known. But it was time to turn the chairs round and open for business. Immediately a group of ten young people approached us asking if we were open. 'Huh! Who, us?' I thought, hoping they were speaking to someone else. In an attempt to look like we had a handle on things we hastily arranged chairs as they informed us that two of them wanted a reading and eight of them wanted to watch!! Thanks God, why ease in gently when You baptize in a frying pan?

We waited for God to speak to us in that deafening silence with twenty eyes watching us, perhaps expecting us to light up in a cloud of purple smoke. That was the moment we knew nothing we could come up with ourselves would help, no learned antidotes that worked in our familiar Christian circles would suffice. It had to be Him. All I could hear was one word, 'politics'; I reasoned with God for more but only one word repeated.

'Trev, you can go first', I said graciously.
'Oh no Charity, you can go first, you're the team leader'.
'Really, do I have to be today?', I thought and saw the abyss in front of me, deep and foreboding. Now or never, faith or failure. I offered that I had just one word to start with and we would see if that meant anything to the young man sitting in front of us expectant and waiting. 'Politics' I said with phony confidence, 'Does that mean anything to you?'

A loud gasp rippled round the group. 'They are really good! I want a turn next', someone said. 'Me too, me too', others joined.'"They are really good."

Are you kidding?!', I thought; I have one word and the other two haven't said anything yet! Something strange just happened.

'I have just been accepted to study politics at university', said the young man.

BEGINNINGS

It has not become the classic introduction to encounters since, but for that day, it cracked a ceiling and the flooding burst through. Now only one person wanted to watch while the other nine took it in turns to wait urgently for their encounter. God gave us words of encouragement, destiny and life for each one of them. The queue formed, a never-ceasing line for two days after that. Stunned by what had just taken place, we trudged back through the festival at the close of our time there, through the litter and bodies, suddenly aware of the murky atmosphere around us. Inside our pop-up haven, the presence of God had grown thick like honey, pouring out tears, healing and new reality; but out here, just a few steps away, a very different atmosphere pervaded. Silently amazed, I heard God ask me to come back, to train up the laborers and come back with increase, for I could see now for I could see now the harvest fields were ripe, and actually we did have the most magnificent tool possible up our sleeve: God!

What we needed were some lessons in how to work with His Spirit out here in the wheat fields, and thus the journey began.

The queue that formed at that hot baptism in prophetic evangelism has never ceased. The journey has woven many of us through a totally unforeseen quest of learning, going into places where books cannot take us and where the many keys of faith unlock doors to previously confounding situations. We find ourselves agreeing to crazy things at His request because relationship with God can be wholly addictive; and we learn to trust that, in the abyss before us, He is there waiting to jump together, catching, protecting, directing. Life was meant for the alive.

IDEAS

What followed for a whole bunch of us in Scotland and beyond was several years of fast track: learning prophetic and creative evangelism on the job, and we are still at it. In Scotland, however, we have seen the most unprecedented rise of various types of evangelism such as Street Pastors. Reverend Les Isaac, the founder of Street Pastors was awarded an OBE in June 2012. Pioneered in Brixton, London in 2003, it has had stunning effects characterized by a reduction of crime in the areas where the teams serve.

In 2013, it was estimated there were approximately nine thousand trained volunteers in around two hundred and fifty teams in the United Kingdom.[1] These Christians go out onto the streets in the wee, small hours to help people in practical and caring ways without trying to proselytize. They demonstrate Kingdom values without a pushy agenda, thus finding that many are drawn to ask about their faith; after all, why would anyone want to be out in the middle of the night, in all types of weather, just to help other people? It has grown hugely - teams in schools, colleges and other nations work with the police and government at their request; the massive positive impact is impossible to deny. The Kingdom of God's love advances. Prophetic evangelism teams have multiplied rapidly throughout Scotland.

In 2006, when the early beginnings of groups like ours set out with quaking boots, this type of evangelism was almost unheard of in the UK. Little groups unaware of each other in the early days have now grown into a relational network of many hundreds of labourers frequently in the fields, tools sharpened, confidence growing and taking others with them.

In their embryonic state, these ministries were people's creative thoughts, seeds from the Spirit of God that seemed like good ideas at the time. I can remember many people not understanding what on earth we were doing, yet providing the food of encouragement, because they saw something of new life, a little ember, a potential bonfire. Many thousands of encounters later, the laborers have seen countless incredible works of God - just like Jesus going to the poor, the lost and broken, those searching and desperate for purpose and value. The expedition has resulted in an abundance of healing, miracles and souls connecting with their creator in radical ways to begin or continue their journey with the one who made them. It changes you in a thousand ways, but for the best possible reasons. The religion of men no longer seems very important; the line between the true religion of God and the empty traditions and impositions of man's religion become more defined as the Spirit teaches you what love and power really look like. We begin to realize that we do not just have a few boxes that we have confined God to, but we have a few warehouses of carefully carved tombs labeled 'not for today', 'too risky and uncomfortable', 'not decent and in order' and 'not like church on Sunday'.

RELEVANT

Yet before the creative embryo of prophetic evangelism sparked life in me, I had sat in church as a young Christian knowing I was probably the worst evangelist in the world. I often felt torn between the all-consuming energy of my passionate journey with God and the fact that failure loomed in trying to convey that to others in the big scary 'out there'. I remembered the 'out there' in the life that ignored God very well, as I had twenty-seven years of it to remember. I knew the harsh realities of a life suffocating in the world, of choices made to trace happiness and freedom that seemed only to lead to deeper trenches of anguish and limitation. I was not disconnected from the experience of those who did not walk with God, yet having tried the archetypal models of evangelism, I was often met with scorn for being old-fashioned or odd, and in the end the rejection wasn't worth it and I gave up trying. But guilt settled in. Meanwhile, I was training with fervor in the pursuit of understanding how to hear from God, how to understand the ways of the Spirit in visions and dream-interpretation, and joyfully disappeared into the deep hole of exploration.

Then one day at a Christian Conference called CLAN Gathering in Scotland[2], a speaker put two words together that I had never before considered in the same stratosphere: 'prophetic evangelism'. What! We could use the revelatory gifts of the Spirit to convey God's heart to others? But that sounds possible – interesting and adventurous even. The flash-backs of dread at clearing a room with obligatory preaching moved to the back seat and eventually left the car. It was one of those life-changers, and Belladrum followed shortly afterwards.

Much excellent training has been developed on learning how to progress in prophetic gifting, prophetic evangelism and many other forms of evangelism now in use; so what follows is not intended to replace, but merely to point to some marks in the road that have been identified so far. We are not just doing outreaches, but preparing harvesters for the great harvest Jesus talked about.

Then He said to them, "The harvest truly is great, but the labourers are few; therefore pray the Lord of the harvest to send out labourers into His harvest". Luke 10:2

How can we expect to bring in a huge harvest of souls if we are not ready as God's church, if we have not learned to be relevant and ready to receive it? In recent years, the effects of prophetic creative evangelism in Scotland and various places around the globe has been astounding. Therefore we must ask why God is moving so powerfully through these tools and reaching thousands of people who would perhaps never walk into a church. If we, as God's church, will not go to the places that are full of seekers, where will those seekers go for answers? In Daniel's day, Babylon was full of spiritual sages worshiping a plethora of gods and idols. They looked for answers and meaning everywhere, building their culture on false deity and its iniquitous influences.

Then the king gave the command to call the magicians, the astrologers, the sorcerers, and the Chaldeans to tell the king his dreams. So they came and stood before the king. Daniel 2:2

NEW AGE

The Babylonian sages were given endorsement at the highest level, with permission to operate as valid sources of answer and revelation for the lives of the people. Throughout the ages this has continued to various degrees, but the 1960s and 1970s saw a resurgence in popular culture with the advent of the New Age Movement. This is a western spiritual movement with its linchpin professing to be a complex combination of some eastern and western spiritual principles combined with self help, motivational psychology, holistic health, parapsychology, consciousness research and quantum physics.3 Its aim is to produce spirituality without restrictions, focusing on the mind, body and spirit and the interplay of these with spiritual and environmental influences. It encompasses both science and spirituality. Inspiration is often drawn from the practices of other world religions. In fact, to try and define a lynchpin or set of standards would be impossible, as all that comes under the banner of the New Age seems to be almost borderless, ever changing and growing, like the altar to the unknown god that Paul found in Athens:

'For as I was passing through and considering the objects of your worship, I even found an altar with this inscription: TO THE UNKNOWN GOD'. Acts 17:23

Engaging the services of clairvoyants, healers and the like was a very strange and suspicious thing to do when I was a kid. You didn't hear of everyday folks dabbling in that stuff – it was considered dark, and even dangerous. But now it is thought of as normal, and it is available in many places such as festivals, parties or through the internet. It is seen as an acceptable practice to seek these sources for wisdom and help. You can tie your wishes to a tree, paint your grief on art forms to try and cleanse the pain, take your hungry heart to someone who seems able to tell you scraps about your life, pay large sums of money for coloured liquids that will apparently release the presence of angels; and it is all becoming very 'normal'. TV programs, magazines, telephone hotlines and the internet reveal an astounding rise in the popularity of such diviners and an astonishing increase in hunger for the supernatural across the western part of the globe, particularly, and so we must ask 'what's happening out there?'.

Joel 2:28 reveals to us that in the last days:
I will pour out my Spirit upon all people. Your sons and daughters will prophecy, Your old men will dream dreams, Your young men will see visions. Even on my servants, both men and women, I will pour out my Spirit in those days.

The Spirit of God is awakening a great appetite for spiritual dimension in the earth. People are evacuating the barren experience of man's organized religion and searching for substance. The true religion of God extends outwards to connect with love through dreams, visions and experiences that cause the urgency of answer. Out there, in their droves, people are stirred to seek for authentic spiritual experience. Many times, the volume has overwhelmed us on outreach as we find people will wait for hours to gain an appointment. However, opposition rarely sleeps, as the enemy musters his cohorts into position to feed the hungry with entrapment. Many people are seeking in all the wrong places, shopping in the supermarkets of New-Age philosophies to conjure remedy and resolution. If the church will rise to provide spiritual food programs where the people already gather, and lay down the well-worn biscuit tins for some fresh substance in relevant packaging, not only will we attract them, but we have the opportunity to prevent them opening all sorts of doors to dark entanglements that masquerade as the answer.

In the previous chapter of this book, we found that Joseph, Daniel and his three friends were taken captive then educated to understand the culture they lived within. They did not decide to emotionally distance themselves from this culture because it was not the Hebrew way of life. Instead, they had to learn compassion and understanding for the civilization God had called them to reach, so that they could be highly effective. Their close relationship with God guided them to offer their best, to serve where they were positioned – right in the center of worldly culture, close to the heart of power, and not in the confines of the church. Divine wisdom is not intended for church circles alone; its turbine was also destined to collide with world culture, so that transforming Kingdom ethics can manifest God throughout the globe.

Their example reveals that we cannot live utterly disconnected from the world, then pop in now and then for an outreach or a rant about our beliefs. There is no evidence that the currently anticipated Holy Spirit awakening involves a conviction for people to flock to the nearest church building - but instead the Spirit stirs His people to equip and advance outward to the various areas of society, to the places where famished people gather. We must depart from vague, directionless Christianity and prayerfully ascertain specifics as to where God is positioning us; what culture, what neighborhood, what people group? Next, with the steadfast guidance of the Spirit, we must find out what the people need there, what is happening in that area of culture, what the issues at hand are and where the open doorways are. Then we need to ask God for great divine ideas and wisdom to bring Kingdom transformation to those places, just as Jesus did.

We have got it wrong if we think success only looks like those who stand on stages preaching to great seas of people. That is one consignment, but if we all did that then who would fill the other roles prepared for God's people?

We work as a body, each of equal worth. If we begin with the sharing of our God-given gifts to fulfill the great commission, if we start to reach towards one person at a time and are faithful with the day of small beginnings, God promises He will take us from glory to glory. Heaven's eyes value faith and faithfulness. We just need to do everything for the audience of one.

AN ENCOUNTER

Recently our team were doing an outreach at a New-Age fair, and we were asked to come and chat to one of the other stall-holders about her dream. She was a well-dressed lady, upbeat and sparky, yet strangely she seemed only partially lucid, and heavy-headed as if medicated. It was easy to see the foreboding millstone around her neck – now we needed the cause. The dream God had given her contained some answers. I saw a concertina of open doors behind her head, and through each loomed a degenerate darkness. In her quest to gratify her hunger she had consumed a smorgasbord of suspect spirituality, inadvertently washed down with the spirit of fear. Dread was now a constant companion, and the foggy confusion of her mind had become the default clarity of her normality.

We asked permission and her agreement to disconnect her from the injurious influences; as we did, I heard loud slamming as the doors shut, and lucidity returned with each closing, until she exploded with a joy and sense of freedom she professed never to have felt before. We were then able to explain that not all doors lead to truth and that there are repercussions to a lack of discernment. That in itself is a concept that seems to come up repeatedly during ministry to seekers. We live in an age that encourages a 'taste and see' mentality; but with each tasting, evil propagates and entwines its grip a little tighter

We were also able to share that God had given her the dream to offer this wisdom because He loves her deeply and cares about her fears. In that encounter, He allowed her hunger to taste something completely different: the utter rejuvenation of alignment with her Creator and the refreshing of freedom. She still had decisions to make – to choose to walk the narrow path towards light and remain disentangled from the multitude of other paths she had deeply entrenched her life in. We gave her a connection card so she knew where to find us in this new journey. All who taste truth will never find anything like that sense of calibration with their Father God – they just need a little time to discover the compass and orientate a new life direction. We love to dictate that that must look like attending church the following Sunday, but then we limit what success looks like and forget the creative processes of the Holy Spirit.

GOING TO THEM

It was when Jesus went out to the people and sat with them, listened to them, loved them, that many others followed.

Now it happened, as He wus dining in Levi's house, that many tax collectors and sinners also sat together with Jesus and His disciples; for there were many, and they followed Him. Mark 2:15

So often in our western culture, we expect people to come into our churches; but on the whole, they do not seem to appear in our midst on Sunday mornings in large numbers yet. So, we must find out about our culture and how we can become relevant; in the world yet not of the world, as the Bible instructs us (Romans 12:2). We do not seek to compromise principle, but to understand and bring compassion and humility to the table as Jesus did. He offered the wine of radical love and forgiveness that simply melted hearts before Him. The thing is, He has not changed, and now we carry Him to people outside our happy church family camps – we carry His essence.

The very quest of this book is simply to investigate and share more of who God is because, as we draw a little closer, we see more; a little closer still and we see more and more; until we can tip off the continental shelf and plummet to new fathoms beyond our limiting imaginations, and we experience the saturation of His presence. Then we take this to others. Creative forms of evangelism allow us to explore what this might look like and the paradigm to draw on the unlimited resources of God for flexible and inventive ideas, so that we can be relevant manna for a slice of culture rather than the size six shoe that is expected to fit all.

WAVES

After my vision at Burning Man, when I was given a sword and the word 'creativity' to ponder, I began to see a huge wave in dreams and in prayer, and I assumed this was the great wave of creativity that was coming. But one day while pondering this, the Lord said 'It's not the first wave of creativity that you see, it's the second'. Astonished, I asked what the first one was then - did I sleep through it? I was shown that we were already submerged in it, water lapping all around. Its effect was the deluge of creative ideas and strategies for mission that enable a new bridge to be built from the church to the amassing hunger of searching people. The wave carried an initial outpouring of spiritual appetite, dreams, visions and experiences, and brought the creative, symbolic messages and riddles of God. It impassioned unity across churches and the action of many laborers and commissioning of evangelists.

Street Pastors was someone's good idea one day; so was Healing on the Streets[4] and all the other expressions of prophetic and creative evangelism that have surged through Scotland and other places. I still remember when none of it existed; now it is hard for us to imagine its absence, so far-reaching is the change in less than a decade; and it continues to cover distance at speed. What I had not recognized was that this was not just a few great ideas from heaven, but celestial tactics in an extensive plan to release creativity.

154

The next wave is an outpouring of God's new creativity for the arts and media; it is the activating of the creative DNA in God's people and the gathering of a creative army, the calling out of those willing to come. Encouragement can be drawn for us from the incredible results of the first creative wave and its significant effects. I see Kingdom impacting specific arenas of the arts and media with various intensities, as areas begin to change dramatically and be used for God's purposes.

As we explore different concepts in this book, my intent is to suggest that we consider the various methods of evangelism currently thriving and connect them into the wider arena of creative solutions beginning to open before us. A progression into increasing creative latitude is explored in these writings. Divine creativity needs critical understanding, or it will be overlooked and lie dormant again amidst the dried out paintbrushes and forgotten ideas of time. The circle returns to the thought that, if God is the Creator, and we are made in His image, then why does creativity merit such a small place in our faith? Seeking understanding of its true meaning will provide some large slabs of a missing foundation, as well as an abundance of colourful tools and gifts within God's church that are the very things we lack when trying to understand some facets of who God is – facets that we also need so we can be relevant, powerful and beautiful as the bride, conveying the nature of Jesus to others.

COURAGE

The creativity of the Spirit cannot be premeditated. It is wild and free; a weapon that breaks the dry repetitive restraints of man-made religion. It brings fresh dynamic through the creative expressions of the Holy Spirit. If we sanitize God and recoil from the supernatural side of His nature, then we can so easily miss what He is doing and the vibrant Christian life available to us.

As God's people open up to new possibilities and the intercessors clear the path with faith for change, we will see a surge of new innovations, inventions, illumination, art and idea through God's church - a bank of ingenious weaponry, a raw firepower rising to break the religious spirit off God's people and the nefarious influences in the world.

It has taken bravery, obedience and perseverance to go out and reach people, but the heavy prize tips the scales without question. never experienced a time when God did not show up and astonish when we stretched outward, sometimes with subtle softness, sometimes like a meteoric missile. In the reaching, we grow and find our spiritual fervor flamed to new degrees; we comprehend better who Jesus is and how He feels about people. To get out there and 'do the stuff', we must join with many biblical characters and show courage; but it changes us in a way that decades spent on a pew cannot replace. Jesus demonstrated to us spending time in the temple and time out there with the people; He taught His disciples on the job, because you cannot replace practice with theory. You cannot feel the hiding, shattered heartbeat of a person and experience the Father's curative care for them unless you position yourself for use.

I used to dread trying to evangelize, years ago, because I just couldn't seem to drum up the kind of compassion the Bible talked about or to love people I didn't know, or care enough about their messy ball of life to want to get tangled up in there with them. Then I felt guilty, like I was a bad Christian. However, I had another of life's epiphanies as I plonked myself down in mysterious obedience in front of these 'messy people' and asked the Lord to use me to bring words of revelation, wisdom and healing. I tried to interpret the messages God had given them in their dreams. They were strangers to me, but suddenly they would become the most important person in the room – my heart spilling across the void to grasp their pain and torments, and their frail hope faintly breathing. I could feel the rush of the river of God surging to fill their desolation with the unconditional embrace that surpasses all understanding. So many people are just desperately seeking acceptance and worth in a world that values life so conditionally and nurtures it even less.

As numerous young hearts have collided with God in the chairs in front of me and my team mates, we have seen their initial protective bravado melt in the safe place of relief, enveloped in the Father's approval. Hope gives defibrillation, then connects with new purpose through the offered words of personal destiny. The imprint of these encounters remains upon your spirit and soul, making it almost impossible to live in a shallow pond of faith, as you encounter God in some of the most tangible experiences. We have become convinced that Christians have so much to give that is relevant and real; the journey leads us only further into hunger to see more, to loot Heaven's storehouses for what is yet to come.

There are notable side effects to this addictive pursuit: I have watched so many Christians germinate new confidence, distinguish and develop gifts and become a fearful force for good. Many creative and prophetic evangelism teams are inter-church, often supported at the core by a particular or agreed collective of churches. They encompass believers from many Christian communities, a leaven giving rise to remarkable unity. In such collectives of purpose, denominational divergence and squabbles over ritual are replaced by relationship, the joy of co-operational discovery and the nourishment of others. As we ask God to help us become less judgmental of the people we are to reach, we must also extend this olive branch to our brothers and sisters. Their differences are trivial compared to what we will encounter in the world, when our newly polished 'non-judgmental button' will be tested out in some of the most unexpected ways. Jesus knew what He was doing when He took His disciples 'out there'.

SPACE FOR GIFTS

The other radical discovery on the mission journey is a new place for gifts. We can be disappointed with church on Sunday because we cannot see a space to use some of our gifts. Sometimes prophetic gifts are not well understood or explored within a church family. In churches where they are, there is simply not always room in the service for another word of wisdom or another prophetic offering. Perhaps your gift is music, but there seems no more space for another musician; you want to pastor, but the positions seem filled. The church is full of wonderfully gifted people, and outside our church walls people are ravenous for divine words and acts that are inspirational, affirming and medicinal to help with the escalating tensions of life. They seek illumination for the recent dream that feels so Important, yet needs explanation. So they reach for the horoscope page or the clairvoyant hotline because, for them, it is the most obvious choice for finding spiritual enlightenment. They look to the art and entertainment of the world to soothe their soul and seek the sagely advice of well-meaning friends when they need the wisdom of God.

Sadly, most people would no longer associate a church with providing spiritual answers. I do not write this from a critical personal standpoint, as I have found many answers in the church, but I am conveying our experience of being out among people distant from God – information gleaned from many conversations and observations with fellow Christians. Sadly, there is a perception that church and its attendees can be out-dated or strange, even judgmental. It is rarely beheld as volcanic and receptive, yet that's exactly what we are supposed to be. In some churches, the activity of the Spirit is charged and meaningfully eruptive – the key is to direct the lava flow out the door. God's church is sitting on stored dynamite, and the Bible clearly shows us we have been given all we need in terms of our inheritance in Christ and spiritual gifts.

For to one is given the word of wisdom through the Spirit, to another the word of knowledge through the same Spirit, to another faith by the same Spirit, to another gifts of healings by the same Spirit, to another the working of miracles, to another prophecy, to another discerning of spirits, to another different kinds of tongues, to another the interpretation of tongues. But one and the same Spirit works all these things, distributing to each one individually as He wills. 1 Corinthians 12:8-11

So why do we often feel as if we have little to offer or stay mute? No fingers pointed here - it happens to us all. There is fertile soil in the fields all around us; it is most certainly time for us to investigate these gifts and spiritual weapons that God has already bestowed. It is time to pick them up off the floor and find out how to use them with competency and power. Taking the time to learn about our spiritual gifts, how they operate and their role within the church and for the Kingdom should be foundational for all Christians. A plumber with a spanner is useless if he has no idea how to use it. The leak in your bathroom will flood your house if he just stands there with his bag of tools and apologizes for the fact that he knows he has some tools somewhere but is not really sure what they are or how to use them. Peoples' houses are flooding. It is true that the more we practice a skill or gift, the more it increases our level of capability. The mechanisms God demonstrates for us in the natural apply also to the spiritual gifts. Those who claim to have high-level gifting with no effort or education are alarming at best, and negate the biblical model of prophetic schools, character training, perseverance, patience and studying to show yourself approved.

Why are the gifts so important for evangelism? Because Jesus used revelatory gifts to tell people about their lives, to bring healing and express the force of the Kingdom, to create a bridge between man and God. He left us with a weighty concept to chew, that we would be able to do greater things than He had (John 14:12). People need to feel the contact of a living God, inhale an intoxicating Spirit, melting into the heart of the Father. When they do, they so often break in His presence.

Pursue love, and desire spiritual gifts, but especially that you may prophesy.... But he who prophesies speaks edification and exhortation and comfort to men. 1 Corinthians 14:1 & 3

Why would God say this? Because He knew that, as well as building up the church, this tool would be vital in the world we live in, a world full of criticism and discouragement. We are made to compete like tadpoles in a jar for worldly levels of accomplishment, with little encouragement along the way. The starving need the pronouncements of heaven through God's people.

Though I speak with the tongues of men and of angels, but have not love, I have become sounding brass or a clanging cymbal. And though I have the gift of prophecy, and understand all mysteries and all knowledge, and though I have all faith, so that I could remove mountains, but have not love, I am nothing. And though I bestow all my goods to feed the poor, and though I give my body to be burned, but have not love, it profits me nothing. Love suffers long and is kind; love does not envy; love does not parade itself, is not puffed up; does not behave rudely, does not seek its own, is not provoked, thinks no evil; does not rejoice in iniquity, but rejoices in the truth; bears all things, believes all things, hopes all things, endures all things. 1 Corinthians 13:1-7

This says it all – love forms the bedrock. We can be supremely gifted and perpetually reaching out to others, but without the love of God at our nucleus igniting motive, it can all be of no significance.

"People are illogical, unreasonable, and self-centered. Love them anyway. If you do good, people will accuse you of selfish ulterior motives. Do good anyway. If you are successful, you will win false friends and true enemies. Succeed anyway. The good you do today will be forgotten tomorrow. Do good anyway. Honesty and frankness make you vulnerable. Be honest and frank anyway. The biggest men and women with the biggest ideas can be shot down by the smallest men and women with the smallest minds. Think big anyway. People favor underdogs but follow only top dogs. Fight for a few underdogs anyway. What you spend years building may be destroyed overnight. Build anyway. People really need help but may attack you if you do help them. Help people anyway. Give the world the best you have and you'll get kicked in the teeth. Give the world the best you have anyway."
Dr Kent M. Keith in the Paradoxical Commandments[5]

These famous words have been pinned on the walls of Mother Teresa's shelters and in the rooms of presidents and great leaders. Dr Keith's point was that we should live like this because we do not live for man, but we do this for God and live in the source of His goodness and reward

I took part in an encounter that demolished my heart for the right reasons. We were running prophetic teams in a popular local pub/restaurant in Inverness. A couple of friends, we'll call them Peter and Samantha, came in requesting an encounter appointment together. I had an initial sense that he was gay, although there were no obvious factors to conclude that – it was just something I sensed when he entered. We gave words for Samantha, and she was greatly encouraged. Then it was Peter's turn.

I was training a fellow team-mate at the time, who was fairly new on the job and still defaulting to religious paradigms and language, tending towards preachy. He launched into a light, well-meaning sermon on Peter's need to turn to God because of 'some things' he was doing that he shouldn't be. I watched it happening in slow motion: Peter's expectant eyes dulled and lowered, and lowered, until they wouldn't engage past the floor as the heavy cloud of condemnation fell and asphyxiated. I listened, watched and panicked! This was going horribly wrong and this man was now haemorrhaging hope in front of us. 'What can I do Lord, what can I say to change this? I have no ideas of my own, but we can't leave him like this.' I pleaded.

Desperate for life-saving tactics, I felt I should simply start calling out the good things in his life: he was an excellent friend (Samantha nodded emphatically); he had integrity and great kindness with rare compassion for others (more nods from his friend, and the eyes were lifting, reaching the table). More words of wisdom and knowledge came that revealed that God had seen his kindness to others, that God was proud of him and some of the choices he had made to stand for good values and protect other people. The words resonated and his eyes were now staring at mine with disbelieving hope. I could see the God of the universe at work, streaming love that cures and words that can only come from Him.

II continued to share that I saw one very important friendship in his life, it was with a man, and I saw Peter's loyalty to him. I discerned it went beyond friendship, but I was not being given liberty to say that at this point - only to extend the compassion and connection of Jesus to this man who clearly struggled to believe he could be loved and accepted in the eyes of God.

He was still with me now, eyes wide with anticipation and agreement. In that moment of safe acceptance, I was able to share that I also saw wrestle, confusion and distress connected to the relationship, but that God was reaching out to help, that He loved him and cared about his life.

Peter left agreeing to begin a dialogue with a God he had not previously known, a journey that would seek for Him. He departed laughing, shining and hugging us exuberantly, thanking us over and over for this incredible experience. I was undone – what a roller-coaster of nerve-wracked, heart-wrenching wonderment. Our job is not to name and shame, or judge what is not ours to judge; our job is to move in the spirit of prophecy and love, obedient to deliver the words of the Father.

But he who prophesies speaks edification and exhortation and comfort to men. 1 Corinthians 14:3

It is so much more effective to allow the imaginative freedom of the Holy Spirit to show us precisely what people need in the moment and not to unleash a pre-designed Christian sales package because we believe that, if we can talk them through the information, we have success, another box ticked. I cannot tell you what that encounter did to my heart; I still well up when I think about it because I got to appreciate something of what that did to Peter's heart that day. I got to see the incredible grace of God in action that meets us where we are at.

We have met too many on outreach who have felt urged into the fold of man's religion but have then struggled to reside in the required mold, hungering for dynamic spiritual experience with creative diversity. Some people have left bruised, perhaps offended after conflict – now they are scared and skeptical. We have some history to undo, a new reputation to sow: to show Christians as radical lovers of Jesus who do not have a religious agenda but a creative mandate that allows people to be more unique and imaginative, and the Holy Spirit to be innovative.

Recommended resource on prophetic evangelism training[6]

THE GREENHOUSE

Ripe fruit can be harvested with ease, but if you try to yank a green plum off the stalk it will require force and remain green and hard. As Christians, we can feel pressure for results that must be evident before our eyes. However, if we pull out the standard Christian package and coerce, hurting people can easily feel pressurized to say something in an emotional moment, but it can lead to resentment and lukewarm believers.

In an age of hard-nosed selling, we need to be careful that our good intentions are not equated with such methods. We have met people wandering lost and hurting from the religion of man and its control. They used to attend church, but now they are seeking answers from clairvoyants. We must take an honest look at some of our methods.

Our role is to discern where the fruit is in the ripening process. Discernment is one of the most important gifts to sharpen and use on outreach; it allows the ingenuity of the Spirit to direct us. If people are not ready to make a commitment, then our job is to help them soak in the 'Son' as much as possible, helping them to ripen further. If they seem ripe, we can explore gently, following the lead of the Spirit, to see if they would like to take the jump.

The Engel Scale of Evangelism[7] is vastly helpful in understanding the process of maturation and helps our expectations to carry balance and wisdom. A religious spirit needs to control and force the situation, whereas the Holy Spirit leads people to freedom with patience and love.

THE ENGEL SCALE

+ 5 Fully committed

+ 4 Reproduction

+ 3 Growth

+ 2 Church involvement

+ 1 Initial discipleship

NEW CREATION

- 1 Repentance and faith

- 2 Decision to act

- 3 Personal problems seen

- 4 Positive to Gospel

- 5 Consider Gospel

- 6 Understand Gospel

- 7 Heard of Gospel

- 8 Awareness of God

- 9 No awareness of God

And Jesus went about all Galilee, teaching in their synagogues, preaching the gospel of the kingdom, and healing all kinds of sickness and all kinds of disease among the people. Then His fame went throughout all Syria; and they brought to Him all sick people who were afflicted with various diseases and torments, and those who were demon-possessed, epileptics, and paralytics; and He healed them. Matthew 4:23-24

Then he made them all say the sinners prayer and promise to come to church on Sunday? Not really; sometimes He just healed the crowd and walked away, leaving them to ponder. We need to trust God to direct their next step and show us where we play a part. Our focus should be on our relationship with God; drawing close, training our gifts and hearing instructions. As we carry them out, we hear some more and the adventure leads to the astonishing.

I came to God through a whole series of encounters (often in connection with Christians), some dazzling, many full of warm mercy. I thought some of those Christians were plain weird then, but there was a sense of safety, something awesome that you could not fully figure. Like so many of us, I took wobbly steps across the stones until I finally found the other side. In hindsight, we can often see the impact such Christians had on our searching journey, and how that helped compel us towards commitment. We must not underestimate the substance of God working in peoples' lives; we cannot control that or make it happen at speed, but we can find the wisdom of heaven to guide us through timing and role when reaching others.

Streams Ministries International[8] have pioneered in the field of prophetic evangelism for many years, carrying out many radical encounters with unripened fruit, facilitating the greenhouse. Now they are experiencing a wave of people coming into the Kingdom who profess to have been deeply touched through one of their teams at some point in the last decade. Sometimes, when people taste the best (the Love of God), they may have to go back into their lives and actually realize it is matchless and they cannot now live without it.

Raise the Barn

In recent years in Scotland and other nations such as Sweden, we have experienced the resonating call of the Lord to pioneer, and many have felt the tug to the front lines and trenches of evangelism. We have looked at its promising impact on the church. This evolution will continue to roll and gather momentum. Now there is another group of Christians who are also engaging with God's awakening, yet they do not see themselves out on the streets with the homeless, interpreting dreams in a bar or face-painting, for example. Many are grappling to see their place in the rising tide of conviction that it is time for God's church to reach out effectively. But if we are all out in the fields, who will care for the wheat in the barn? Who will disciple, aid and spend time with the bruised, helping them to understand the ways of God?

If we think of the barns as facilities within the church family where new seekers can be nurtured through developing connection and enlightenment, we can see the clear distinction between this vital resource and the calling to evangelism which can be the initial contact or encounters people have with God – the gathering of the wheat sheaves. For years we have been industriously trying to meet the challenge of training laborers, accommodating outreaches and pioneering new territory, but I have come to realize that there is simply not time or stamina for the evangelists to be the ones building the barns and trying to disciple all the seekers as well.

I believe we are beginning to glean the edges of the great harvest (Luke 10:2), and as we glimpse the acres of golden ears our need for determined preparation becomes clearer. Some vastly exciting and fruitful, but hugely energetic, years have left me convinced that we need to activate a bigger army if we are going to receive a great harvest. I am persuaded that God's church holds many superb hearts with excellent skills waiting for the opportunity and timing of God to prepare and then operate barns. It is certainly evident that if we do not prepare for a harvest, we cannot expect one anytime soon. In these current times, we should encourage the rise of the barn builders and incite the church to inquire of God for new, creative ideas on evangelism and discipleship.

FOLLOW

The conundrum we face is that, although people may have an extraordinary experience with God at a festival on Saturday, they are still not keen to frequent church on Sunday. Some have little God grid, others have been sadly burned by childhood church attendance. Memories of frustrated containment, boredom and squashed spiritual gifting are still fresh. They do not want to return to a religious structure, but their empty confusion leaves them browsing the clairvoyants and searching for spiritual snacks to ease the hunger.

I hasten to add balance: some people left churches offended, and made little attempt to mend a small rip before it became a deep rend;

166

others abhor authority or did not stick church and God through tough times or adolescence, perhaps switching focus to the consumerist attitude that dulls the embers of the Spirit until they barely twinkle. Yet they stay lit, reminding, drawing, until one day their owner encounters the living God again in such a powerful way they not only remember what they lost, but sense a new land of possibility. Others, battered and broken by life, young and fragile or old and frost-bitten, unfold before the light of the Son in some of the most touching, remarkable experiences we ever get to witness.

But while many of us wade deeper into the fields of wheat, we are painfully aware of the need for new barns to be raised and for existing barns to be furnished and armed, and of the fact that there is often a huge difference between what people encounter on an outreach and the experience of church on Sunday. I am not trying to knock church on Sunday – great things happen at many churches on Sundays – but we also need to acknowledge and address repeated evidence. Bridges need to be built.

It is not a case of debasing what has gone before or throwing away our identity, our services and our buildings completely, but there is a glaring need for some new interpretations of church that allow new seekers and existing members to delve and probe in more creative ways. The rise in creativity is already seeing new innovative variety and ideas coming from God's people to reach out further than we have been able to before, creating stepping stones all the way to a healthy life in Jesus. And this will increase alongside the connection and construction of barns to gather and care for the incoming harvest that are free from unnecessary structure and restraint. But all these things will not blossom within a religious stranglehold because they will require creative latitude for the Spirit. We will need to expand the dimensions of our faith and collaborate to a much greater extent with the supernatural side of the Kingdom, asking God constantly for ideas and solutions.

SEEDS

At times we have limited the embodiment of church and evangelism, leaving many breathless in the compression, afraid to share the Kingdom message outside the sanctioned methods that have been measured for specific outcome. Some techniques have surely yielded favorable results, but even so, our limitations limit God – then we wonder why we are not seeing the power we desire. Where people seek the new fire of freedom and diversity, there has been a swell of new laborers and outcomes: love gifted in different packages that cause the starving to throng. The treasure hunt for creative ideas must rise. How can there be a great harvest unless someone first plants the seeds that will then need time to grow and ripen? We are in the time of sowing and more sowing, watering and catching the first fruits; but there are barn-loads to come.

MEDIOCRE OR EXCELLENT

But solid food belongs to those who are of full age, that is, those who by reason of use have their senses exercised to discern both good and evil. Hebrews 5:14

Would someone read one medical book and expect to be a qualified doctor? Would you want your child treated by that self-appointed doctor? There is a place for believers to explore, to see how the shoe feels; but it would be sad to think that nursery-level gifting is all we can offer as ambassadors for God (2 Corinthians 5:20). My observation is that grace is lavished like a milky river on Christians willing to face unfamiliar outreach ventures. Some of the first exploits yield unimaginable sweetness. But we must graduate from working in the milk bar to the steak house with some dedication (Hebrews 5:12; 2 Timothy 2:15).

We find proof of those maturing the gift–character mix by the quality of fruit. Those willing to train gifts8, seek scripture, wisdom and ethereal relationship begin to offer a more excellent meal, and are able to weave expertly through encounters using an assortment of salient tools and inspiring team mates to standards of merit. So there is a place for the application of education, but then there are things we can only learn on the job. Jesus took His disciples with Him, and taught them through holy escapade; we need both.

OUT THERE

There are many different mission fields and roles within the church, at home and abroad, so it is imperative to define where God wants you in position. Who are the people, what is their culture, their language? It may not simply be geographically foreign, but also culturally foreign: street, high school, Goth, New Age or upper middle class. People come in all sorts of packages; if we cannot connect, we seem inconsequential to their lives. We have often found ourselves sent to those with little framework for God or who explore New-Age practices, hunting for meaning. They do not favor religion or understand our in-house church language and well-meaning antidotes; sadly, some do not even respond well to the name of Jesus yet, because they can have such wrong perceptions of who He is. When a heart is bolted fast it is hard to persuade it open – it requires the experience of a connection with God.

The world is full of information, but most people do not readily respond to God on the basis of information alone. The Word is living and they need to meet the author. We can use the tools that God has given us to partner with Him in the process. Religion defines its parameters so tightly that only certain phrases and practices are acceptable. On the other hand, the Holy Spirit's creativity offers a plethora of colourful and unique ways to connect unique people to God.

LANGUAGE

Most groups and organizations have a common language; the medical profession, for example, uses many abbreviations for complex terminology that sound like Taiwanese to the average person, but it is efficient for the medics who understand it. Church communities are the same, with biblical terminology and well-worn phrases. But we cannot simply extend that outside church and expect people to translate it, as if our church language will cause salvation on the spot. It actually does the opposite, triggering exclusion. We must normalize terminology and facilitate junctions. What's wonderful about the arts and expressed creativity is that they can transcend words in visual form, or use words in a way that allows more latitude for personal application to the hearer, like a song or poetry. Thus we return yet again to the importance of symbolism.

Words are powerful (Proverbs 12:18; 18:21; Ephesians 4:29). Negative words voiced over a life can fetter and decay a person. So many live amongst the amassing rotting rubbish of their effects. God's people come armed with affirmation and prophetic declaration that changes the outcome. A word of holy encouragement, a destiny defined, and the power of words have the opposite effect and bring renewal. Prophecy can be spoken, painted or danced; destiny declared through poetic license, layers of message procured through creative depth.[9]

COMBINE HARVESTERS

God loves teams – they are designed to establish unity. God has little interest in stars and stages; the more gifted or experienced we become, the more it is about furnishing others.

As we forgo individualism and embrace the challenges of team work, we sharpen the blade and increasingly keep our eyes on the prize of Kingdom advance together. Mission involves courage and a dollop of jolly hard work. However, when we find joy and relationship at the nucleus of the vision, the sheer exuberant fun of the Spirit is close at hand, fortifying us in the wrestle and the encountered pain of others. We are stronger to give again and enjoy life in the Spirit. I am also learning to take the lid off what even this looks like – God's sense of fun would catch us off guard if we would let it. It gurgles and sparkles from passion-filled people. He is full of joy.

ADVANCING EVANGELISM

Although familiar with leading evangelism teams up to that point, my first year at Burning Man hurtled me down the rabbit hole into wonderland. It was typical of many outreaches in some ways: many different walks of life gathered there seeking escape from social restraints and expectations.

They came to discover their spiritual journey or travel another mile in one well traveled. I witnessed so many tumble straight off the edge of the cliff into the outstretched hands of God. There was the pastor's daughter, who had fallen out of the nest having struggled with suppression in a traditional church and had taken the long descent into the carnival of carnality. But she missed God. She sat in speechless shock at the revelation that we were Christians, stunned to find God reaching out to her in this way, and here of all places. She reached back, offering her young life again to Him - her box for God was blown up with holy explosives and she was undone.

The Spirit was unshackled and allowed to run wild and free through us and around us, and I experienced a creative spiritual velocity that set a course for the unexpected, mingled with familiar landmarks. The outcome was full immersion for many. One man slid off his chair to the floor and peacefully slept in the Spirit - he had a dream and met Jesus there. He hadn't had the peace to sleep well for a long time. There were many filling with light, expressing astonishment. There are tipping points that take us into new dimensions of God. One day I tipped.

THE OCEAN FLOOR

A young couple came to the encounter tent; she was looking for healing, he was looking for a destiny word about his future. She experienced the beautiful curative connection of God. Now it was the young man's turn – my spirit felt exuberant about the unforeseen that was about to take place. I saw over him the future of a prophetic warrior, a Samuel-type calling. As my team mate and I spoke out the destiny and revelatory gift we saw over his life, he engaged intensely with God. He shared that this was what he had waited for all his life, as the words resonated with something dormant within him. He was manifesting vividly as power surged through his body; sometimes we were both laughing so hard in the Spirit that the neighboring cafe tent formed a curious audience of awe. At one point he cried out explosively 'Wow, you can't buy this stuff! This is amazing!'.

For about an hour he progressed through many waves of healing and encounter. Then I saw a vision of him on the ocean floor; God was a figure bathed in incandescent light walking towards him, arms open. I shared what I saw, and his reply contained details that made me realize he was seeing the same vision. I asked him if he knew who the figure was in front of him, but he did not; so I was able to introduce the Father of complete acceptance. Exuberant manifestations changed to floods of healing tears in that moment, with a heartfelt uniting of Father and son. As the vision progressed, so did its clarity, and we could see the same things in the spirit, sharing details - now this was creative! I'd had no notion of this possibility before, but it opened a locked door in my Spirit that impelled me to consider that the creative potential of God lies available for us in uncharted volume.

The power and presence of God in an encounter like that is almost impossible to illustrate to the reader. But many of us can remember a tipping point when we heard the unexplained click of the light switch; so we must seek to understand what just happened. The young man found his Heavenly Father that day and his spirit rose to meet and accept his calling as a follower of the one true God. He renounced all darkness, and accepted the Creator into his life to teach him and change him. It was one of the most joyful encounters I have ever taken part in.

It is a slice of the mission field. It is certainly not the only slice, but certain principles cross-pollinate. One is the passing of the torch. When someone is sent to catch a flame, they can bring it back to a location and ignite others in turn. Sometimes the deposit we are given through adventures in God seems only to multiply when it is shared, like yeasty dough.

FACILITATING FREEDOM

We often ask for more manifestation of the Spirit and then we offer Him a narrow, familiar channel through which to arrive. We would all love to see more healings, more miracles, more power; but the danger is in presenting the desired empty container to God, then expecting Him to fill it - disappointment can often follow, leading to frozen faith and frustration.

We allow the concerns of comfort to rise high above exploits. But Moses drew near the thick darkness where God was, to find the blueprints, to seek the next stage - the thick, weighty presence of God; then he came out shining with the glory (Exodus 20:21). It is time to allow the Spirit a much greater freedom. As creativity is restored to the church, and the people of God activate their creative and imaginative DNA and then combine this with wisdom, I see two things happening on the mission field:

1) New creative ideas and strategies for evangelism
2) Increased freedom of creative expression for the Holy Spirit through believers

STRATEGIES FOR SEED

Prolonged restriction generates lack of fresh vision and the cement of sameness. The Holy Spirit moves with creative fire and lacks no imagination. God wants to release His people from the confines of the constantly neat, tidy, restricted and repetitive. As the church ascends to seize its creative DNA, new master-plans will emerge - new ideas to prospect and creativity to reach people-groups. Fresh ideas and expression will come forward as God's people engage their own gifts and creativity, essential for the sickle that strikes the harvest fields. We will see all sorts of problem-solving projects and teams ignite where the fire has been previously dim. We may also see a rash of smaller ideas that do not work so well; but it is far better to try than never to have tried at all, and for some of these people it will not be about success or failure – it will be about growth and maturing.

'Keep trying' would be a fitting mantra in the lengthy season ahead, encouraging one another's ideas where we see the Spirit alight, even if they are embryonic and unusual. The early pioneers are the ones who hack a way through the undergrowth, before a small path materializes with some footfall. Eventually a road will appear where many can travel more readily and in greater numbers. God is stirring pioneers and the adventures on their hearts that may have looked impossible before, but gracious timing is opening up a land of possibilities before them. The barn-builders, the ones who will disciple tender new Christians, need to be given latitude to emerge and establish. The barns need to be raised along with them - the structures and new ideas for nurture, preparing for the golden crops of tomorrow's harvests.

STRUCTURE NOT STRANGULATION

As we learn to minister creativity at higher levels, good structure is essential. Like the multi-directional tendrils of a magnificent climbing clematis, a solid framework underpins and encourages well-formed expansion. Without structural support a chaotic mess can develop, and the undoing of knots damages parts of the delicate growth. The lattice looks like good training in foundational faith values as well as gifts, skill and character. We are used in the process as we continue to grow, while the Holy Spirit can move with increasing uniqueness and variation from this safe frame. Man-made religion feels the need to control, to know the outcomes, to diminish all risk; control, repeat and continue until the creative manna goes stale. In creativity, if you truly want to keep things fresh, you are always learning new things. To soar within this arena, clear biblical guidelines of what is and what is not OK are needed, together with good training and practice. It is also very important for people to understand the pot of gold contained within their Bibles, and that it is highly relevant to the ailing world around them. Accountability to good leadership, the canopy of capable intercessors, the support system of peers and friends in a church, and oodles of encouragement will go a long way in allowing the creative army to ascend with health and vigor – warriors in position where timorous beasties once stood.

STRATEGICALLY PLACED

In prayer one day, I saw a network of God's people across countries, stretched out in their hundreds of thousands; they were in their workplaces and neighborhoods, and I realized this was the army of God, already strategically positioned - but they needed activation. For the last few years we have seen an acute focus on outreach teams that gather and go to do events or go to the streets or the homeless, etc. I believe this is an absolutely valid expression of evangelism that God has greatly blessed. It has marshaled and motivated many laborers and generated heroic courage, new certainty and zeal. These expressions will continue to climb and mature on the strong frameworks that have been carefully built and fought for, and they will see advance in their creative ability.

However, we are all called to a missional life, and I sense the next stage will also focus increasingly on energizing people in their workplaces and where they live. Before the Street Pastors and prophetic evangelism teams exploded into being, the Christians involved were still Christians in churches.

My point is that many hundreds of thousands of Christians in the secular environment have lots of Christian teaching and church experience, yet many do not seem to feel greatly empowered or equipped to share Kingdom in their working environment or locale. Often they distinguish people working in some kind of church ministry position as more 'spiritual', so jobs can even seem like a waste of time for some or a waiting room to a more spiritual post. Some great teaching for Christians in the workplace has already been released, so I do not seek to diminish any of that, but just to add what I see in connection with the release of new creativity and the sovereign timing of God.

Although the emerging outreach teams of the last few years have consisted of people already Christian, specific equipping was needed for us to learn how to use our spiritual gifts in different contexts and to offer them in a form that was culturally pertinent. Much was learned on the job about the practical nuts and bolts, and improved training systems are being developed over time as a result. Part of the creative upsurge will activate new instruction and intelligence to help Christians feel more influential in their workplace or life situations. Before working in ministry, I worked in a secular environment for years. I found that what I had been taught about evangelism up to that point was too difficult to transpose to the real world, so I gave up and resorted to being just nice. But I felt powerless much of the time by comparison to the power Jesus said we would wield. While this may not be the experience of every believer, we would all welcome more firepower and insider heavenly data on how to make a difference.

In her book "Invading the Seven Mountains with Intercession", Tommi Femrite says:

'The workplace holds the power over resources that are either consecrated for the Kingdom of God or captured for the powers of darkness.....our God may own "the cattle on a thousand hills" (Psalm 50:10), but in recent seasons the enemy has worked hard to steal as much of the church's inheritance as possible. And as Wall Street's corrupt leaders continue to be exposed, the need for a revolution of righteousness in the business arena becomes more and more apparent. Until intercessors will step up and stand in the gap for those who desire to operate upon this mountain with integrity and holiness, we will continue to find the church robbed of the resources that rightfully belong to us.' [10]

That is an interesting thought, when we see churches so often struggling for finance and wondering where all the resources are. It is time to empower to a greater extent those whom God has sent to the market place.

A strange imbalance seems to be forming in church culture for the people who work full-time in the secular arena, whose call is found in the trenches of demanding career environments. Time as a commodity is inflexible, but it seems that so many in this category can feel that they cannot measure up to those with more time for 'Christian activities'. We have produced a legion of Christian weekly huddles that require time on top of the expectations of work and family, yet they rarely equip specifically for strategic Kingdom advance in the plethora of workplaces that consume much productive time. They are not 'waiting rooms' but callings, God-given vocations, strategically positioned for Kingdom impact. We can wear people out with the expectations of club attendance or 'outreach activities' without addressing the real considerations of their daily work place, and cause them to carry a sense of missing the mark in the squeeze of time and energy. Failure debilitates.

Imagine those same Christians armed with new strategy, commissioned and encouraged to make their workplace their mission field and, released from time-pressure, to concentrate on the people around them, supported by a network of other Christians in similar circumstances. When I say 'the workplace', that does not just represent people in offices or similar; your workplace could be at home with small children. It is just where you find yourself on a daily basis doing your business. I know some remarkable hard-working Christians who have vital jobs, yet they feel lesser than the people who have microphones at church or who evangelize in Africa. This can be the result of a lack of focus on specific kingdom strategy for the workplace, the exploration of ideas, the use of the five-fold ministry and the gifts of the Spirit in the work environment. Teaching and equipping on this subject has become a specialization, yet that's where millions of Christians are everyday.

People are now surrounded by many rules and regulations that limit traditional evangelistic methods in their workplaces. What's needed are new creative ideas and resolution for diverse situations that rise above all these restrictions; the Holy Spirit is not restricted. Ideas should come from God's people on the ground, not repetitive 'one size fits all' programs, because one size will not. There are heavenly strategies to come that will revolutionize this area, mostly through people who already work in situ. There are Christians who already have strategy but have not seen space to share it. God is shifting pieces into position to open the stage of favor for these ideas and the people who have the messages of new hope and empowerment for the market place workforce - the kind of revelation that sets people free from wrong expectation, prescriptive evangelist antidotes and dictated outcomes - a standpoint where we assume the position that leans heavily on the King of Kings.

I think we can look out in disbelief at where on earth the great harvest is going to come from in the West and indeed where the army of laborers is to gather it? But much of the army is already strategically positioned in the workplaces, and in the next season we can see a new force of creative innovation in this area as we pray it in together. I am sure that, if many of us better conceived what the advancement of the Kingdom looked like from God's context, we would be liberated into a new confidence that we have already been doing great things in the environment around us.

Joseph and Daniel didn't see anything ground-breaking happen for a long time, but quietly chipped away, sowing Kingdom and modeling Godliness in an environment that worshiped everything else but God. But they were also ready to step up to the platform with razor-sharp tools when the door of time opened before them. Their perspective of their God and their position was intact.

If we grasp we are limitless when we collaborate with the limitless Father, we will begin to expect solutions and innovative ideas that transform; our grid for what evangelism and Kingdom growth looks like will magnify and become liberating and diverse. Trailblazing revelation, teaching and practical implementation are coming in this area to mobilize God's great army to be highly effective for the Great Harvest. With the progression of these things, a restoration of the distribution and balance of time will occur, and a sense of increasing significance for all roles in the Kingdom will help restore vision and value to people for where they are already strategically positioned.

The Seven Mountain Mandate

Many years ago, Bill Bright of Campus Crusade for Christ and Loren Cunningham, who founded Youth with a Mission, were on their way to meet together. On route God gave both of them the same revelation, which indicated seven mountains or areas of society that define a nation. It also revealed that capturing a nation for God would require apprehending all seven areas.

Ask of me and I will give you the nations for an inheritance. Psalm 2:8

The work of Dr Lance Wallnau[11] and prophetic insights of Johnny Enlow[12] are exceptional in developing that seminal vision. They greatly contribute to the enlightening we need to mobilize an army of believers in these times. The seven-mountain message outlines the seven areas of culture as: media, the arts and entertainment, education, government, economy and business, religion, and family. Our technique has largely been to go into all the other mountains, then attempt to bring people back into the mountain of the church. This was seen as the best evangelistic plan. Johnny Enlow sees a revolution coming: God is scouring the earth for Josephs who will rise up into the mountains of society so that we can go after the nations in an unprecedented way.

The material in this book intends to explore what part the upsurge of creative DNA will play within this mandate. I believe it will be one of the key ingredients to taking the nations once we have a clearer rendering that the creativity of God is a part of our inheritance to spark powerful change. As the world continues to tremor around us, God's people do not have to be alarmed because it is our time to transcend, to conspire in His amazing mandate to reach people and nations in these heady days.

In the Spirit I have seen a gap closing these last few years. The generous accommodation that allowed us to nestle comfortably in the sleepy armchairs of half-hearted conviction in our churches is diminishing. The Spirit stands, stirring the beloved to arise into what they were made for. They must either draw closer to the King or become keenly aware of the shortcomings of their faith experience so they are challenged to make a decision. That gap continues to contract. The outer edge is not a safe place to hide – it will not protect you from the current shaking or that which is to come because 'from him to whom much is given, much is expected' (Luke 12:48). We have been given so much that the world needs. The confrontation of conviction to deepen can simply begin with some letting go of the parts we thought were safely hiding.

The warrior King intends destruction against the spirit of religion that opposes the church through His formidable creativity. Like the four craftsmen of Zechariah 1:18–21, it rises to destroy forces that oppress the nations. A multitude of religious beliefs and traditions have certainly brought much oppression. The religious spirit causes dry, controlling, repetitious faith - the kind that ruins relationship with God yet masquerades as His very character. It is time for us to see the real character of God, the one He portrayed for us in the Bible, not the cold God of religion that lacks life, colour and variation.

The enemy has sought to form a paradox. On one hand he has aimed to make church an uncreative, rigid environment wherever he can through the spirit of religion, trapping God's precious and much-loved people; on the other hand he has rocketed creativity in the world making it so seductive and diverse that it draws people's attention away from the church in droves. Yet God's people are not powerless, and in this time of redemption for the creative gifts, God will redress this situation and reverse diabolic systems. His heart is to see the church as an eminently creative, supernatural, power-filled place, leagues above the temporal dark entertainment of the world.

Interestingly, Enlow shares a vision he had of Joseph's coat of many colours, and the Lord called it 'The Seven Mountain Mantle'. He was shown that Josephs will carry the authority to displace the enemy and his darkness from the seven mountains of society. In relation to what we looked at in this chapter and the qualities found in both Daniel and Joseph, it is important to note that they both moved in a high level of spiritual creativity. It was in their ability to interpret the dreams of Kings and to live at a high level of creative wisdom (the Master craftsman).

Colour is also inseparable from creativity and art - it is one of the main ingredients. You could not say that of mathematics or sport to the same degree. So it is no coincidence that the coat was made of many colours: God was trying to highlight a vital component. I believe the revival of creativity will be an absolutely integral key in the seven-mountain mandate. It will take heaven's annotations to bring revolution to every mountain of culture. There will be little room for one set of rules, one set of teaching tapes to show us all what to do. What will be required are varied resources and a mature level of ability to work with the Holy Spirit closely and allow Him creative freedom for respective situations, as Daniel and Joseph did.

We must learn to hear God's voice as close as our own, to clasp the commission for us as individuals and as a collective. It is time to embrace the spiritual gifts He has assigned to accomplish the directive in these times. I believe the coat of many colours also represents the manifold facets of God as we come into a time of the increased defining of their identity. Some facets just need restored, others discovered as we search through the folds of a colourful and diverse God with surprisingly creative characteristics.

Another interesting point Enlow makes is that, in Joseph's journey up the mountain of society, he is no longer looking simply for individual decisions to follow God, but his mission extended beyond that. He was on his way to reforming society, and if he had not kept his eyes centered on the target and gone destiny-hunting, civilization may not have been able to continue. Some of us will be conscripted to focus mainly on individuals or communities, but it is also time to arm and consign the ones who are called to be influential in the other mountains. They need support for that charge. We need to broaden our scope of thinking of what evangelism looks like and how it can be carried out.

Lance Wallnau's teaching on the seven mountains makes the following points: he looks at the royal priesthood (1 Peter 2:9, Hebrews 7:1) and helps us to examine what we have access to. He expounds that the royal priesthood is when someone is operating in a kingly anointing and a priestly anointing combined. The priestly anointing is about intercession and intimacy. In the Old Testament, the priest was someone who offered sacrifices and opened up a gateway from heaven for man's redemption.

The kingly anointing is about being able to vanquish and acquire territory that once belonged to the enemy, and adjudicate that territory and bring about kingdom rule. The priestly anointing opens up a pathway for heaven to come and invade the earthly realm. As the two anointings work together, the priestly releases an anointing to the kingly; the kingly dominates and occupies, and then the priestly administrates for the benefit of the kingdom. God's royal priesthood has the two anointings working in synchrony.

We have separated the two, not wanting to administrate worldly territory, because we presume that would distract our focus from the more spiritual concerns and activities, and we do not fully understand what an advance of the Kingdom looks like. If we are to move forward into culture, then we need to understand the roles of the five-fold ministries - the teachers, pastors, evangelists, prophets and apostles —and their roles within culture. It is vital that we bring together both sides of Christianity - the mystical and the practical out-workings such as social care and justice.

When the Israelites went to survey the promised land, they found established cities with huge guarded walls. The land was not vacant, waiting for them just to move in; it was populated. Systems were in place for life, administration, work, military and defense. But Joshua and Caleb had a splendid attitude of victory; they knew they would not be alone in the conquest because they knew their God and that He was able. God is looking for Joshuas and Calebs to pioneer new paths into the mountains of culture. Our challenge is to be so utterly convicted of God's goodness and love that we can display it in the nations through places of cultural influence.

And He changes the times and the seasons; He removes kings and raises up kings; He gives wisdom to the wise And knowledge to those who have understanding. Daniel 2:21

One of the precepts of the 'seven mountain' directive is a primal shift to the demonstration of Kingdom principles as a way of advancing Kingdom, rather than only proposing to impact individuals through evangelistic methods. In the western world this concept carries not only powerful potential but a very liberating direction for evangelism. The Bible actually bears no record of Joseph or Daniel trying to convert anyone. Instead they lived as credible examples of Kingdom standards. Through this life-code they were allied to God's sovereign power, enabling them to do things far beyond natural facility, such as administration and governance at the highest level, and dream interpretation. Their example reformed the minds of kings and thus affected multitudes, elevating God high above their surfeit of confusing gods and beliefs.

One of my most personally-enlightening discoveries was that evangelism does not only look like preaching to people and telling them they should come to church. This propelled me to action. I realized there was some value in my evangelistic offerings and I was free to learn of stepping stones and the inestimable part they play in helping others keep moving towards the other side. If we are to reap an entire harvest, then we need a flexible horizon encompassing a wide spectrum of ways to share God with people and draw them to His Kingdom. The narrow channel of recommended past evangelistic methods has actually nullified some believers, because they do not seem to work anymore in certain environments. This can leave Christians feeling like frustrated failures.

Statistics show that the number of Christians in the world has grown hugely, but Kingdom-thinking among believers has not grown very much. This reveals a problem: too many Christians are worldly-thinking rather than Kingdom-thinking. Many out there in the mountains of culture are just not sure what to do because old evangelistic models are forbidden in their workplace or have little effect. For some people, the constraints in their workplaces define a place where expressions of faith are rarely tolerated or understood, and so preaching a good sermon to your colleagues is seen as unimportant.

Thus we find ourselves in an age where a new scope of creative methods is needed to further heaven on earth. We can honor the evangelistic channels of old for their effectiveness in their time, but some have become unwritten law through generations, the uncompromising acceptable standard – some of it to the exclusion of biblical methods even. Following the examples of Jesus, Daniel and Joseph alone, we are being given diverse, creative and powerfully supernatural scope to progress into a new season of evangelism and church. As believers explore, they are being shown many techniques that take them under the radar of cultural strangleholds – insights such as the ability to affect a spiritual atmosphere, divine appointments, stepping stones and the beginning of advancing freedom to try creative methods that not only embrace the supernatural presence of God, but cannot work without it. This is the model Jesus gave us.

New revelation of the power-tools we have to hand will spark new ideas for specific environments and situations. God's freedom always brings advance. We should consider that one of these tools will be dream-interpretation, and the understanding of enigmas and the language of God. Through the tool of dream-interpretation, both Daniel and Joseph were able to travel from what must have seemed like the bottom of the mountain straight to the top because they could translate the dreams of kings. We can ask God for divine connections and inroads, without any sense of failure for not closing deals and having rooms full of colleagues at church by the following Sunday. We can relax in the sovereign timing of God for their life and enjoy our part. Increasing liberty will help and motivate many in the work place actually to spread the good news with effect and break the stalemate.

Joseph never had to strive for success, but he did strive to stay close to God even within a Godless environment. He did favor the road to Kingdom ethics, and God released great power and authority through him in a very different way than He did with Jesus - Joseph didn't work within an environment that gave him liberty to preach. What Joseph and Daniel did was determine proof of the existence of God and His power so that many believed.

In western society today, some no longer believe that there is a God; for those who still do, they can often have a very poor image of His relationship with us and view Him as cold, uncaring and responsible for anything bad that happens. These are exactly the right times to be demonstrating we have a magnificent God full of love, kindness, answers and power. Some believers will be managers or business-owners, people with substantial authority or favor who can take larger steps to help Kingdom break out in their work environment. Let's consider that teams could be equipped to go into such places and use creativity through art and other expressions specifically made for this arena to bring about intercession, altering atmospheres and bringing heaven's interaction.

The greater the commissioning on our lives, the greater the cost to get there - as also modeled by Joseph and Daniel. A significant destiny will not be handed to us on a plate, because our plate would crack. We see this all the time in the world of famous people: with great fame and responsibility, the existing hairline cracks deepen into downfall. Character, obedience, tenacity and inseparable relationship with God are the stalwart protectors that help us to run the race (2 Chronicles 16:9a).

If some of us are called to influence kings and queens (men and women of influence and power), then who are the kings and queens in our sphere of influence? Let's pray that God will give them dreams and spiritual experiences that we can interpret. What skills do you have already that you can combine with the rest of the 'creative combination' so that God can increase what you have? Pray for doors of favor to open, doors of influence, and for the ability to understand the supernatural language of God.

THE ARTS OF EVANGELISM

The arts themselves can also be used as a preeminent tool in the coming days to connect people to God. With a new understanding of divine creativity, art-forms can be made that will perpetuate change.

Already we see the evidence of this at work. People have been healed emotionally and physically by simply looking at art-work or being in its presence. (We will examine this area in more detail in the final two chapters.) The conduit of the Spirit-fueled arts can transmit healing, life and miracles. Many people in the world think Church is boring, but infectious fun is to be found in the waves of the Spirit – creativity is bursting with exuberant delights. All we have to do is start with who we are and what we have in our hand already, offering it to God and asking for the 'creative combination'. This is how mission movements started in the UK and in many other places.

Blueprints + Spirit + Wisdom + Creativity + Existing skill/ability + More skill/ability added by God, joined with Character, Obedience and Perseverance

Years ago some of us went out as tiny groups of people around Scotland, sometimes even just in twos and threes, and took 'the combination' where we felt the path of the Spirit leading us. Very little was polished and no one felt like an expert - there were no gurus on the ground to lead us, so we just had to get a sword in our hand and start hacking a path in the undergrowth. Now the soldiers are many and the fruit so undeniable that prophetic evangelism has become strangely 'normal' in many sectors where we were once labeled risky and on the edge – but then little paths often look like that. As one of our leaders quoted, 'I am doing things now I would never have approved of a couple of years ago!'. Sometimes that's just part of pioneering, and it is logical that many times some fruit needs to be evidenced before many will join. Pioneers do not look for numbers to begin, just a small group of adventurers willing to pursue the vision. God will build the house if we are in His will; we do not have to fear smallness. As the biblical story of Gideon exhibits, God likes to reduce our natural odds so that His ability is ever before us and we cannot be tempted to congratulate ourselves with all the triumph – but instead repeatedly experience that He does awesome things through normal people, like us, to reach a world He loves.

Consider if the arts and other expressions of creative worship and message were more of an acceptable norm in our churches. Seekers would be drawn to explore more freely, contrasting with some more regimented environments they have previously experienced, where they may have felt exposed and out of place. We can focus on practicalities over spiritual depth and exploration, and wonder why God's presence is like a faint shadow in our midst. He longs to break out in the creative power that lies dormant. Many people have had their innocence robbed at some stage - some when they were very young - and they need to become a much-loved child when they encounter Father God. It takes time and some space. Children absolutely love to be creative - the hard evidence of that is undeniable. Again God examples something for us in the natural so we can draw lines to the spiritual environment required for seekers to burgeon.

As the Spirit's blades whir to life in the season ahead, ingredients that have settled in certain pattern and acceptance are being mixed into new substance, new positioning, forming the intensity of an atmosphere that craves change. We must respond personally and as a body. God is beginning to ignite the artisans and the many dynamic facets of His creative DNA available to all His people. He is looking to see who will pioneer and construct bridges for transition.

RELEASE

The leading step is to deliberately undo the bolts, dust off the webs,
take a deep breath and open the door.

So in practical terms, what is required to release new creativity in God's
people and how can we take steps towards that? Each Christian community
or individual needs to start with an authentic decision to work with God,
allowing the facility of new creativity for any area of life, any calling, any gift.
Then we must allow the intertwining purpose of the arts to come forward
and take its place in this process, helping to activate spiritual creativity for
all God's people. It is wrong to think that, if we bring back a few banners
and a painting in the hall, things will just happen. Restoration without
reason will be short-lived and will meet the same reception from others
as previous creative attempts. Art may be seen as superfluous or 'nice' at
best - and annoying at worst - as it has so often been perceived as carrying
little revelatory reward in the past. New creative ideas and strategies will
also require a welcome space to come forward, with encouragement for
exploration. Gifted teachers who will study, grasp and convey this message
will bring much enlightenment to the church, helping it to explore different
shapes and forms of Kingdom growth.

The objective is not simply to obtain another rainbow pool and then use it until it is arid, with no continuing cycle of sustenance. Dry repetition will eventually set in again. But as in the vision of the rainbow pool, the intent is to go after what is contained in the chasm underneath the initial surface realizations; or little will be changed and the asset will still remain hidden and unopened.

OPEN THE DOOR

The doors have stood shut and growing cobwebs for a long time, bolted against the deeper creativity of the Spirit. It is like discovering a secret walled garden that was there all the time, but the realization is only just dawning that there is a door. The first step is to undo the bolts deliberately, dust off the webs, take a deep breath and open the door. Imagine a vast and exquisite garden, largely untended for many decades. In amongst the inevitable weeds are many beautiful plants, flowers, trees and birds of many species and colours. But they have been neglected for an age and need some assistance to be set in order again - given boundaries for their species, so they can thrive together in a synergized garden.

This is not the garden of a new-build house with little but grass. Creativity and the arts have been progressing for thousands of years. It would be a mistake to treat them like a grass patch. The key is the willingness to find the mature plants and gifts that have wandered with a lack of guided aim, like resplendent rambling roses. Large plants, like mature gifts and significant callings, need some tending and a frame of healthy support and direction. If they have it, climbers climb high and cover large areas with great beauty.

When weeds are removed, flowers can emerge no longer choked with misunderstanding and rejection. As the prolific weeds of scorn, criticism and the forgotten value of creativity are addressed, there will be room for the new shoots and species to be planted and to grow in a secure environment. When the guiding framework (comprising of character and a grasp of the purpose of gifting) is restored to the different areas of God's creative DNA, they can learn to co-labor in harmony for the intended yield of beauty and strength. Watered and tended, this garden could be glorious: filled with a great variety of new life, scented and fruitful - the fresh air of heavenly breath that breathes the new into position.

A significant volume of our creative DNA lies choked by the weeds of history and perception, imprisoned by the lie that it is superfluous, low in power and treasure, and that much of it is simply owned by the world. But the Holy Spirit is an amazing gardener who does daring deeds through people. Even one heart that decides to start with prayer and Spirit-led action can begin to change the neglect and rediscover beauty. A team of gardeners can make even more impact. If we take down the walls from around the garden, we will stop treating it as a specialist area that requires sectioning for the minority group of artists, and see it instead as a life-force for the whole church through which the river of God flows, distributing fresh genius for all.

GATHER THE GARDENERS

Once the decision is made to unlock the door, the next step is to start tending the garden with prayer, asking God to gather the gardeners, the artisans and God's people who respond – all those with illuminated eyes at this juncture – so the adventure can begin. There is strength in numbers, even if they are geographically spaced far apart. It is important that some leaders and people with authority affiliate with the gathering groups – if not initially, then eventually. Prayer is a prerequisite for the clearance of negative weeds, preconceptions, lies and criticism that have choked the Holy Spirit's creativity in God's people. Directive paths will begin to emerge for specific groups, as the heart is willing to follow. Truth breaks lies, so a surge of new light through resources like this one will clear more weeds piece by piece. Remember: creativity goes hand-in-hand with wisdom, so it is necessary to pray for that along with new revelation and divine understanding.

EMERGE

As the misconceptions clear, people in your group or church will start to emerge with their brand of ingenuity, because they will feel the advancing spiritual freedom to come forward. They will sense new safety from the gardeners; the shading of prayer will alter atmosphere from exclusion to acceptance and protect the new foliage from thorns. Claiming that creativity and the arts are merely shallow forms of beauty or embellishment is equivalent to saying the same of flowers and plants. But in God's ecosystem they are vital, producing the oxygen we breathe. Some hold healing properties, some are food, and can you imagine a world without the exquisiteness and radiant colour and smell of flowers? They symbolize the fragrance of God, and indeed this is waiting to be released in greater measure through His people. There are many different varieties of plants and flowers in the garden, with different properties. We will examine different types of creative people, and the roles they are called to, in this chapter and the next. For the artisans, it should be noted that specific artistic gifting also carries specific commission, so that artisans can disperse what God has given them and stir inspired DNA into the whole community of believers.

RIVER AND WELLS

This first stage of new freedom for creative manifestation and exploration will strongly influence the wider radius of people within the searching Christian community. New hunger for a multiplied depth of God is already surfacing in the pioneering communities on this expedition. We are beginning to see this happen in Scotland, where churches and larger ministries glimpse the gap and the need to restore the arts and creative liberty as part of a larger divine move. They have made fundamental steps with intention as they seek to comprehend what this all means and what lies ahead. Multiplication is coming to break the weariness off plodding journeys of parched faith, to lift the struggles of smallness.

In the river we can swim, splash and, when we've had enough, climb to dry shores with relative ease. If God gets too close, if He goes near those areas of our heart that remain guarded, we can jump out, dry off and go right back to the way we were. The plunge pools of the Spirit hold a different outcome. Sinking densely into the spaciousness of the Spirit, the weight intensifies; we see the surface getting further away and, with it, the option to resurface and jump out. As time ticks we will fall further and further into the thick waters of the deep, until we have remained there long enough to drown, to lose our own breath and all the striving and self-effort we do not need. In that place we allow God to put to death the things in our life that are superfluous, the weights that beset us (Hebrews 12:1) and the mindsets that keep us going in circles.

As we allow God an extended period of time to take us into the deep and cleanse His church, we will also find things down there that we cannot find near the surface. Saturated and steeped, we will discover new wisdom and creative genius activated for solution, strategy and purposeful artistry. We will discover parts of God's nature we had previously missed or misunderstood and the revelation for the gifts and five-fold ministry roles we also currently miss. For ourselves as individuals, we will obtain progressively significant relationship with God, with fresh freedom and healing for new creative expression long repressed. New direction and innovation can ignite the faith journey again, as the season ahead contains the fulfillment of dreams long hoped-for and the permission to dream far bigger with realistic hope. The wells contain joy-filled healing and unity of purpose with new vigor. But we must not quit quickly, or before we know it we will be paddling again. The real depth that God has intended for us lies below, in the deep, heavy waters. Each community of believers will find that the voyage holds variety, as God unfurls his specific plans for areas and churches, leaders and communities.

From the season of wells I see the church emerge aflame with new force and the growing certainty of a rising warrior. This will not be about railing against the world, but about taking back ground in great strides from the enemy with new bravery, wisdom and the razor-sharp solving abilities we found in the well. With a new conviction of our creative DNA and capabilities, we will turn the tables on the enemy's influence in many areas of culture and model this for the next generation. As new life invigorates the church, it is then crucial it is directed outwards to those in desperate need of eternal life. In this way the wells will continue to fill, the rivers to rise, as its source is intended to heal the nations.

Then the angel showed me the river of the water of life, as clear as crystal, flowing from the throne of God and of the Lamb down the middle of the great street of the city. On each side of the river stood the tree of life, bearing twelve crops of fruit, yielding its fruit every month. And the leaves of the tree are for the healing of the nations. Revelation 22:1-2

PEST CONTROL

The creativity of the Holy Spirit is advancing to confront the religious spirit in God's church that masquerades as His identity. This is an effective weapon because in its very nature it cannot be rigidly controlled. It requires the profundity of the Spirit and preeminent trust in God's ability to bear life. It will therefore collide with the religious spirit head on, and we need to be prepared for some people not to like change – they will oppose and argue its presence. We must see past flesh and blood to the spiritual forces at work behind the aversion.

The enemy will particularly harass something in its infancy because it is easier to stop a few children than a fully formed army. But if the pioneers will stand together and pray with conviction, it is possible to break the strongholds of religion at work in some Christian communities, which suck the very life from their midst. We must be galvanized by the many examples of biblical courage where the few brought great change for the better in their time. Jesus is a good example of this. He often contended with the religious spirit that sought to stifle people's lives through control. If we respond with love, sensitivity and prayer, then inroads can be made by intrepidly following the Spirit's navigation.

We need to survey the creative garden in our communities and nation, take a deep breath and make an assessment; some areas need some work, being covered in weeds, overgrown and neglected. We cannot expect to open the door to this forsaken garden and find a botanical paradise in precise arrangement with paths in place. But we can begin to work with the head gardener and learn how to reclaim, preparing it for the changes soon to come and the generations of the future.

TWO AREAS

There are two areas to consider:

1. The general release and stirring of the creative DNA in every believer that can energize any area of their gifts and calling; this has been discussed previously.

2. The Christian artisans, those who show substantial gift and passion for an area of creative skill and possess significant Kingdom calling to use it.

ARTISANS

I believe the role of mature Christian artisans is multifaceted, but primarily to help agitate the waters and assist the release of the creative DNA in all God's people again. There are Christian artisans at all levels of development and so we must consider how to help them progress so they can fully contribute to the body.

Many Christian artisans have been trained outside the church; and the framework of the world is based on performance and self-effort. With very little education on how to transpose their skills for the church arena, some will probably feel rejected, or their skills have been dormant so long that they will need time to pick them up, dust them off and believe in a safe canopy to try again. There are currently few Kingdom artisans who have a high level of excellence and a sense of determined destination. Because of this lack, a struggle has evolved as these artisans work in positions in the secular arena; they can feel little link to Kingdom creativity. Thus their gift for heaven's use has become obscured within the mass of worldly, high-level talent and its value system.

Alternatively, their journey has been altered by discouragement or misunderstanding and so it has been put in the hobby box, resigning the pursuit of a more substantial role. On the other hand, some Christian artisans have battled hard for a healthy perspective and we should look for them, learning from the wisdom they have found in God. It is time to turn the tide and cultivate enlightened direction and location for God's artisans and all His creative people without disparaging the day of new beginnings.

MUSIC

Music has been greatly championed as the creative epicenter of church worship; it is essential, and contains many opportunities for artisans to contribute. Either it can take us into a euphoric glory cloud or we can find ourselves endlessly singing the same songs that feel dry and repetitive. There are a few reasons why we experience the latter; sometimes the hearts of the people are amiss individually or collectively, and we must be careful not to criticize without checking out the plank in our own eye (Luke 6:42). Another consideration is that worship is a priestly anointing; the worship band is not called to the mechanics of song and music alone, without adding the freshness of prophetic creativity and diversity.

If creativity means to produce something new or a new combination of factors, then in order to lead other people into a place of worship creatively, musicians need to wait on God and seek anointing through relationship with Him in order to inspire others to a heavenly focus. This goes beyond the simple execution of good skill. No matter how heavenly a song is in its inspiration, it can switch from distributing life to feeling dull if mechanics replace anointing. We are all God's vessels and responsible for seeking good condition and enthusiastic service. A half-hearted effort will rarely yield a melody of holy power. The priestly hearts of worship leaders who have prepared their lives in the secret places with God ignite worship with compelling potency that clearly engages the presence of the Lord. The distinction is tangible to the participant.

MISSING

Now, what about worship through the different forms of creativity? What depths does God have waiting for us to discover as we develop the other areas in worship, intercession, mission, discipleship, teaching, prophecy, etc.? Enlightened education and underpinning are needed for God's creative people to blossom.

At the beginning of such restorative work everyone is learning on the job and forming a bank of knowledge and experience. We must allow for the nursery before we can expect high school; but God blesses beginnings and loves them just as we love little children. We do not discredit their enthusiastic efforts when they thrill to present the picture they have just drawn or the messy sheet of sums they have completed. If we never let this develop again in the church, we will close the door to this prophetic powerhouse meant for God's people.

I hasten to add that there are churches already on the road of recognition, exploring and developing new innovations, ideas and the arts (particularly media) to demonstrate Kingdom and convey the message of the gospel very successfully. Such churches often attract and stimulate younger people, and the generation gap between teenagers and young adults is not so pronounced. My hope is that the information in this book will help continue the good work they have started.

THE FRAMEWORK FOR FLIGHT

Setting good standards and expectations from the outset helps people find biblical boundary. This applies to everyone and to the ingenuity that will come forward from any of God's people. Artists, particularly, are often labeled as rather alternative, disorganized people. Many of them have heard this so often they have accepted this box for themselves; but the truth is that, in the Kingdom, they need a good structure to support them and Kingdom standards to live by, just like everyone else. Weak character and lack of vision do not produce powerful Kingdom artistry with distinction.

TRAINING

Beyond good teaching of the foundations of the Christian faith, there are other areas that need development for all God's people. A foundational training course in learning to hear from God and understand the different ways He speaks to us would be the starting point. Courses like 'The Art of Hearing God' by John Paul Jackson include clarification on many other areas such as character and the spiritual journey; that would be invaluable to anyone. Gaps left in any foundation will weaken output and so we must all seek the foundations of durability for any gift. The creative people of God must be taught their purpose within the church and the mountains of culture to enable them to move beyond where they are now. This book and other emerging materials in this field can be used to equip people. Teaching on subjects like the language of God and the use of our creative DNA in the mountains of culture will deepen understanding for wider purpose.

SPIRITUAL DNA

The chapters called DNA Part 1 and 2 outline some important things for the people of God to grasp before new creativity can be maturely released. An understanding of 'the combination' will release new patterns of hope and spiritual productivity:

Blueprints + Spirit + Wisdom + Creativity + Existing skill/ability + More skill/ability added by God, joined with Character, Obedience and Perseverance

THE MAGIC LIQUID

I had what felt like a pivotal dream on this journey of digging. I was in a bedroom that contained a whole wall of sliding mirrored glass doors that I assumed concealed a wardrobe space; my husband was in the room fixing something. I was at the top of a step-ladder looking in a section of the mirrors. An older gentleman came in and told me to say the words 'I am German'. As I did, I was amazed to find that the doors slid open to reveal the reception area of a top-secret, high-level scientific company; I understood that it made something exceptional that was not yet publicly available. My husband Alan and I went into the reception and we were politely asked to go to the waiting area. We were told the scientists would be with us soon. In the waiting room we found a cup with a clear liquid; I explained to my husband that it could turn from a clear cold gel into a hot cup of coffee instantaneously. We were waiting for the scientists to come and explain to us more about what was being developed in this confidential facility.

I understood that this dream was about the release of creativity, that it was being hidden, but had the ability to do extraordinary, supernatural things; and that it was not just for the arts, but was available for any area – for science, maths, etc. However, it took me a while to figure out what the code was about, with no obvious links to Germany. Then one day I felt to look up the main traits of the German character, since this seemed to have had a bearing on access to the wardrobe.

5 TRAITS OF GERMAN CHARACTER[1]

1. Creative energy: On a large scale, the Germans have always been great builders and inventors. On a smaller scale, individual Germans are some of the hardest-working people on the planet.
2. Thoroughness: The Germans have a much-used saying: if something is worth doing at all, it is worth doing right. It seems that the Germans never do something half-way; they are masters of organization and give great attention to detail.
3. Orderliness: Another famous German saying is 'There must be order!' They are neat and punctual.
4. Sincerity: Germans pride themselves in their honor; they generally do what they say.
5. Loyalty: This trait is so strong that it has worked to their detriment at certain points in history; but in the positive it is to be admired.

What God was showing me in this dream was that a key to access the hidden realm of creativity was to aim for a standard of excellence; and not just in skill, but also in attitude and character. For the artistic people of the Kingdom, this would mean throwing off the label of being undisciplined or lacking order. This is not to say that creativity is to be constrained or controlled within unrealistic expectations, but that the important traits of Kingdom character should apply to all of us; and we can seek God's enabling to become stronger in weak areas.

WEIGHTY FOUNDATION

There are no magic shortcuts, because training, development and maturation are just part of the journey; and the Kingdom of God is all about journey and not just destination. When I took the 'Art of Hearing God' course,[2] I was shaped for the future by learning the fact that character was the 'single greatest enhancer of our gift'. I also learned that there is a time to be called, trained and commissioned. Sometimes being aware of the calling on our lives can be rapid: a prophecy, a season of destiny-driven navigation. From this steerage we rarely land in the arena of public ministry on a regular basis. It is not the instant qualification for a specific career or role; instead we often find ourselves in the lengthy and mainly hidden years of training – the grounding of our character, the practice of obedience, the grapple to understand the Word and the ways of the Spirit. Because I was shown the process ahead, the long years of hidden training were joyful for me; I understood that they were about evolving relationship with God. The focus is never on performance or public opportunities to demonstrate our spiritual prowess, but simply on knowing God extremely well.

We never stop growing, but there comes a point when the Lord can reckon us ready for commissioning; this is often clearly marked by an increase in favor, opportunity, anointing and authority to carry out a certain function. This follows the example of Jesus, who matured for thirty years before being released into ministry. Jesus illustrated an exemplary character for us: he was never above servanthood and loving the least of society with acts of simple kindness that displayed the in-workings of pure gold. He was gifted beyond belief, but He never put that above listening to, and being obedient to, the voice of His Father. He warned us not to be deceived with pride – pride in our gift, pride in our status - but in all things the Kingdom points to love, priesthood, obedience and humility.

I have learned, and am learning, so much from the excellent ministries of those who have walked before, and have infused regularly in the places of the Spirit to uncover wisdom and revelation amongst the instructions of the Word and the presence of God. Without some instruction, without taking the time to quench our spiritual thirst, we live on the surface of the Christian experience. If we stay there long enough, we think that's where God also lives; we fail to realize that, if we are lukewarm, we will begin to resent the Kingdom of God and those who are passionate and searching.

Not only so, but we also glory in our sufferings, because we know that suffering produces perseverance; perseverance, character; and character, hope. And hope does not put us to shame, because God's love has been poured out into our hearts through the Holy Spirit, who has been given to us. Roman 5:3-5

Humility keeps us open to what God has to say. It keeps us willing to learn and produces the vital combination of hungry, humble and teachable. When we elevate gift above character-progression, our senses become dulled to our sliding attitudes and actions; we excuse ourselves because we are 'gifted', and there are people around us confirming the fact. Character keeps us strong for the long haul. It plants our feet on the rock and helps us stand when people treat us nice or when situations are rough. If the focus is on gift we begin to seek the approval and applause of man. Some do not notice the slip until a storm hits and the gift alone is not enough anymore. Gifts are endowed by God, but character must be worked in a person to bring a measure of experiential insight that can grasp the things of God that release change and force. Some may keenly feel the long years of refinement and the tests of varied size, but what remains is a pure, fresh canvas on which the Lord is poised to paint a new picture. There is inconceivable intimacy with God available on the journey.

HEALING: PRESENCE NOT PERFECTIONISM

As a young woman, before I knew God, I tried for many years to conform to the standards of the world, particularly in my art work and in my appearance. Although happily consumed with art college, I was full of striving and desperate to find worth, seeking the approval from the world that I had lacked as a child. I worked relentlessly to achieve a place at an esteemed college in London to study fashion and textiles, and for four years I endured the cold, hard iron of what it is like to be a student at that elevated level, jostling for position. Tutors were unhelpful, fellow students were often cruel and constantly competitive. About eighteen months after graduation I finally let God rescue me from the mess and begin to unravel the tight coil of an utter lack of self-worth. During that time I had a vision that brought the most extraordinary healing I could have imagined.

I was in a bright board-room, sitting at one end of a vast table with my portfolio in front of me. In the stage of life shortly after graduation from art or design college, a student's portfolio often represents the pinnacle of personal creativity and effort up to that point. It is excruciating to take it round potential employers while braced for criticism and rejection. God appeared beside me as a figure in white light, and He asked to see my portfolio. Instead of rushing with the half-hearted interest that I had expected, He wanted to linger on each page, discussing the projects, posing questions, perpetually affirming, enraptured with the details others would miss. We stayed there a long while – in reality my eyes were closed, but I became aware I was sobbing deeply as layers of rejection fell to the ground. Here were the patriarchal qualities I missed – the empty space was filling fast. He had time for me, He was attentive to detail, He saw every effort, every brush stroke, every idea, and He wanted to convey that to me. I was so undone by this unexpected encounter, it so deeply touched my young life.

A primary step towards progress is the healing of God's creative people. Many have been shut down as this area has been devalued in our churches or within a world culture that offers a form of esteem through vicious competition. Many creative Christians are caught between the two worlds. I believe a grace is being released for accelerated healing in this area. It does not have to take years – sometimes it will take minutes, sometimes a little longer, depending on the journey, but the goal is to get healed and move on into the new productivity of heaven. Shawn Bolz said that there would come a time when we look back on this era of the church with disbelief that there was so little colour and creative expression, and probably call it 'The Dark Ages'![3]

God wants to exchange the rejection, the belief of failure and hopelessness, the weariness, the sense of smallness and limitation for new expansive vistas. Although many people have suffered at the hands of ignorance, there is nothing to be gained from holding resentment or projecting blame. We need to understand this is a timely shift and that history has been largely responsible for the perceptions of this area within God's holy house.

We must also fathom that some of our experiences have been caused by the opposing ranks of the enemy, terrified of what God's creative people could do if they rose up. There may be many situations you felt were unjust, but God in His sovereign wisdom was trying to remove the personal hindrances that would keep you from the greater plans He had for you. There is the death of performance, so that presence takes precedence. Some of our experiences have been training for reigning, the etching of character, toughening us to stand and answer the call to be warriors. It is imperative that we move on without bitterness, and woo the arts and the ingenious DNA of the Spirit back into the church.

CLEANING THE PIPES

As we reposition to receive, we need to be clean vessels. Have we drawn from erroneous wells - wells of the world, of the soul or from the dark well of the enemy – to inspire and feed our inspiration? Have we compromised and had a foot in both camps, perhaps confused by a lack of guidance?

Have we used the gifts God has given us for purposes outside His Kingdom? Have we been lazy and ignored the prompting of God to cultivate the gifts He gave us? Have we settled for mediocre and not pursued an excellence of character or call?

Such activities can be responsible for deficient inspiration and original thought. If you have longed for visions or dreams from God and desire a heightened experience of the Spirit – but struggle to get there – allowing God to wash you clean from the build-up of these activities will surely help. We can ask God to bring to mind the debris that needs to be placed on the altar of repentance, so that the spring-clean can invigorate our ability to hear the voice of God more easily and catch a new spark. Let's offer Him all that we are and have, clean and set in order. Reach out with new hope and curiosity.

For behold, the darkness shall cover the earth, And deep darkness the people; But the Lord will arise over you, And His glory will be seen upon you. Isaiah 60:2

We carry the light inside - we carry God's glory, which will shine brighter in this age because thick darkness covers the earth. There is more revelation available to those who seek it. So let us allow God to clean us up and position ourselves to catch and radiate intense light.

We can commence the journey at any time. God will receive you as you are to begin the tutoring process of listening and collaborating in creative accord with Him, which in itself brings healing. As we learn our unique composition and the benevolent friendship of our tutor, we see that the expectations do not lie in faultless mechanical masterpieces, and a new freedom enters the process. When we finally learn to let all our gifts, talents, hopes and dreams land in the hands of God we will be astounded at what He will do with them. It may not happen overnight, but embarking on the process is utterly worthwhile and life-altering.

DECLARATION

Within the area of The Arts, it seems acceptable, more than in most other arenas, that our creativity is wide open to critique and the assessment of others. If it was all constructive criticism said in love it would be fine. However, in the world it is mostly just people's opinions, their preferences and sometimes clawing criticism that are seen as wholly permissible. We are told to get used to it because, after all, 'It's a tough world out there'. While this may be true, it is not the Kingdom's way. In the Kingdom, iron sharpens iron out of love, lifting up not ripping apart. But as yet, there is limited practical training for Kingdom creativity, so Christian artisans and creatives are mainly channeled through the world system. They are frequently beaten down by cold criticism, until the joy of innovation is greatly diminished and the fear of experimentation anchors the sails of progress.

Creativity becomes tainted with the fear of rejection. What felt delightfully sacred at the naive outset of the journey can so often become the heavy yoke of sheer survival that tries to hold on to inspiration and purpose. We can begin to adopt the pattern of constant judgment for our own work and, without noticing the seeping shadow, we allow the dark voice of condemnation to become the constant companion of our efforts, masking as constructive appraisal.

To break this pattern we need to repent of inadvertently or intentionally agreeing with the enemy's commentary and assert positive pronouncement over our creativity. Freedom follows so we can create in the joy God intended. Let's also break off from our memory and spirit all the counterproductive words that others have spoken over us. We should include those words we cannot even remember, because they can also strike like flaming darts and land with ill effect. Repentance should then be extended to all the damaging words that we have spoken over ourselves and our gifts, and ask God to forgive us and liberate the abilities that He has given to be energized with a sense of new value. Now determine not to create to please man, not to live tossed to and fro by the opinions of people; but seek only to please God and aim all your creative works for the audience of one – He will take care of everything else.

Clean up the Oil Spill

Repentance is also required by God's church for having rejected the creative gifts of the Spirit and having handed them to the world, even unknowingly. They have been used to bring harm to the church and greatly further the schemes of the enemy. Then repent for rejecting the artisans as a people group and for wasting the resource that should have been empowered by the embrace of the church; this will help to shift the concrete boots of dull ritual and wrong perceptions, allowing life to breathe again.

Like all historical changes, this can start with a few humble hearts willing to fill the gap with prayer. It is not about blame, as we have discussed, it is about change. As artisans and creative people, we can posture ourselves in prayer. We can make the first move to forgive and determine to present an excellence of attitude and character to our fellow believers. God is unlatching doors of favor. They are swinging open for those who are ready, but if we remain bitter at misunderstanding we will squander the new favor of God and sow more destruction for future innovators. It is a case of rising high to gain perspective, far above our own wounds on the battle field.

The vision is to gather as God's creative army for the greater good. In that place we find the new healing of acceptance; it will not be found in the rehearsing of personal afflictions. Artisans also need to repent if their behavior has been less than desirable. Are we a great blessing to our leaders as creative people? Or are we demanding, touchy, unreliable and lacking in character, excusing it as the 'artistic temperament' or wearing the badge of rejection as an identity? If we want to see things change, then first we must humble ourselves in the sight of the Lord and He will lift us up (James 4:10).

SANCTIFIED IMAGINATION

God has the most prolific imagination. When the Hubble telescope was launched in 1990[4], it took a picture right beside the moon of what was thought to be empty space; but what they found were images explosively full of kaleidoscopic colour and light, just hanging out there in lonely space. There will be many more such spaces we will never see.

Apparently we know more about space than we do about the oceans right here on earth. So far, 230,000 species have been discovered in the oceans, including some of the most alien-looking works of art, and they are all alive and thriving far beneath the deep dark waters. Some radiate an internal lighting within mysterious shapes, and again we see so little of what is there - a sliver of His creativity. And apart from those, there are the millions of species of birds, animals, plants and trees. We can hardly comprehend even a small fragment of His expansive creation.

So why create all this when we can see so little and wrap our heads around even less? Because He is the Creator, utterly creative at the core of who He is, and we are made in his image (Psalm 107: 22-24). If we are like Him, then our imagination must be connected to the infinite dynamo of God that can 'see' something before it is created. Imagination is the gift, the tool, He has given us to bridge the unseen realm.

For by Him all things were created that are in heaven and that are on earth, visible and invisible, whether thrones or dominions or principalities or powers. All things were created through Him and for Him. And He is before all things, and in Him all things consist. Colossians 1:16-17

Just as with our gifts, we can choose to connect to the work of the enemy or the life of the Spirit. Let's equate imagination to a computer program for a moment. When the computer is off, nothing is happening; but switch on the machine and, within it, a program starts that is designed to form pictures, build worlds and compose scenarios at our command, creating dimension from flat thought.

This is just like our imagination. We choose what we feed into the program. When we feed it with the murky fodder of enemy inspiration it creates fearful scenarios of danger, failure or rejection. When we fuel it with our fleshy aspirations and carnality of soul we will orchestrate images that feast those desires and lusts. If, however, we connect it to the Spirit to be nourished with God's essence, it can be used as an instrument, networking us to the transcendent realm of the omniscient God. Faith is the substance of things not seen - connecting it with the mechanism of imagination can help us to 'see' what is possible through God (Hebrews 11:1).

Creativity and imagination are inextricably intertwined, and both need reclaimed and sanctified for heavenly productivity. It is time to extract this gift from the jumbled perceptions of its mechanics and view it as a gift or tool. As in any other gift from God, the choice lies with the owner as to the destination of its use - much like revelatory gifting, which can be used to tune in to the tree of the knowledge of good and evil (clairvoyants and similar) or the tree of life (prophetic gift). Imagination will respond to whatever we feed into it. Like creativity, we have also watched this tool be used by the world to devise evil.

Imagination also has a powerful effect on will. What we imagine of ourselves, or the outcomes of particular events, we can begin to believe, and even move towards that belief as if it were fact. We can then allow our actions to align with the process. For example, think of yourself traveling to an interview for a job promotion you would love to achieve. If you entertain constant images of failure, perhaps rehearsing past defeats, this can form agreement with your current fears. If you then imagine the interview as a negative scenario, this can actually affect your actions in a negative way, leading to more real-life failure. The more people fuel their imagination towards a repeated direction, the more patterns of imagination become entrenched, and they can become strongholds for sin and fear.

There is an interesting analogy in the movie 'Green Lantern'[5]; and they protect their power source of 'will' from their enemy, Parallax, who uses fear as his primary weapon. Their job, of course, is to be protectors of the galaxy, and they use their imagination as their capital weapon. What they can imagine, they can bring into being for the power of good against darkness. They are only limited in power by their imagination, and if they allow fear to enter their being they will be defeated.

Our imagination can be used as fertile soil for the enemy's tactics of fear, or we can choose to stand guard and allow only the Spirit and faith to alight there, deliberately and actively swatting any fearful flies and dark thoughts, denying them a landing site. One fortifies the fetters of fear - the other enables Kingdom intervention (2 Corinthians 10:5). Let's not allow our imaginations to restrict our destiny in God.

Let us consider dark and violent computer games or horror films as an example. They were fabricated in the realm of someone's imagination; when played or watched repeatedly, such visuals pull the participant into that realm, affecting their own imagination. The degree to which that happens will depend on the amount of time spent absorbed in that sphere. With enough absorption, the spiritual dimension hidden in such media will eventually seep into the perceptions and actions of those engaging with it.

Technology has accelerated to enable the composition, with astounding clarity and dimension, of magical lands with mythical creatures and animated adventures of survival. It can take the tools of human creativity and imagination to dizzying heights of global impact. Many of us are inspired by the creativity of others - it can draw out our own creativity and engulf us in fascinating escapades.

Aside from the positive adventures into creative worlds, we also need to discern where the enemy is using such tools increasingly to pull people from the world of the five senses into the realm of soul and shadow, praying on the weak and those disappointed with life. His message seeks to bring the illusion of power, or the temptation to engage with dark forces, to people who feel disempowered. Simulating superheroes that do superhuman things makes some people feel empowered in the moment, negating their shortcomings or the sense of smallness in their own lives.

In contrast, some heroic figures can inspire and remind us we have the ability to tap the superhuman power of God to do exploits for His Kingdom. Indeed the Bible is full of superheroes, and the example points us towards our connection with our Creator. The identification of source and motive is imperative. As God's people, we are to be guardians of our imagination, and thus our creativity, nourishing them with faith and Spirit so they are electrified. They connect to our perceptions and actions and inspire us to seek the legitimate force of heaven that has substance in this life and eternal consequences.

God gave us imagination to be a powerful tool for a life of faith. When our imagination is cleaned up, sanctified and devoted to God, He can bring healing and growth to this gift. Many of God's people have a limited imagination because in some sectors of Christian life we have been taught it is 'not real' and therefore wrong, or it is 'just imagination'. I find that it can be treated with suspicion or lack of understanding, so we do not talk about it much. But, like creativity, it needs to be redeemed and restored to God's people. Like every gift, it needs to be practiced and matured. When I pray, I always come with an expectation to 'see' into the realm of the Spirit and connect with God in a visual way. Some would say that, because artisans have a strong visual gift, imagination is only really meant for them, but imagination is a huge part of every human life. We all imagine things, and frequently. It is available for all of us to see into the realm of the Spirit in different ways.

A few years ago, God asked me if I would like to see what my spiritual journey looked like and where I was on that passage. He took me to a spiritual location that I could revisit, explore and fly through with Jesus. It became an adventure in installments and the discovery of many things that provided extensive wisdom and comfort at times.

One day I was told I had moved to a new place or level on the journey. A new chapter began and, along with it, a realm of absorbing investigations in my prayer times. In my current level I found the rainbow pool described at the start of this book, and a land filled with colour, musical notes, exotic gardens and a library filled with golden books that illuminate wisdom. Practicing the connectivity of sanctified imagination and Spirit sharpens the tool and opens an expressive visual language. God can show us things that blow up boxes, revealing crisp panoramic perspective, filling our heart with the Kingdom of Heaven and its beauty. We can be transported from the ordinary world surrounding us to a place of such divine wonder that we are left with a sense of eternity. What does your journey 'look' like?

A well developed, submitted, and sanctified imagination can be shown eternal things of the Spirit that can then be released on the earth and shared – through a dance, a sculpture, a teaching, a business plan, a medical breakthrough, a new engineering method, etc. When we practice, we mature in this ability and are more able to reach deeper into the storehouses of heaven and bring that wealth to our creativity on earth. We could argue such things away by stating that they must line up with scripture, and then claim that this does not. However, we must be careful to ask if our own thinking aligns with the evidence: the Bible is jam-packed with supernatural and strange events, with dreams and visions, with enigmas and the symbolic language of God. We should not immediately look for more 'logical' teaching that aligns with our opinions and allow cynicism to stifle creativity.

When Laban tried to con Jacob out of taking flocks as part of his reward for many years of hard work, Jacob used a visual aid to connect his imagination to heaven, and a supernatural outcome ensued (Genesis 30:37=39). Biblical characters frequently saw into the realm of the Spirit – Daniel, for example, and John in Revelation. Jesus spoke with stories. There were no films or printing presses in those times, so art as we know it would not have existed. Stories are altogether different from preaching a sermon - they require us to engage our imagination. We cannot help but do so; as we depict scenes and characters in our mind's eye, we sense emotions through the weaving narrative threads. Jesus taught us how to engage our God-given imagination and bring visual life to the Word of God; it is another vital and God-given tool for our use, and an inseparable component of creativity.

IMPARTATION

Impartation is the transference of spiritual things from one person to another. It means to make known, to tell, to relate, disclose, communicate, to impart knowledge. So we can impart or give away what has been given to us in different ways in a spiritual transaction. The Apostle Paul wrote of wanting to visit his friends so he could 'impart some spiritual grace to them' (Romans 1:11), or release blessing or gifts through laying hands on them. We sometimes presume this is only for inside the church, but Jesus went out and laid hands on the sick, calmed the storm and converted water into wine. Therefore, just as Paul transferred spiritual anointing through handkerchiefs (Acts 19:11-12), we are able to impart what we hold into the creative works we form in alliance with the Spirit, effecting change in a person or environment through grace.

Testimony is a great example of this. It is an impartation through words, or the telling of a story. Many years ago, when I had Chronic Fatigue Syndrome and was wiggling my toes in the waters of Christianity, I began to hear multiple testimonies of extraordinary healing for the very illness that plagued me. Contagious hope landed and remodeled my thinking - I could be healed; it was possible - and in a few more months of feeding on hope and testimony I was healed. There are many different stories and voyages to healing, but the point is that the power of the testimony is through stories that seem to transfer power for hope, faith and rescue. At times people have been healed on the spot while listening to a testimony. In these embryonic days of understanding creativity's powerhouse and the inclusion of its release through the arts, stories are accumulating of people being healed simply by looking at or being surrounded by art, without even being touched by another person. The impartation came through the art.

Last year at the CLAN Gathering event in Scotland[6] , one of the leaders on our creative team had painted a picture of a beautiful big tree. On returning from a break to continue work on the painting, she found a lady just standing and crying, absorbed by what she saw. It was ministering deep inner healing to her, which she shared with the artist. There are growing numbers of accounts of physical and emotional healing coming through the arts and transferring life to people in profound ways and sparking new creativity within the recipients.

The film 'The Passion of the Christ'[7] impacted some people so deeply that they left the cinema seeking to give their life to God. Its creative genius portrayed the cost paid for our salvation and the incalculable love of God for mankind, and this stirred the desire for connection and salvation. Paintings that are intentionally created to release healing can do so. Dance that deliberately moves to change an environment to one of faith can do so. I have repeatedly watched art affect an atmosphere in the way that God showed me it would beforehand; without a word being spoken to the participants in the room, I simply watched amazed as it happened. As we intentionally seek to design with the author of our DNA, commanding forces are released. Therefore we have to understand that we can affect the spiritual environment around us individually and collectively.

Realizing what we carry within us is the key to imparting it. If we have £1000 in the bank, but do not know it, how can we give it to someone in need to assist them? All of Romans 5 is the revelation of our freedom obtained through the death of Jesus, but also the resulting realization that His Spirit lives within us and has released us from death to life. We must develop creativity that releases the true life of who Jesus is. He is the person of the Godhead who helps us come to the Father, and so our innovation must reflect that dynamic. So how do we do We attract anointing by steeping our heart and spiritual eyes in the Word, by spending time with God in adoration and search, allowing the rhythmic tides of the Spirit to wash over us. From this place we discover innovation and metamorphosis, and we release prophetic creativity through any area of life or gift as we are directed; then we impart that to others. Prophecy declares; it changes and releases something of the ways of God on the earth.

Lives that are constrained by man's religion will produce imagination and creativity that is subject to its asphyxiating parameters. It will want to convey its own message and its own theology. It will not want to create the pure, living water of the Spirit that will carry out revelation. We must not be scared to look for God's unveiling or frightened of what is to come. Let our creative works be part of a witness to a dying world that only the life of Christ can save – not tainted religion, not idolatrous gods, not their flesh and blood. As the pride and idols of man fall, the Spirit of a loving God rises, and those who know Him can engage with abundant possibilities to convey the message of Christ.

Spiritual Atmospheres

As we become more aware of what we can carry and dispel, we can affect the spiritual climate around us, rather than let it affect us. We carry the Holy Spirit and also the gifts and anointing He has given us. We can learn to affect specific settings in specific ways as directed by God. Dawna DeSilva, the founder of the Bethel Sozo healing ministry[8], has written some ground-breaking teaching on this subject from her experiences. She discusses how we can walk into an environment and become affected by the spiritual atmosphere there without realizing it. We might enter a shop and suddenly feel tired or fed up, even though we did not enter with those feelings.

When ministering to people using Sozo, she realized she was being affected by what other people were carrying, such as anger or bitterness, and thus there was need for cover. We need to check that what we are feeling is coming from ourselves; and if not, we reject it and the spirit from which it came. We refuse to engage with it, and in that way we are alert and protected.

I am on a compelling journey, where I find God teaching me about setting an atmosphere through creative works for specific purpose like a mission setting or conference. But this could equally apply to a workplace like a school or office. Most teams will pray before they run a Christian event, to set a spiritual tone for such things as healing or breakthrough. Taking that a step further: if artfulness and creativity, in combination with the Spirit, can carry a presence or anointing upon it for a specific reason, then that can be transmitted to people in that environment and we can use creative works to activate intercession, healing, etc. This is 'atmosphere design', and it can be conveyed through combinations of space layout and the various methods of artistry and spiritual creativity.

After my initial qualification in fashion and textilele design, I added subsequent training in interior design; I worked in the industry for many years, in a variety of countries and contexts. I am very aware that what you install within a space, and how you position it, can greatly affect the 'mood' of the environment. A dim, cluttered and grimy room feels oppressive, but a light and clean space with interesting objects and decor brings repose or inspiration. Colour, light, form and space interact extensively to create the mood of an environment.

God began to speak to me about combining my education and experience with the spiritual aspect. The choice of colours, objects and layout of a space can be made using a combination of skill and Spirit. The intentional placement of specific works, because of the anointing they carry, can take us into a wholly new concept of atmosphere. These considerations fascinate me.

As I studied the tabernacle of Moses and the temple of Solomon, I sensed the Lord speaking about the formation of 'tabernacles' with Him – I was to take assorted collections of creative works and artisans into various situations and locations, like outreach events and conferences. As I attempt to collate repertoires of works (which include the gifts of musicians, dancers, poets, painters, writers, etc) for specific teams and events, God is bringing together different combinations for designed purpose.

The first time I attempted this was for a mission event I co-led at the Belladrum festival in the Highlands of Scotland for several years. We would set up a station and offer free prophetic ministry in diverse forms, dream-interpretation and healing. In the first year there were three of us on team; by the fifth year there were sixty people from five nations, and three hundred square meters of tents at our station.

By the fifth year, I felt it was time to experiment with what God was showing me about tabernacles. The talented team were up for the exploration, so we designed and brought together the interior of the tents; this included wall and ceiling coverings, large sculpture, paintings, lighting and distinctive pieces made for the event. There was a dance team, a live music team and an art team that would draw or paint the message they had from God to give to inquiring seekers. We made each piece with prayer in the embryonic beginnings of learning to create with the Spirit in a more definitive way. Hundreds of people poured through our doors for close to five hundred appointments in those two days as we worked to maximum capacity most of the time, just to keep up with the demand.

So many engaged with God through the imaginative menu on offer, with many tears of healing, salvation and submerged connection. The annual festival theme was 'Space' and, while avoiding the inevitable green martians, we asked God for direction; I painted a large image of an explosion of stars and power in Space with another team artist. The painting evoked unexpected emotions for one lady; as she stood captivated before it, she asked to speak to the artist. She wanted to know what the explosion represented, and I was able to point her towards her Creator. He was undoing her heart that day without anyone touching her, just the painting. God became real to her.

Since then, I have been involved in leading creative teams and bringing collections of creative works and combinations of artisans into outreaches and gatherings. I have been awestruck many times as I watched these 'tabernacles' release the spiritual dynamic we had been shown before the event, without any spoken instruction. The sculpture of the angel's wings seems to stir people into new creative freedom wherever they are placed. I also built a large sculpture of gates that I sensed was to help people crave for, then cross into, the next season of deeper wisdom and understanding.

Wherever these works of art go, I watch people become impassioned to take the plunge and realize that the season is changing. I have seen paintings, music, dance and poetry do the same thing within an atmosphere. I am not implying that these bring change on their own; but they contribute to what the Holy Spirit is working in the people within that environment. So we can craft works with intention for what they will release.

Let us consider again that the arts of the Spirit are meant to intertwine with the Body of Christ and help to stir the creative DNA for the benefit of all. Specific works and artisans already affect areas of culture in the same way as the example above, but this is rarely well-understood. Artisans could be inspired into making a much greater impact. For example, they could assist believers who work in secular environments, helping to change the spiritual temperature. Believers working in the mountains of culture will be able to release new ideas and answers that also bring a higher spiritual dynamic where they are positioned, as they rise to grasp their own creative DNA.

As an interior designer and artist, I think of the whole space as a canvas. I think in terms of the question, what 'atmosphere design' is required within a space or spaces to expedite God's agenda? The ideas start to develop within the team for lighting, art, fabric, room layout, etc. This process moves beyond a nice bag of tricks to jolly up a dull space. It is a holy preparation, a priestly calling to bring intercession through our creative works, so that the presence of God can increase and the Spirit can bring unrestrained creative delivery.

Some older church buildings are exquisite in architecture, yet are somewhat austere inside and could be greatly enlivened with the release of more creative activity from the community there. Although we should preserve the precious history of church architecture wherever possible, we do not always have to match it with the interiors of a bygone era. Many creative people have faithfully produced banners and fragrant flower-arrangements that have lifted the spirits of many – wouldn't it be wonderful to release such people into new realms of freedom and encourage new gifting and idea?

Even though modern-built churches can be brighter, boxes with plain white walls reveal nothing of the innovations of the Spirit or the uniqueness of the community. Indeterminate neutral plains imply a blank canvas crying out to be written upon. Left without personality, they frequently hold the dispassion of an office space rather than the heart of a people. However, when we walk outside into a beautiful garden bathed in sunlight, we find it full of different flowers and plants. A multitude of colours and light play-dance in brightening hues; there is texture, form and smell, and such a sense of emancipation we want to take off our shoes and run barefoot on the grass, or linger in peaceful rest to absorb the delicious environment.

Little kids adore such a garden; the first thing they want to do is play and laugh their heads off. The presence of God is so like being in the garden; its phenomenal life-force leaves us in motionless wonder at times, and worry dissolves in seconds as we slip off our shoes and rustle barefoot through His garden.

If this is the essence of His presence, let us consider that our faith communities should more closely reflect this type of lively, colourful environment; they should encourage greater freedom of expression, so that we can express ourselves in creative worship and wonder. We do not need to attack the past to embrace the future, but if we do not at least consider the need for change, we will not achieve it; the seasons of God will shift around us and we will feel the void with increasing certainty.

We can make a start by asking the Lord how to construct, or facilitate others to configure, atmosphere-design that will encourage people to find freedom. You may not have the budget or the skills you would like initially, but remember 'the combination'. When we move and start, God adds to what we have; as we continue to try, He helps us advance and mature. Favor, provision and like-minded people will gather with the momentum of a holy rolling snowball - all we need to do is start and follow the imprints of God.

UNITY

When Moses and Bezalel teamed up to undertake the construction of the tabernacle, all the people of Israel were asked if they would bring a contribution, but only from a willing heart. Such was their generosity of spirit that they brought too much! This powerful act of unity under-girded the project and blessed its outcome.

There is always power in unity. As we pray for the renaissance of creativity, others in our communities and groups will start to apprehend what God is doing and champion the vision with time and patronage. A network of believers is already appearing as action is birthed. God blessed his people greatly with His presence and leading when they supported His vision for the tabernacle. He will do the same with those who would support this restoration.

Then Moses called Bezalel and Aholiab, and every gifted artisan in whose heart the Lord had put wisdom, everyone whose heart was stirred, to come and do the work. And they received from Moses all the offering which the children of Israel had brought for the work of the service of making the sanctuary. So they continued bringing to him freewill offerings every morning. Then all the craftsmen who were doing all the work of the sanctuary came, each from the work he was doing, and they spoke to Moses, saying, "The people bring much more than enough for the service of the work which the LORD commanded us to do." So Moses gave a commandment, and they caused it to be proclaimed throughout the camp, saying, "Let neither man nor woman do any more work for the offering of the sanctuary." And the people were restrained from bringing, for the material they had was sufficient for all the work to be done - indeed too much. Exodus 36:2-7

ENCOURAGEMENT

As opportunities arise, it is important for us to support and encourage each other - even in twos or small groups to start with. As people of common vision gather, they can pray for and inspire one another to keep going, developing ideas and networks. A collective purpose builds backbone. As the imperative to fortify people for their workplace roles gathers momentum, interest will also increase. New understanding and creative teaching will be required for this, as well as a good guiding framework. Many Christians have a sense of standing alone in their workplaces outside of the church environment, with only passing conversations about the challenges they face. Supportive collectives of like-minded adventurers can go a long way in sustaining success; people dive into deeper relationship with God to release their creative DNA, pursue solutions and change, and galvanize for kingdom impetus in their spheres of influence. Let's pray for these things and for God to assemble the leaders who will guide and motivate such change.

BREAK THE MOULD

Another key to clearing the blockages to creativity is to position ourselves for something new and be open to a wholly fresh approach. During my very first project at art college we were asked to draw an object that we had brought in, so I dutifully got out an HB pencil and some A4 white paper and began a careful composition of the bunch of rose-hips in front of me. The tutor approached and, drinking in my painfully tight rendering, patiently suggested that I should chuck away the white A4 paper and the HB pencil and use something else – anything else. Something strange broke wild and free in that moment, and I found myself ripping paper, blowing paint through drinking straws and layering materials with massive brushes, as the confinements of my high-school training snapped and along with it the need to control the results. Fear of failure in the exploration was broken, allowing the floodgates of joyful creativity to flow. I realize now that that was a pivotal experience in releasing my creative DNA.

If we keep repeating the same patterns we will get the same results. 1 Corinthians 2:9 tells us there are still things to discover that we have not yet seen or heard but that God has banked up, ready to show His people. Are we up for a spot of adventure, where we stop anticipating the same familiar outcome from ourselves as well as from God? We are not confined to our current condition, but we can progress in many directions as we plug into the source.

Sometimes the simplicity of changing the natural helps to change the spiritual - a different environment, mixing with new people, even just a new route to work can be sown as faith for new direction. Listen to new teaching, read areas of scripture you are not familiar with, invite people for dinner you wouldn't normally ask; just follow the nudges of the Spirit until the road materializes before you with new clarity. We are creatures of habit, and sometimes just breaking out of the repetitive grooves that take our lives round in familiar cycles can set us on new paths that cultivate expectation. Changing a habit allows God to speak to us in new ways. It refreshes life and breaks off dry repetition and weariness. The process takes some courage, trust and willingness to accept change when it comes, but it could also open a pivotal moment for you.

PRACTICE PRESENCE

Evolving thriving communion with God leads us to learn how to invite His presence, but then we need to learn how to receive it and treat it with the utmost esteem. He is always with us, and the sweet sense of His presence is tangible and glorious; but we must understand how to host it, so it remains and intensifies. If we practice this in our private times with God and in corporate times of worship, prayer and mission, it will increase. When the Spirit starts to rain down, we can ask how our participation can fulfill His objective. Sometimes the answer is simply worship or intercession. At other times there is a prophetic mandate.

Each soaking is for a different purpose; sometimes it is to bring healing or strength, but always it seems to include the purpose of pouring lavish love in reciprocating action. Artisans must also discover how their creative works practiced within worship and presence can contribute to what God is doing in such times. In the age ahead, learning to host and work with the presence of God is imperative for us all. The Holy Spirit is a teacher who loves to answer questions, so we can learn on the job as well as in the prayer closet. Let's ask Him to teach us.

We can learn much from people who model what regular saturation in God's presence looks like. We can glean from their wisdom and experience. There are to be no jelly-molds that shape all, but we should look for the places that are seeking to facilitate wells and pilot new flight.

HANDS

What skills do you have in your hands already that you can combine with the rest of 'the combination'?

Blueprints + Spirit + Wisdom + Creativity + Existing skill/ability + More skill/ability added by God, joined with Character, Obedience and Perseverance

We have to start somewhere. At the end of this chapter is the outline of a process that can be used by anyone seeking to move in Kingdom creativity. Understanding and working through this process will lead to new direction and blueprint. Once the patterns start to appear, we combine them with the rest of 'the combination', praying for the interaction of the Spirit and asking for acceleration and multiplication. As demonstrated by Bezalel and team, supernatural skill was added as they faithfully provided the components on their part, showing perseverance, obedience and character. We can pray for favor and opportunity: the next time we find ourselves in an outreach situation, a conversation at work with a colleague or another with Mum at the nursery, or wherever there is a problem that requires answers or action, simply ask the Holy Spirit for a creative solution. Offering prayer and inviting people to church are great things to do, but we can also widen our spectrum of response by asking the Lord for understanding for their specific situation, and offering spiritual insight and solution. If we practice, confidence and competence will grow.

UNDERSTANDING WHAT YOU HAVE

If you understand what God has given you, what gifts, what strength and what areas of the five-fold ministry you are best equipped with, you will be a lot more effective and the process will be a great deal more enjoyable! If you know you have a shepherd's heart, then you may be called to be a pastor to the people in your workplace, and you can seek the insights and ideas needed to help them. You may be apostolic in the business world, or prophetic and called to help people in the New Age, or a teacher within the field of science. When we truly understand that the five-fold ministry operates through all believers, and not just in the church building on Sundays, then we may be revolutionized.

Do not be put off by tests of faithfulness. As we determine to move onwards and upwards, like Daniel and Joseph, we will be tested for promotion. Do not be surprised and do not give up!

Some are called to influence kings and queens (men and women of influence and power). If that is you, then who are the kings and queens in your sphere of influence? Pray that God will give them dreams and spiritual experiences that you can interpret. Pray for plans and concepts that will be exactly what they need. Ask for the divine circumstances required for you to demonstrate what God's Kingdom looks like right in the middle of culture.

HOUSE OF PRAYER

There are many types of intercessor. For years, I felt a bit of a failure in this area because I never seemed to get to the hours on my knees with the long list I thought I was suppose to pray for. When I come into the presence of God, I just want to hear and see His creative conversation for that time-frame and respond. Finally I got a revelation: this is prayer! We may all do it a little differently; some people are called to be intercessors, because they love to pray - it is not that hard for them to remember to pray for people, details and situations continuously. Some love a quiet room, some love to walk outside, some love music playing; but we should allow ourselves creative freedom in this department too and not dictate what it should look like for all of us.

However we pray, we need to pray this shift into place, to pray for our churches and lives to be filled with freshly inspired originality – for all the reasons already stated in this book. For many years I have been praying for each stage of this restoration along with the swelling numbers who also see its implication. We have been amazed – beyond amazed – at the things God has made tangible since we started; we had nothing on the ground, just a vision, a sense of what's coming and a response to God's request to intercede.

Prayer and worship should be at the core of this move. But it is also necessary for the arts themselves to be restored as a vehicle for intercession. This will help us to remove constricting boundaries and enable many to enjoy prayer with energetic fervor, through vehicles such as dance, art, poetry and prophetic music.

David worshiped and prayed to God with wild, exuberant creative worship. In some communities we are quite far removed from this, and save exuberance for outside church walls, where it seems acceptable. We refer to David's dance in our worship songs, but no-one moves; everyone feels awkward. To be fair, it is hard to leap into action across the void in creativity. David allowed creativity to be all around him, in dance, in song, in playing the harp and in his prolific plans for the temple that Solomon would build. It is not so hard to get up and dance when an atmosphere of creative freedom is the norm.

THE CREATIVE PROCESS

Here is a practical guide to the creative process, drawn from an education in art and design, but fusing that with the examples of God's Word. If this method is unfamiliar to you, it can be used to engage your creative DNA and help you start to cooperate with the Holy Spirit. Sometimes we do not start because we do not understand the creative process. Or else we give up at a certain stage and assume failure, not understanding that we had genuinely reached a natural and essential stage that required pushing through. This will outline the process in its entirety for any gift, skill set, calling or work environment.

STAGE 1: THE CREATIVE SPACE

In the beginning God created the heavens and the earth. Genesis 1:1

First this: God created the Heavens and Earth—all you see, all you don't see. Earth was a soup of nothingness, a bottomless emptiness, an inky blackness. Genesis 1:1 The Message

God moves out and gets creative; He has a new project in sight and He lays out the blank canvas before Him. First, we need to get 'in the zone' to embark on a new project, and collect the materials we need at the inspirational stage. This may include art equipment, setting up new systems on our computers, making space in our calendars, etc. We might be hoping for a new medical solution, poetry, a new teaching series, a book, a painting or new strategy for business. At this stage we know we want to get creative with the Spirit, but we cannot yet see the outcome; so we prepare in faith and pray for divine inspiration and wisdom.

STAGE 2: AN ATMOSPHERE OF CREATIVITY

The earth was without form, and void; and darkness was on the face of the deep. And the Spirit of God was hovering over the face of the waters. Genesis 1: 2

God was brooding and percolating over His creative project. This stage usually begins with a sense of lacking direction. You are ready for action, but ideas are vague and formless; you have questions and you cannot see the finished outcome. This stage is the beginning of the creative process, and is perfectly normal. Position yourself to receive and expand your thinking on what God can give you. If we just expect more of the same, then perhaps that is what we will receive. But if we expect something else, where are the limits of the Spirit? This is not the time to give up if you do not receive a blinding flash of inspiration that delivers the whole project on a plate. This is where you start to dig and explore, collecting fragments of the picture. If we do not understand the process, we can expect the entire picture in one bite - when it doesn't come, we think we have missed it.

Time spent seeking God's direction will yield gravitation towards things that inspire and catch our attention; these can be written, visual or aural. He comes to meet us in this moment, because we have stepped towards Him and moved in expectation and faith. We are finally saying to Him that we cannot create apart from Him. We recognize our need to allow the Spirit's teaching and instruction through the process. We humble ourselves, submitting gifts and goals. Now we ask, wait and seek for inspiration and assignment.

Start to gather the fragments that appear. They may come through pictures or words from God, scriptures, conversations, experiences, dreams, visions, or through being prompted by the Spirit to do some research for more information and comprehension of a subject matter. Once we start to work with the Spirit to glean inspiration for a certain focus, He can speak to us through anything, even through the actions of the family dog! God loves relationship and conversation. Open your eyes and ears to a wealth of possible communications to help you; catch the pieces and bring them together.

Artistic people are accustomed to this stage and its productivity. Dancers start to experiment with moves and music, musicians begin to experiment with notes, sounds and combinations. Designers will construct various boards to explore amalgamations of mood, colour and concept, and pin them up on the walls in their creative space. The same principles apply to anyone: gather the things around you that inspire, gather the communications of God and the results of directional prompts, and a spiritual concept board will begin to emerge. Sometimes God shows us new combinations of the familiar, or He can give us completely new thought processes to investigate. Sometimes He outlines the skills, gifts and resources we already possess and how they could be used with fresh dynamic; a bit like painting fabulous colour in a room that felt tired: new vigor is breathed and felt.

STAGE 3

Then God said, "Let there be light"; and there was light. And God saw the light, that it was good; and God divided the light from the darkness. Genesis 1:3-4

At this stage there is increased clarity and revelation. In your collection of leads, research and fragments, you start to see patterns forming: combinations that work well, or the direction of a message. Continue to bring the parts together with intention, looking for connection and orientation. Too many of us have lots of fragments from God, scattered and seemingly random; but until we bring them all together, we cannot see the synergy between them. As we fit one piece with another, something magical happens and they spark fire and ideas; direction grows stronger. At this stage, let the Holy Spirit surprise and delight you with new revelation for solutions, creativity and strategy.

STAGE 4

Thus the heavens and the earth, and all the host of them, were finished. Genesis 2:1

In this stage the ideas are coming together: the canvas is taking shape, the dance is forming, new business solutions and programs are binding to take shape. Now keep working and pressing in until you finish the project or complete the outcome, arriving at the intended goal with God's help. God brought all the parts together and worked at the Creation until He was finished. This process can even be used in discovering your calling, gifts or life-direction.

REVIVAL IS MESSY

Leaders who are willing to let this restoration take place in church communities and ministries will need to be prepared to let people start to paddle, bearing in mind that it may look more like the order of the nursery to begin with. It has been said that revival is messy; it is not neat, orderly or controlled, but it is usually wild and a little chaotic. As God begins to move through the new creativity and wisdom that is coming, then it is best to be open to the radical and the power-filled. Charles Finney (1792-1875) preached outside the church to working men, and multitudes were saved because he swam against the direction of the norm. What he did was completely revolutionary and contrary to the church culture in that day, but look at the outcome. God will use the innovation of His nature as part of revival because it cannot be pinned under man's government and control. He is longing for places to break free. We live as though He has a floor and a ceiling, but He has none. He longs to show His people the inconceivable, the spacious rooms of new trust. As creativity meets religious restraint head-on, a little turmoil is guaranteed. A little blood will be spilled here and there, but the results of revolution bring new vistas of vision and fields of faith.

THE IMPOSSIBLE

We always look at what we have already, and struggle to engage with what we consider impossible. Perhaps we cannot imagine Christian art and creativity to be any different from what they are now. How could a painting heal a broken life? How can a dance bring transformation? Yet these things are already happening. What if a sculpture could help to change the hearts of people in positions of great authority because it carried an anointing so impacting that words were hardly needed? A well-known phrase says that a picture is worth a thousand words. A hundred people can see hundreds of different things in one painting, unrestricted by the boundaries of finite words. Only a few years ago, it looked impossible for prophetic words and dream-interpretation to crack open thousands of hearts before God in the festivals, cafes, pubs and streets of Scotland, but it has already happened. New creative dynamite awaits the asking for all the mountains of culture. He is the God of the impossible.

POSITIONING

"The light that is about to be released through the arts will be unprecedented."
Excerpt from the Morning Star Bulletin

In this final chapter we will focus on the Mountain of the Arts and Entertainment and the characteristics of the artisans who can permeate this arena with Kingdom force. This mountain affects all our lives in numerous ways. As a Church, we can greatly aid the revival of God's artisans by recognizing their significance in the wider restoration of the creative DNA in God's people. This concluding chapter aims to begin a dialogue concerning this mountain, and propose a strategy for advancement with orientation. It is time to raise up the missing army of creative warriors and establish their purpose in the church and the mountains of culture.

CREATIVE WARRIORS

"Art is a basic form of prophecy and worship, and there is a beauty and anointing about to come upon a host of holy artists whose prophetic art will burn away the fog that is now over it, just like the sun burns away the fog in the morning. Artists who worship the one true God, who keep their souls purified by the singleness of purpose to glorify the Lord, will be

given a greater power. They will become like prisms that refract the light of heaven and give colour and meaning to the world. As deep as art has plummeted into darkness, the light that is coming will be even greater. Beauty, meaning, and the elevation of all that is good will soon be seen in an extraordinary army of artists. This is the time when everything that has been sown in man, the good and the evil, the light and the darkness, will come to full maturity. The light that is about to be released through the arts will be unprecedented. God will not force people, but He will give them an opportunity to see His light. It is not our job to make men see the light or want the light, but it is our job simply to walk in the light and reveal it."
Excerpts from the Morning Star Bulletin[1]

I had a vision in December 2012: I was on a stage looking out across thousands of people seated in a Christian conference setting; they were waiting, expecting something to begin. I took a ram's horn and blew; the sound reverberated through the auditorium. From amongst the people I saw some who were dressed as soldiers begin to emerge and rise from their place to come forward. I knew they were the creative warriors, the artisans who were willing to answer the call. They wore pieces of armor like those from biblical times, but not complete suits; some pieces were missing. The commanding presence of God was so overpowering in that moment that I felt infinitesimal by comparison, and deeply humbled by a sense of great privilege to be allowed a part in calling the creative warriors into position, in the timing of God. I also realized this was an imperative part of what was coming next as the Kingdom moved forward in the earth. It seemed essential that these warriors were shown who they were and that they had been made ready for this time.

As this journey has progressed, I have come to understand that there is a definite call and directive for the artisans of God; the prophetic, artistic people who have felt the need to spend time and personal resource studying, practicing and evolving areas of artistic gifting. This is a different mandate from the general release of creative DNA discussed at other times in this book.

CAUGHT BETWEEN

At present, many believers who have felt that their life-commission involved specializing in artistic disciplines are stuck between two worlds. They have often trained within world systems to gain technical skill, which holds great merit, but then they have also been taught the philosophy of the arts from the world viewpoint. This creates a framework that is not Kingdom, and encourages artisans to draw from a variety of wells and sources, to build personal stages and to seek man's approval for validation. However, if they attempt to bring their creativity into the church arena, they often meet little understanding of the contribution creativity has to offer, or what the creative DNA of God actually is; so their contributions and gifts struggle to see a place to settle. We are supposed to flow from the life of the church out onto the mission field; sadly, however, because it is not developed extensively within a Kingdom setting very often, the mission field is also missing a great wealth of creative input from Christian artisans.

FIRST THINGS FIRST

To begin change, we must first discern the road we are to follow. Are we to develop our artistic gifts at a higher level as an artisan for specific purpose, or are we to use the general creative DNA available to all God's people for another focus, such as teaching or youth work? Once we see who we are designed to be, we can cast off the shroud of rejection and forge ahead as pioneers ourselves, or join with those who have that calling. The artisans are gifted to serve within many diverse areas for the Kingdom of God, and we will examine some of these within this chapter.

PRIESTLY ANOINTING

We have looked at God's desire for His people to dive deep for wisdom and to trigger the creative DNA at a profound level so that excellent strategy, and more, can be acquired. Parallel to this, the prophetic artisans have a very important role. Where they have grasped the revelation of coming reformation for themselves (practicing access to deep caverns), and where they have allowed the purification of gift and heart, they have an essential role in helping to open and sustain deep wells in God's church. Theirs is to agitate the waters of the Spirit with sound and anointed art forms that offer prayer, worship and prophecy, like the artisans who formed the tabernacle of Moses.

Then the Lord spoke to Moses, saying: "See, I have called by name Bezalel the son of Uri, the son of Hur, of the tribe of Judah. And I have filled him with the Spirit of God, in wisdom, in understanding, in knowledge, and in all manner of workmanship, to design artistic works, to work in gold, in silver, in bronze, in cutting jewels for setting, in carving wood, and to work in all manner of workmanship." Exodus 31:1-5 NIV

The temple was filled with art forms, gold, fine linens, embroidery, jewels and objects of great value, as we looked at in an earlier chapter. Even the priests who were separated to serve the Lord were to be adorned in symbolic holy garments.

Now take Aaron your brother, and his sons with him, from among the children of Israel, that he may minister to Me as priest, Aaron and Aaron's sons: Nadab, Abihu, Eleazar, and Ithamar. And you shall make holy garments for Aaron your brother, for glory and for beauty. So you shall speak to all who are gifted artisans, whom I have filled with the spirit of wisdom, that they may make Aaron's garments, to consecrate him, that he may minister to Me as priest. And these are the garments which they shall make: a breastplate, an ephod, a robe, a skilfully woven tunic, a turban, and a sash. So they shall make holy garments for Aaron your brother and his sons, that he may minister to Me as priest. Exodus 28:1-4

The garments were to be 'holy' or set apart for God, but they were also designed at His request for 'beauty'. Here, we find again that beauty holds considerable significance for God, not just to delight the eyes but to serve a spiritual purpose. The garments were to be woven together in beautiful threads and 'artistically worked' (Exodus 28:6). There were different parts to the costume, with engraved precious stones such as sardis, topaz, emerald, sapphire, diamonds and more. In fact, the whole setting of the temple, along with the robes of the priests, was a feat of allegorical beauty, craftsmanship and artistic excellence. The artisans in that day most certainly had a role of value in the house of God. The designs and directions for this project did not just stem from the good ideas of man or a passion for art; they came in the form of detailed instruction from God Himself. How distant we now seem from valuing beauty, art and craftsmanship as something holy and sacred.

Looking back into history, we can see that before the reformation the church did indeed champion the arts of the day; and great artisans like Michelangelo were used to demonstrate the character and beauty of God. But the graveyard void since that time has lasted so long that we line up to see these historical places on tourist trails; they are from a bygone era. We can certainly learn from and respect the changing seasons of history, but the development of the arts within the church has been painfully slow since those days. Hundreds of years ago it flourished and led the way in culture, greatly influencing it for God's Kingdom. The void is now so wide between those times and the current influence of Hollywood, for example, that we struggle to know where to start and how to redress the balance.

Again, it is important to impress that God did not tell us to ignore the Old Testament when the New Testament came along - it reveals much of His character and those things sacred to His heart.

Neither did Jesus oppose the example of a creative life-style. What He did oppose was art and creativity being used in the wrong spirit: to build great temples of man's religion, to take from the poor to fund extensive projects for the wealthy in the name of God. He opposed people placing their faith in great structures, as if they could earn some merit of God's approval and bargain for His love. When He came to the earth, He came to facilitate a shift so that man could live in personal, close connection with the Father without the mediation of a prophet or priest. Despite this transition, it is true that, at times in church history, the emphasis has still been placed on building great structures for the wrong reasons (for example religiosity); quite rightly, the Reformation revolted against that.

However, somewhere in the mix of man's wrestling and journey to find intimate relationship with a loving God, art and creativity seem to have been injured: caught up in the heat of religious battle and been left with a faint heartbeat, hardly breathing. They have been seen as a distraction, even pernicious at times, resulting in the danger of worshiping created forms rather than the Creator Himself. Books have already been written on this subject to define history and the journey in detail, but I want to present another angle in response to past events. From the excesses to the purification and near extinction of creativity in the church, God wants to restore a new balance and bestow fresh innovation through His people, for the central purpose of demonstrating His wonderfully manifold creative nature. In turn, we can use this fresh creativity to increase effervescent worship which will then take us deeper in to cycles of further divine release.

The aim is not to fill the earth with church buildings over-stuffed with art. The aim is that our believing communities would become hubs of Kingdom creativity; and what is formed within them, through the instruction of the Spirit, can find worth again. Where ingenuity and artistry are ignited, they can be used to go and reach the mountains of culture. The aim is for artistic forms to carry the presence and anointing of God so they can bless the church, but also be used to flow outwards to a world where people are desperate for an encounter with the living God, like the woman at the well (John 4:1–42).

There is a role for artisans who are pure in heart and who are called to create works that carry holiness (this includes all the areas of the arts: dance, poetry, painting, film, etc.). There is a commission to release prophecy and bring edification and declaration. This is about working with the other areas of the five-fold ministry within teams and communities. There is absolutely no room for personal agendas or stages. However, I see these artisans helping, through this level of sacrificial service, to invite and host the presence and purposes of God that lie on the horizon. They will be able to make all kinds of art forms, beyond their current natural ability, that carry layered messages and important mysteries. Many different insights will be seen within one piece, because the art forms will carry something of God's multifarious nature. The prophetic declares, it changes atmospheres, and these art forms will change the spiritual atmosphere in communities within the church. Some artisans will also be commissioned to arenas outside the church walls and used to change the spiritual environment there so that Kingdom activity is greatly enhanced.

MUSIC

We have taken verses like this glorious account in Chronicles to see that music certainly has a part to play in leading God's people into worship in the church:

And it came to pass when the priests came out of the most Holy Place and the Levites who were singers stood at the east end of the altar, clothed in white linen, having cymbals, stringed instruments and harps, and with them one hundred and twenty priests sounding with trumpets- indeed it came to pass, when the trumpets and the singers were as one, to make one sound to be heard in praising and thanking the Lord, and when they lifted up their voice with trumpets and cymbals and instruments of music, and praised the Lord saying; For He is good, For His mercy endures forever, that the house, the house of the Lord, was filled with a cloud, so that the priests could not continue ministering because of the cloud; for the glory of the Lord filled the house of God. 2 Chronicles 5:11-14

However, we usually stop there – forgetting that the tabernacle was also full of all sorts of creativity and craftsmanship that was considered equally holy. Music is indeed a wonderful way to invite the presence of God and for His people to bring worship and focus on Him. There is a mandate for this area too, not just to continue existing but to come higher. If prophetic art works are to be crafted through training and a heavy reliance on the Spirit's input, then the same should apply to music.

While we all enjoy worship songs, it is true that without effort we can easily fall into merely singing words for the sake of them; there is little challenge in a sing-song. However, the presence of God is meant to challenge us, to provoke us to plunge, to help us to hear and catch what God is showing us as we assemble together. If we are simply playing a song set, with methodical skill alone, then we must take an honest look at how deeply this runs.

How much do we engage the Spirit in the process? Using songs written by others in inspired moments is obviously not wrong, and part of musical culture. Many songs are anointed for such use to great effect. But we must be careful not to hide behind the safe, rigid parameters of their pages alone, without creative deviation or prophetic flow; these are the things that stretch and grow us from the inside.

Worship leaders who know how to plummet into the presence of God and take others with them with anointing and skill have paid a cost, if you ask them their stories. Their lives have allowed character to be sculpted, they have taken narrow roads and many risks, and have sold out for a God full of mysteries; they have found treasure, and you can hear it in their music when they play.

Music has had center-stage for worship in the church for a long time, with only a little input from the other areas of artistry – another product of our Protestant history. Where restoration begins to surface for the other areas of the arts, we must be alert to the appearance of a territorial spirit that seeks to work through musicians with indignant agitation over ground long held by them alone. But this rises up because we fail to see the great perspective of the creative DNA of God's people and the priestly role of the artisans, and it will actually block what God is doing with competition and pride. Just because the area of music is firmly in place does not mean it has reached the level at which God intended it to operate. It faces just as great a challenge for change as the other components of art.

As musicians embrace the missing areas and artisans and are willing humbly to explore new concepts in unity of vision and friendship, a new power-house of God's Spirit will hit the Body of Christ and ricochet back into all the areas of creative expression, including music. We must aim for distinction and lay down our arms of competition and territory. The territory belongs to the Lord, and when creativity is fully restored in the church, we will be able to rise and challenge the filth we see it used for in the world more effectively; a higher blessing awaits. The way forward is to take the low road with each other, to forget personal agendas and seek the Lord together for a whole new dawn of the arts in the church.

INTERCESSION

Another role for the artisan is that of intercession. We are familiar with the use of music for prayer and worship (Joshua 6:1-6), but it is perhaps a leap for some of us to think of using art as a valid form of prayer beyond words. But words are certainly not the only thing God has given us to pray with, and artistic people often find themselves frustrated by the limitation of words alone; they long to make something, or move. Although there are already some believers using art as intercession, I see this becom more prolific as a reformation of the arts within the church gathers force. Artisans will be moved to pray through many types of expression, on a completely different level than we have currently recognized; these will include prayer through drama, creative writing, sculpture, etc.

Some creative works will be taken into the mountains of culture because of the weight of intercession and anointing that rests on them; works made in prayer for specific schools, neighborhoods, workplaces, geographical areas and places of influence. Some of these pieces will be formed in worship within the wider body of the church, and they will be blessed to go out and impart what they carry – this could be a dance team, a film or a painting.

I see whole Christian communities beginning to understand the power of impartation while praying over pieces in collective faith; they catch the vision that these art forms can help to change the atmospheres of culture, to change hearts, or to bring healing and restoration and provide opportunity to share the Kingdom. If this sounds farfetched, I have already seen this beginning to happen, as perhaps have some of you – people transfixed in the healing power of anointed art, seekers flocking towards Kingdom creativity with fascinated open hearts, engaging with their Creator.

Those of us in hot pursuit of this revelation are being shown wild new blueprints loaded with symbolic significance, and are being asked to form them. Momentum is gathering and we stand at the beginning of a new path, with eyes fresh for more to come.

The Mountain of the Arts and Entertainment

Many artisans have a call to The Mountain of the Arts in culture. If we are going to redeem our creative inheritance to gain Kingdom terrain within society, we need creative warriors with the right equipment who are ready to invade this mountain. I am not just talking about the Christian artisans out there surviving, but about them being valued, schooled and sent out by the church with prayerful backing. It is difficult for people in our Church families to go and invade culture for God if they do not feel worth much in the Church family home; it leaves them vulnerable. Children who do not feel esteemed at home tend to go out into the world feeling damaged and rejected and can be hit hard out there. With prayer and some action, the Church can become a place of supportive and informed underpinning for God's people who are endeavoring to let the creative DNA loose in the mountains of society.

The Mountain of the Arts and Entertainment has towering impact on the cultures around us in the western world and beyond. To be able to bring change, we must first understand the mountain and how the enemy has used the talent within it to broadcast his message. There are two trees from which we can draw: the tree of the knowledge of good and evil, and the tree of life. The tree of life is accessed through our spirit in connection to God's Spirit; it brings us revelation from Him. However, God told us not to eat of the tree of the knowledge of good and evil, because it is accessed through the soul and also provides information sourced from the enemy.

And the Lord God commanded the man, saying, "Of every tree of the garden you may freely eat; but of the tree of the knowledge of good and evil you shall not eat, for in the day that you eat of it you shall surely die." Genesis 2:16-17

The entertainment industry draws from this tree. A tree's roots are wider than what is seen above the earth. As people engage with certain films, books and computer games, they do not realize they are engaging with far-reaching roots into devilry, soul and deception. They do not see the cord pulling them into addictive pursuits that in turn cause their flesh to hunt for more; so they watch more evil and see, hear and absorb more darkness, because it anesthetizes the pangs of the flesh. It is a cyclical incarceration. Many people 'feed' themselves in their leisure time with a form of entertainment, but there are many forms in the main stream that offer gratuitous violence, dark spiritual influence, hopelessness, twisted themes and wrong sexual influences and appetites. A substantial part of the entertainment industry has become marked by a lack of purity, and what is now morally acceptable is low in the mire.

The antidote lies in holy, powerful creativity – untainted by worldly greed and the need for fame, not chained by the desperate human cry for affirmation; pure artistry that can only come from God.

Part of the remedy is to make art forms that draw from the tree of life; and to carry this commission we need artisans who walk in great purity with an unshakable focus on God - the Bezalels and Josephs. The roots of the tree of life are also far-reaching; they run through the Word and the Spirit, into the fire and passion of God and access the heavenly realms. For this reason, artisans must become masterful at listening to God and learning His language, intensely dependent on the Spirit to collate works of influence and intercession. The battle is on; not so much for the conviction of God's existence, but for the portrayal of His identity. He is rarely represented as His true nature, but often shown as callous, detached or muddled with the character traits of the enemy, until there is no clear distinction.

Lance Wallnau teaches that the Arts and Entertainment mountain can release the glory of God more than any of the other mountains because it can capture things in music or in a visual state. Believers in this mountain are in gold-mine positions, but he says that we are not teaching our people to be relevant in positions of influence in this mountain.[2]

To better understand the Mountain of the Arts and Entertainment, I have outlined some main themes that dominate this area of culture at present, and have examined ways in which they manifest in the world. Then I have added a Kingdom perspective to show how we can counteract negative influences with Kingdom morality.

THEMES OF DOMINANCE IN THE MOUNTAIN

POWER & GREED

WORLD: Power is a dominating theme in many of the arts. Physical beauty, intellect, money or physical strength are often used to achieve it. Power is used to control situations and outcomes, frequently with lawlessness. Sometimes that is shown to end badly, but equally the outcome is one of achieving success or vengeance. It is sometimes portrayed as the power of 'good' or man's power within himself, but rarely as God's power for a positive outcome.

KINGDOM: God is the highest power over all. Power can be transferred from God through us, as our lives are submitted to Him. There is no ladder-climbing in the Kingdom, no success of the flesh in its own strength; but as we humble ourselves, He will lift us up (James 4:10).

FLESH

WORLD: There is a huge increase in the acceptance of more explicit sexual material in the arts, but also anything of a sensual nature; whatever is pleasing to the flesh. Moral standards seem much lower than just ten or twenty years ago. The most common thread is the portrayal of women as sexual objects and adornment, devaluing them and setting standards for them that are based on outward appearance and sexual availability, rather than skill, intelligence or human value. Some music videos have taken a leap into the realms of soft pornography. Proverbs warns men of such snares and their road to death, yet many men are trapped by the sliding morals of the culture we live in. It is little wonder we have seen a horrifying increase in sexual abuse and the sexual trafficking of women and girls.

KINGDOM: God values human life so much that He sent His only son to suffer and die for us, so that we could be saved and have a personal relationship with God as a greatly loved, protected and enjoyed child of the Father (John 3:16). This goes way beyond the exceptional kind of love we feel, even for our own children. Each one of us was redeemed at high cost. Forgiveness is extended to all of us as we come and bring our struggles to God and seek a holy life to guard us from the influences around us. God has made provision for the desires He gave us within the context of marriage, and the Bible gives us healthy guidelines for relationships of purity and unity.

VIOLENCE & HATRED

We have seen an increase in violent content within the arts, promoted by technology. Although not wrong in itself, technology has made graphic dark and violent imagery more widely available, particularly to a younger age group. Gone are the seemingly innocent days of Pac-Man. The disconnection from real life can numb people to the real value of human life and the emotion behind acts of violence. There are endless movies where many are murdered to achieve a goal - the glorification of power through hatred and destruction.

KINGDOM: As said above, God values lives. In Kingdom we are taught to live in the power of the Spirit and that God will fight for us and with us. We are to put on the armor of God (Ephesians 6:10-17). Our fight is not against the flesh and blood of mankind, directing hatred and disdain towards people, but we fight against principalities and powers, rulers of wickedness in heavenly places (Ephesians 6:12).

THE SUPERNATURAL

WORLD: The increasing hunger for all things supernatural and connected to a spiritual world beyond our natural world, combined with the advancement of computer graphics, has caused an explosion of film and TV programs about vampires, witches, supernatural settings and abilities. Harry Potter opened the floodgates to the popularity and acceptance of supernatural gifts and powers as cool and desirable.

But the source of power in many of these programs is confusing. Sometimes it seems a mix of good and bad, but the lines of distinction have been blurred, leading to confusion in people as to the difference between God and the devil. There is a widespread deep deception that draws many into a fascination with the supernatural and leads them to develop an affinity with darkness unawares, without the discernment of dark from light. Thus doors are opened to many nefarious influences that ensnare people. This all seems to create, in some areas of the religious community, further suspicion of all things supernatural.

KINGDOM: In Joel 2:28 God said He would pour out His Spirit on ALL flesh in these times, that people would have dreams and see visions. The increase in hunger for all things other-worldly is in response to God pouring out His Spirit, waking people up to see that there is more than just the world of the five senses. The enemy seeks to take advantage of that, but ultimately God's people have the greater power in their hands.

In Daniel 4, Daniel was proved more outstanding than the greatest diviners and clairvoyants because he carried the Spirit of God in him. So do we, but we have to take that out there to where there is spiritual hunger, because most people do not associate church with the kind of supernatural power they see on the TV.

Yet God has equipped His church with many spiritual gifts and supernatural abilities, and He has called His people to heal and do miracles in His name. A life in God is full of the supernatural when we acknowledge it and work with it. Initially created by God, supernatural gifting is being counterfeited by the enemy, and it is time for the church to address the spiritual hunger out there with the tools we have already been given to do so.

LOVE

WORLD: The human need for love and acceptance is one of the most common themes, but apart from God it is mainly focused on romance and the hope that love from another human being will fill the void; which, of course, it does not. The focus is usually on the 'falling in love' and initial attraction stage, and rarely on the reality of relationship-longevity or mature love; this paints a very unrealistic picture. The shallow perceptions only teach people that attraction is love and that trying a string of relationships is normal. Marriage has become obsolete, or approached lightly and quickly with a fast get-out clause if things do not work. This view of marriage is common in movies, but leads people into endless heartbreak and rejection.

KINGDOM: God is love (1 John 4:8) and, as our maker, He created us to need His love, to need the intimate connection with Him as a Father. When people do not know God closely (even Christians), they search for love in all the wrong places, trying to fill the void that only the immense love of God can fill. God's plan is marriage between one man and one woman as a partnership, bound together with God. When we are filled with His all-encompassing love for us, we can extend love to others: to a spouse, to family, to friends, to strangers even - because we give from that source and not our own strength.

AREAS OF THE MOUNTAIN

Film, television and literature are all affected by the themes we've just looked at: power and greed, etc. They also quest to explore human life in all its complexities. Many times the story-line explores how humans deal with various challenges apart from God. However, the shift is coming in these areas, and already we see works from the mountain-tops that strongly reflect the message of hope and help: films like 'The Passion of the Christ'[3] and 'Les Miserables'.[4]

There are other areas of this mountain that deserve investigation, such as fashion, interior design and so on. We shall explore, in outline, some of these while recognizing that there are many more areas of the arts and crafts to consider. Further wisdom and revelation will come from people who understand them in more depth.

FASHION

The western fashion industry, like many areas of art and design, is influenced from the top down. Styles and seasons are dictated by major designers, and lines and trends filter down to High Street level and mass production. At the top of the mountain there is huge pressure to perform, to remain in favor and success. The world behind the scenes can show little kindness as the fires of competition breed a hotbed of elitism. By the time styles proceed to production levels this becomes more diluted.

However the ethos from the high echelons of the fashion houses have carved the standards of appearance for generations, particularly for women. 'Very thin' has been the most desirable standard of beauty for decades, and statistics of anorexia and eating disorders have steadily risen, with women between the ages of 15 and 30 being the most affected.[5] But, beyond this, the majority of women and some men do not like their appearance, constantly finding fault with it because they will never measure up to the models in glossy magazines. Anorexia is very rare in developing countries like Africa, where it is not desirable to be thin. Mass-production of fashion-wear has also caused the exploitation and unjust treatment of labor in poor countries.

I praise you because I am fearfully and wonderfully made; your works are wonderful, I know that full well. Psalms 139:14 NIV

We are God's creative work, His sculpture; each one unique, individual. Contrary to what the world of fashion tells us, we are beautiful the way He made each one of us. It is our responsibility to steward well the body He gave us and care for our health, but we do not have to measure up to fashion-driven expectations. Jesus paid a supreme cost for us, and He wants us to celebrate and love the way that God made us and be free from the impossible measuring stick.

Freed from the negative aspects, fashion is a highly exciting area with massive scope for Kingdom influence and originality. The anointing was stored in the cloth of Peter's handkerchiefs, and when people touched them they were healed and delivered (Acts 19:12). Beautiful designs and fabrics made from God's blueprints could carry all sorts of anointing for specific purposes. Just as the garments for Aaron's priestly outfit were works of art, beautiful clothes could be designed and made by believers, without the constrictions of unsuitable worldly trends. Clothing can be used to carry messages through visual imagery, words and logo, to display symbolic meaning through colour, pattern and shape; the scope is enormous. God also wants to give His people ingenuity and insight for the technical advance of the textiles themselves. Just as Lycra was a ground-breaking material, there are similar extraordinary advances to come through cloth and fabric combinations.

INTERIOR DESIGN & ARCHITECTURE
Interior design has not suffered the same decline, in terms of the look and focus of a product or interior; this can be refreshing. Some design houses have made increasingly progressive design available to the mass market.

The downside is the focus on materialism: filling our houses with seemingly meaningless objects that we cannot afford and attempting to keep up with cultural standards. Mass-production has a positive aspect, in that is it accessible, but even that can impose great social cost, in terms of fewer small business opportunities and poor working conditions in impoverished countries where wages are very low. Materialism has also helped to create huge debt in western countries, and this is reaching crisis point.

In the Church, architecture was once used as a significant vehicle to mark a standard, like the high steeples of places of worship seen across communities and cities; some are still standing many hundreds of years later. These are examples of the most ornate and spectacular architecture in the world. Lack of resource and vision means the church rarely builds anything close to these masterpieces today.

In this area, there is the fascinating journey of 'atmosphere design' awaiting us. God can give us plans for environments and objects, and help us execute the outcome. They will be designed for specific agendas and will help to invite and increase His presence and glory, to set a particular spiritual climate in that place for others to receive. Heaven is not limited to our perception of interior design and spaces; there are many inconceivable rooms in heaven full of the eternal. We can ask God to show us those rooms and grant us access to share in their bounty, and then release it on earth (John 14:2).

Our homes could radiate a spiritual atmosphere that influences people as they enter. I have seen this happening many times now; art and atmosphere design that affects the spiritual climate, helping people to be more receptive to specific things from heaven. Remember that the tabernacle demonstrated to us the significance of atmosphere design. God loved to fill those spaces with His presence.

Equally, He has plans for new architectural projects that reflect His nature and sovereignty, that send messages to the world of who He is; in buildings created to fulfill all sorts of aspirations within the mountains of culture. He is just waiting for His architects to seek for them. I believe that, as we search the Spirit, we can design and co-create environments that greatly honor God. We do not worship the objects or buildings, but we can seek to make creative forms that lead people towards the message of God and cause them to ponder His ways, His beauty, His sovereignty and His salvation.

MUSIC

Popular music struggles with originality in this era, perhaps more than any other. There was a definite sound to each of the last few decades, but this time-frame seems loaded with a mishmash of repetition from the previous eras, or arduous chanting of simplistic musical sounds. As previously discussed, popular music videos contain a surprisingly shocking slide of morality, and the devaluing of women. There was a day when they were just stories to accompany good music; now they seem to prostitute souls. As a woman, I find it degrading to watch, and it is ensnaring to men. Yet these images are common-place and widely available to young eyes. It seems you cannot just be gifted musically without having to sell your soul. Of course there are many genres of music, and each is open to the influences of world culture and its topics; but it comes back to which tree is the source, and that is usually apparent in the finished product.

Music is a beautiful gift given to us from God; it creates atmospheres, leads us into worship and fills up our senses. Just like all the other areas of the arts, new inspiration will fill this area when there are musicians willing to seek and stretch. There is also much interplay to be explored between music and the other areas of the arts, to produce new combinations from a place of unity.

DANCE AND MOVEMENT

Within music and dance, the more classical forms seem to be affected less by carnal or shadowy themes. However, ferocious competition leads to the pursuit of worldly excellence, which in turn can result in struggle with perfectionism and striving. Although beautiful art can be produced through much training and effort, we have to remember the difference between the excellence of the world and the excellence of the Kingdom. God does not want us to shy from hard work, but striving in our own strength for our own stage can kill; and many have fallen.

Contemporary street dance is one area that is seeing exciting art forms, capturing the imagination of youth. It is highly creative and intended to express the movement of heaven. Unfettered within the church, there is so much ethereal beauty and power that is yet to be expressed through this medium that will carry the supernatural forces of heaven.

LITERATURE

As with all the other areas, the common and dominant influences weave their way through the volumes of literature available, from newspapers to novels, with the outcomes already discussed. Kingdom progress finds exhilarating new vehicles such as slam poetry being used to proclaim gritty messages and prophecy. As we increasingly learn to interplay the various creative forms, writing and poetry could be used to engage in original ways. The incorporation of words into other works of art such as paintings and sculpture is not new, but it could be significantly developed; and with the wealth of penmanship available to us from the Word, the exploration of this area will continue.

Thankfully, like music, this area has not suffered a dearth of encouragement or volume within the church. An almost overwhelming multitude of Christian resources is widely available, with its span greatly increased through the internet. Advancement would see literature written for the mountains of culture – works full of Kingdom values and message – yet cleverly non-religious in language and approach. Such modern parables could intertwine hope for the hopeless through their tales and draw the starving to Jesus, while at the same time cutting through the guarded apprehensions people have towards religiosity. One such example is The Shack by William P. Young.

ADVERTISING

Advertising itself is a powerful medium. It can sell for good or bad, it can alert us to things that are advantageous, and it can sell us false truths and tempt us with products we do not need. Explosive volumes of advertising (together with television programs selling people a life of happiness through materialism, life style and beautiful bodies) have led many to submerge into the grim mire of deep debt. The lure of the quick fix with little forethought has contributed substantially to the crashing economy of many nations today.

The skills of excellent advertising can also help to send emphatic messages for such topics as justice and the fight against poverty. Kingdom skills can be used to develop advertising for righteousness, finding favor through prayer, and for the market opportunities that will be needed. God can bring revelation that helps His people to see things ahead of time so they have insight into what people will require and respond to; this, in turn, will give them breakthrough campaigns. The focus, as in all the other areas, should be on the Father and not about acclaim. He wants to produce ideas that will bring a very different result to the current outcomes of man's campaigns.

INVENTION AND PRODUCT DESIGN

This has become a huge industry; there are products and gizmos for everything, as invention becomes more accessible. There are many positive sides to increased invention. It has helped to fuel mass-production, and we have already highlighted the pros and cons of this. Object and product design reaches into every area of life, from the decorative to the highly practical – and even life-saving. God has many divine inventions to deposit within His people as we seek Him for the revelation of what is needed and what will bring breakthrough solutions to difficult problems.

FINE ART

We have already discussed this area in some detail with respect to wells, sources and outcomes, and we have discussed exceptional skill without Spirit. This is one area within the church that needs revival, having long been diminished and misunderstood. Talented believers hold within themselves stunning ideas and joyful artistry, when given the opportunity to release it. I am discovering that when you uncork the bottle, champagne emerges from people whom God has prepared. At a higher level of skill on the spectrum, there is much to paint, draw and sculpt to unleash intercession, message and prophecy.

PHOTOGRAPHY

This is an area that has actually developed considerably with the aid of technology. Many have portrayed the utterly spectacular Creation and the 'works of His hands' with delightful sensitivity (Psalms 92:4). Earlier in this book, in the section on working with the supernatural, I described what happened at CLAN Gathering when dozens of photos captured inexplicable images of supernatural presence. The images themselves seem to ignite a sense of the tangible presence of God for onlookers after the event. Photography has often captured supernatural activity in Christian meetings that has not been seen by the naked eye, such as circular orbs of light that can even appear to have wheels and circles within them. They have been photographed all over the world, and we have recorded these phenomena a few times on home ground, always in meetings where there has been an intense presence of God.

Photography has an essential part to play in recording such activity in the season ahead, as the heavenly creative dynamic combines with our own abilities. The images will become commanding works of art themselves that carry intention.

How do we Reach the Mountain of the Arts and Entertainment?

I love the arts and I love film. The reason I am writing this book is not to spread disparaging opinions of all things creative in the world; but to help redirect Kingdom values to correlate with forms of creativity, so that we can see ethereal power and beauty released though them upon the earth. Over the coming years, there is still much shaking of world systems to take place. As eternal wisdom is released over the same years, we can use it to influence the mountains with tidings of hope, healing, solution, power, miracles and, ultimately, salvation in God. Every single age group and people type is greatly affected by the mountain of the arts and entertainment, so how do we bring change?

The previous section "Areas of the Mountain" begins to bring understanding of what is actually at work in this area of society on a global scale. This vast arena covers many niches, so I have generalized in order to highlight central themes and bring a foundational understanding of the wheels at work. Greater exploration needs to be done to find the details within areas of this mountain; the nuts and bolts. The point is to have an understanding of what's going on so we can see how to motivate change.

DREAM

I had a dream one night. I was in the central area of an art college, which had a large dome of glass windows. People were carrying out various artistic activities in small groups throughout the main space. I understood my role was to 'sort things out', and as I moved from group to group I was learning and interacting with the various exercises taking place. I interpreted most of the dream's message, but the part that baffled me was a colossal mound of rock within this indoor area. I wandered round the back of the rock and found a horrifying group of demonic entities. The leader seemed utterly intimidating as he scowled at me from the rock's pinnacle, and I silently assessed he was too powerful for me to pull down and that I was lacking enough strength or anointing to do so. Immediately a very thick rope appeared in my hand, and with one swift movement I lassoed him, pulling him from the pinnacle. I then repeatedly beat him off the ground from side to side, as he continuously diminished in size, until eventually he disappeared. When he dematerialized, so did his cohorts. I had no idea what the large rock represented, and prayed until I heard the phrase 'seven mountains', which I confess I'd never really heard of until then. Thus began the exploration of the fascinating revelation into invading the mountains of culture. Since then I have realized that what I saw in the dream was the mountain of the arts and entertainment. I believe it is an encouragement to us that what may seem to be impossible is not. God can place in our hands the exact strategy we need, combined with the weapons of our faith, to bind and tear down principalities and powers over areas where He commissions us to go.

Moving in the Opposite Spirit

To make considerable progress in this arena, artisans must carry Kingdom traits that bring the opposite spirit to the principalities and powers that rule over this mountain at present. One of the main ways we can counteract the darkness is to demonstrate the love of God by showing people they are valuable – because throughout this mountain there is an underlying message that value can only be obtained conditionally, and that whatever is required for one to be regarded as valuable can actually damage. The worth of people is very low; women are mainly measured by physical beauty and youth, and men seem more valuable if they have power and money. People are portrayed as easily dispensable.

Jesus paid the highest cost for the lives of all men, women and children, and the message of God's supreme love can break the low self-esteem nurtured in this mountain. A lack of purity and holiness is rife, which encourages the opposite ethos of promiscuity to seem like freedom; but this is the very road that robs people of their value. The works and lives of God's people, commissioned to this mountain, should be ones of sustained purity and holiness. We are to be in the world but not of the world (John 17:14–18). We are to know our value and the great price paid for our lives. So we do not need to be entangled by what other people are doing, but nor do we judge them.

Jospehs

Many artisans called to this mountain are being chiseled in secret to prepare a Joseph-type character and faithfulness within them. The lure of worldly success and fame becomes dull to the submitted, sculpted heart;

distractions and temptations minimize in the chiseling. Some artisans are ready to pick up their tools and go to war in intercession through the arts. The first call already resonates in the ears of some creative warriors – wired and willing, audacious and ready. Timing means that these first ranks will have to pioneer the roads, sharing what they learn on route.

As the creative warriors come forward, I sense the Lord saying that what has not been recognized will be recognized, what has not had favor will have favor, and what has not been seen will be seen; so that the plans and purposes of God become apparent in this hour. Some are still being prepared in the mold, and it is important for us to discern the stages of others on this journey. Who are the ready warriors, and who are the ones who need a little more time tucked away from front lines while school is still in session?

UNTAINTED

Change will also come through creative works that are conceived through an exceptional heart; some simple in form, others highly accomplished and complex – untainted art forms that carry the power to break off the poisons of evil with hallowed purity. Jesus carried a purity that defeated darkness, to show us it was wholly possible. His tactics were humility and the avoidance of goals such as self-gain or the riches and power of this world. He did not ever use the gifts of God as a vehicle for self-glory and He refused to come under the influences around Him. He taught the people the character of God through love, and displayed the power and sovereignty of God through supernatural signs and wonders.

PRINCIPLE

Creative warriors need to apprehend the principles of identity, value, character, obedience, faithfulness and perseverance. One thing many artisans have had to learn is tenacity: to hold to their brand of artistry and not allow it to become swallowed by the many conflicting factors they face. Some of these tests of stamina make us who we are, and become ingrained in order to form indispensable stamina for the long road of ministry. Solomon began well; God gave him astounding wisdom and creativity, and as a ruler he made Israel a great nation; but he became distracted – who wouldn't, with seven hundred wives?! He was disobedient, marrying women from many nations that worshiped other gods, turning against God's instructions; this eventually led his heart to their idols and his life to the place of despair.

When God gives us wisdom, skill and great gifts for a certain charge, we should pay even more attention to our character and obedience, to keep us from falling and failing. The greater the gift, the more the responsibility. Many artisans want high success but have no idea of the cost. The world is full of the shattered lives of famous people who have paid a great price for their success and discovered that the reality is nothing like the dream.

PURPOSE

In addition to preparation, distinguishing our purpose will set our feet on the path of clarity where focus and detail will be sharpened. If we are unsure of where we are headed, we will wander aimlessly and passion will decline. Being creative for the sake of being creative is not enough; but even the smallest glimpse of a vision can show us the way ahead, even if that is just one step at a time. What land is the Lord calling you to influence? If the Children of Israel didn't know the land they were to take or the cities they were to pull down, then they wouldn't have got very far. What area of the mountains is He asking you to reach? Remember that creativity reaches into every single mountain of culture. Come to God without a box and see where He starts to direct you.

What are the gifts and skills you have in your hand already? Some of us have been trained in various areas of the arts, formally or on the job, or, most commonly, a combination of the two. Artisans rarely put all their eggs in one basket, and are able to cross into different areas of skill and understanding. I spent years training in the area of fashion and textile design, and later interior design; but when I felt God was asking me to lay down my career and focus on developing prophetic evangelism, I wondered why on earth I did all that training and work in the industry.

A few short years later I found myself organizing teams and events that required many of the skills I learned in college and business. Now I use almost all of my training and experience (in art, design and business) to make art forms, to project-manage events and teams, to write and speak, or to do whatever else God asks of me. Your training and experience may presently seem limited to your current sphere of influence, but when we present all that we have to the King, He adds to it, and we find ourselves involved in releasing much greater things than our box determines. Even if that box had been hugely successful in worldly terms, it cannot compare to being part of God's eternal plans.

The perspective of the divine is always to come higher and not settle for the smallness of short-lived worldly accomplishment. In his loss of eternal perspective, Solomon wrote 'There is nothing new under the sun' (Ecclesiastes 1:9); and when we draw from the wells that are earthly and temporal, we will eventually find the same disillusionment as he did (Jeremiah 2:13). If we draw from the everlasting well, our bucket finds the effervescence of the waters of life, which can flow through our creative works and out towards others.

There are many valid assignments for the artisans. Some of us are called to be pioneers – ground-breakers and road-builders. Some are called to help establish settlements and develop them. There are worshipers, with priestly anointing to help the church dive into the deep waters of the Spirit; there are intercessors, who realize prayer through multimedia; there are creative teachers with fresh revelatory messages; there are those called to bring the voice of justice in the struggle against poverty; there are the prophets, declaring messages inside and outside the Church through art forms; and there are the healers, demonstrating the power of God.

There will be apostles to the mountain of the arts and entertainment, and there will be apostles who bring the specific areas of creativity into arenas of culture and the Church, to oversee and help release it on a wider scale. There are artisans called to the film industry and television, those called to write books, to dance and to produce major works of art that are not even labeled Christian or aimed at the Christian market. Their purpose is to take Kingdom ground in culture, and fill environments with His glory. There are so many categories to consider, that resources are needed to help define the areas where the Lord will bring creative restoration.

However, in the day of beginnings, we can ask the Lord to show us what we already possess, then ask where is He directing us to use it. It is the time of pioneers and courage, of unprecedented favor for those who are willing to be prepared and sent. If we all look for a slot in the mountain of the Church, we will be disappointed. Some will be sent there but many will be called into the mountains of culture to make inroads; small or large, but all valuable. Let's not be offended if our churches cannot make room for dozens of creative people painting every Sunday; that may not be what God is asking you to do. Let's take personal responsibility to search the Lord for where we should be positioned and how we should start.

TEAM WORK

One of the strongholds in the arts is individualism. We are encouraged to advance our own kingdom, as it were. We are trained to find our own stage and hold on to it. Self-reliance is encouraged instead of dependence on God; trust in one's own gift and strength to make things happen. We move in the opposite spirit by fulfilling the first commandment:

Jesus said to him, "'You shall love the Lord your God with all your heart, with all your soul, and with all your mind". This is the first and great commandment. Matthew 22:37-38

Other people are seen as competition; thus jealousy, strife and hatred are rife in this mountain. We oppose this when we fulfill the second greatest commandment:

And the second is like it: 'You shall love your neighbour as yourself.' Matthew 22:39

The army of God's creative warriors will have to fight as one, preferring one another, lifting others up higher, training and mentoring the next generation. There is no room for individualism and performance. We must guard against a territorial spirit, where we want to hang on to every sliver of ground and recognition for our area of creativity and our own gifts. God is confronting this within His artisans, and many will sense it rising up within them where it had previously gone unnoticed. Allow the Lord to show you where this is hiding in your life, where individualism and performance have a foot-hold. We need to repent and go all out to move in the opposite direction.

This may even look like a time of being asked to lay some stuff down for a while so that others can come higher. We should meet the testing head-on, as an opportunity to mature and respond quickly. Working faithfully with what we are given, and dropping the diva attitude to think like a team player, will multiply our gifts so they can serve in the army for eternal purpose. This is a crucial key to purifying the creativity in God's people, readying us for work in the mountains.

Iron sharpens iron, and teams gather strength. Many times a little conflict within teams is used by God to sculpt character; so it becomes a guardian for the gifting in ourselves and others, steering those gifts towards safe borders. Teams are not designed to stifle uniqueness. We can often soar at far higher levels of ability and anointing when we play a team sport. It helps to keep our lens focused on the heavenly agenda and alert to the journey of our team-mates and not just our own. As we extend our own strength outwards for the good of the whole, we find an incomparable infilling awaits.

Accountability to others prevents us falling into the unmarked graves of deception. It can catch us at the point of stumbling and alert us to the loose branches concealing the deathly pit below. Lone rangers can be easily deluded within their own universe and are prone to the puncture wounds of pride. Companions on the journey shake our tight perspectives loose from their provincial holds. In short, teams kill individualism. The Word shepherds us to submit to trusted leadership, to preserve and bring wise council on the road to being a friend of God. Your leaders are commissioned by God to keep watch over your soul (Hebrews 13:17).

COMPETITION AND EXCELLENCE

In a society fueled by individualism and performance, we have learned the art of constant comparison. Either we come off worst and feel inferior, or we feel superior when others fall short of our prowess; neither brings life to us. The Master Craftsman seems to have an aversion to the conveyor belts of mass-production when forming His own Creation. No two leaves are identical, no two human beings are, either. The game of comparison can rob us of self-worth and embed in us critical mechanisms that we use to aim fire at others in the search for our own confidence.

Before I knew God I did this for years, but from my own self-assessments I was always left wanting. No matter how hard I worked, I didn't meet the standard; no matter how hard I tried to align with the painful perfections of the fashion arena, I was defective. The constant dripping tap of comparison and cynical assessment of others and ourselves can kill us and the creative works that flow from us.

Our greatest healing is to be found among the waves of God's unconditional love, the layers of learning our uniqueness as His personal art works. These disentangle us from failure and the deathly standards of the world. Over time these truths galvanize us with the strength that stands guard, alert to the enemy's schemes and put-downs. It gets progressively easier to swat the hornets before they settle.

When we focus outwards on the greater purpose and team unity, the temptation to compare is stifled. When we see our moving part in the Body of Christ and our credible contribution, we do not have to be afraid of what we lack; we can celebrate the contributions of others, because the suffocating hooks of competition have been extracted and we are free to compose together.

STRATEGY

Teams require certainty of vision and strategy. We can only go where God is giving us latitude. Heaven's definition must carve the location of our calling into the mountains. Then we need intelligence as to the spiritual dynamics at work within that sphere, and a plan of action to move in the opposite spirit. What are the details of strategy? Where will God give us authority and favor to advance? And what does the task force need to carry with it to break strongholds of influence? We absolutely need God ideas not just good ideas. Many good ideas have made little difference even if they were carried out by well-meaning Godly people. The Spirit holds the eternal tactics. As we move in close and stay close, He will navigate us through shark-infested waters so we can deliver the cargo we carry to the famished.

WEAPONS

It is a real leap for some of us to see that the paintbrush we hold in our hand is a spiritual weapon, just like a sword; but when we really understand the creativity of God, this will not be such a jump. Earlier we looked at the passage in Zechariah 1:18–21 where he was given a vision of four horns representing four demonic strongholds that will rise to crush the nations. God's chosen method of reciprocating assault is to send four 'craftsmen'. This correlates with the title God gives to His limitless wisdom: He calls it a 'master craftsman' (Proverbs 8). Both wisdom and creativity are parts of God's core nature; fused in purpose, they form a very powerful weapon, powerful enough to oppose strongholds over nations. It shows us that through 'the combination', it is possible for man to become a force to be reckoned with:

Blueprints + Spirit + Wisdom + Creativity + Existing skill/ability + More skill/
ability added by God, joined with Character, Obedience and Perseverance

Combining these factors, we can become intimidating warriors against the
enemy's camp. How we carry out that warfare and redeem Kingdom terrain
can look like a whole spectrum of creative activity. It is not restricted to the
format of a traditional warfare prayer meeting. It is more potent to focus on
our eternal General than on the enemy campus. Creative warriors need to
be locked onto God's guiding beacon and loaded with His presence.

Some surprising things may be asked of us on this expedition. How can
painting a picture be warfare? But if we consider impartation and that
what we carry can be dispersed into an atmosphere for divine effect, we
start to change our perspective. In these early days, I would urge people
to experiment: let God illumine new direction and new enterprise; it might
be unfamiliar, or familiar but stirred with the unexplored. Obedience and
trust lead to prize and presence. Victorious personal chapters in our own
story with God can landscape the future. Listening and learning, trying and
transforming, we are called to walk journeys of unique experience and not
of production-line practices. If this is to be a journey to unleash our creative
DNA, then by its very definition it will be creative and full of unique requests
and commissions from God; but that's where a life accustomed to the heavy
depth of time spent in the well is able to soar into the unexpected.

Consider that the armory in heaven is stacked with paint, dance costumes,
materials for sculpting, books with blank pages waiting to be written, and
music sheets waiting for notes. Ask the Lord to enlighten you as to the
weapons you already hold and to reveal the ones awaiting your collection.
There is much to fight for: the advancement of justice, love, kindness,
goodness and mercy, and the healing and salvation of souls. Warriors in
this day do not stand alone, but are flanked by the heavenly host; it is
essential that we awake to their connective mandate so that the earthly and
heavenly armies work in unity. Elijah was not deterred as he stood before a

great destructive earthly force. He could see a greater angelic army poised to destroy its intentions. The enemy of Elijah was blinded by supernatural forces and taken prisoner (2 Kings 6:8–23).

And Elisha prayed, and said, "Lord, I pray, open his eyes that he may see." Then the Lord opened the eyes of the young man, and he saw. And behold, the mountain was full of horses and chariots of fire all around Elisha. So when the Syrians came down to him, Elisha prayed to the Lord, and said, "Strike this people, I pray, with blindness." And He struck them with blindness according to the word of Elisha. 2 Kings 6:17-18

BUILDING A POWERFUL ARMY

God is going after performance, split motives, dirty vessels and egos. If we are to advance to the caliber of creative warriors, then we must allow the time of preparation or we will always struggle within the limitations of our individual margins. Let the call begin to sound, gathering the army of artisans – the call to awaken the lost creative DNA in God's people. We can barely imagine what lies ahead, but it does involve heady days of glorious Kingdom triumph; and it is better to be one who joins with comrades in the fray and enjoys the great spoils of assured victory, than to watch from the sidelines with a timid heart.

DEFINE THE LAYERS - ADVANCING SKILLS

A bracingly realistic stock-take is needed. One of the issues with Christian art, in many quarters, is that anything passes as 'art'. If our perception of God's creative DNA is impaired, and thus its mandate or value, we will move into the default Christian mode that does not want to offend anyone. However, there has to be definition if we are going to reach the mountains of culture and serve effectively in the church. We must make an honest inventory of our skills and their level. The solution is to raise the standard and clearly define the layers.

The following is a suggested overview of what the layers look like:

LAYER 1: There is the general release of the creative DNA for every one of God's people; this can be expressed, celebrated and developed from any level of skill. This layer is the very beginning of the journey for people trying new skills, waking up their creative DNA.

LAYER 2: People training, practicing and seeking to develop in specific areas of creative skill.

LAYER 3: People beginning to emerge with more confidence and individual style in a given area or multiple areas of creativity, but still aware of the need to practice and learn much; becoming stronger in skill and ability.

LAYER 4: People who have trained extensively in their area of skill, much practiced and confident at a high level, from which they will continue to mature. They have invested much personal resource in this journey. These are the artisans with a specific commission to use their craft for areas such as worship, intercession, writing, film-making, fashion, etc. They can be called to any one of the seven mountains. This layer needs artistic people of perseverance and hard work, qualities displayed for us by figures like Joseph.

A TOUCH OF THE X FACTOR

If we are to re-establish value for the arts within the church, then layers need defined. The world does not equate the nursery with a PHD and neither should we. No layer of the spectrum is less valuable than any other. Indeed, through the general release of creative DNA, a scientist may spark world-shaking discoveries. The point is to restore definition to the arts so they can rediscover specific purpose as God intended. We need to shake off some of the confused niceties that are blurring the edges of the artisans' mandate. If people are honestly assessed to be in the first or second layers, then it is not correct to define them in the same vein as artisans who have invested much to reach a good level of skill, just as we wouldn't dream of allowing a low-skilled musician to lead the worship band.

Our uniformed thinking and default niceness hosts a childish mentality in some people. A similarity to the first rounds of the X Factor[6] develops where people are convinced they have great talent, yet do not seem to hear the tunelessness of their offering. Sometimes that reveals the need for healing of hidden issues, such as a lack of self-worth. Sometimes it reveals weak character. When little children bring their parents the scribbled drawings of youth, the songs that wander off key and funny dances with serious faces of determination, they are celebrated with the delight of love for effort and innocence. We fix such pictures on the fridge and clap with booming encouragement. Yet, if they are still doing the same thing at eighteen and expecting the same applause, having invested little effort in progressing their skill or time in practicing, we would be concerned.

Sometimes we encourage creativity to remain at an immature and stunted level in our Christian communities because we feel it is not acceptable to challenge any offering, or challenge someone to invest practice and education in the skill they are so eager to use publicly. But we would not accept that from someone learning to play in the band, or someone learning to preach. We would call them higher with love, encourage training and point them towards presence instead of performance. Equally, children will become discouraged and stop creating if you never make them feel that their creative offerings are valuable and worth calling upward, if you never fix them to the fridge. We have a lot of that around already, so we need to steer through the layers.

Lumping all the layers together has been a mistake that has brought a diminishing of the intended call for excellence in this area, and the enemy has used bad art to distract and detract from the true purpose of the artisans. Artistic gifts need to be matured, just as spiritual gifts need to be matured; it takes time and application. The training for an artistic career can sometimes be harder than for other subjects because of fierce competition for places and accolades, the long hours involved and the weight of its lower value in our societies; many give up. But God calls us to be people of dedication and training (2 Timothy 2:15). If we establish the layers with a practical expectation, then we can define destination for the areas of creativity.

Wholehearted encouragement of exploration and progression for the creative DNA that is installed in all believers will go a long way to ensuring healthy progress. But it is also time to unfetter the artisans in our communities and cheer them higher.

Skill Versus Kingdom

I remember from my first week at art college when a young student declared that whatever we produce is art and that that cannot be questioned. Even in my naivety at the beginning of my art education, I remember thinking he could not be serious! That's like saying that anyone is a dentist if they fancy a dig in your teeth. As that year unfolded, some students worked very hard to develop craft and skill to a wonderful standard. Others rarely showed up, did little, and their work was poor and lazy by comparison. Not surprisingly, they were not awarded the coveted places on the successive honors degree course.

Art history runs from the great masters painting ethereal works to ludicrous toilet seat installations that hold little message, yet receive great acclaim. Through such a confusing parade of standards, the enemy has devalued art again. But we are not to measure the standards of Kingdom art by the nonsensical art in the world. We can see the hand of God connecting with works across the years that leave us awestruck with their depth and extraordinary mastery of skill. These art pieces authenticate the connection between God and the artist in such masterpieces as the Sagrada Familia by Antoni Gaudi or The fighting Temeraire by JMW Turner.[7]

Artisans need to advance in two main areas: Kingdom qualities and skill. Future Kingdom art is to encapsulate divine, end-time purpose. God's artisans must strive for distinction in all that they do. This is completely different from perfectionism. It is a joyfully liberating adventure to work with, through, and in the Spirit of God. We bring the skills we have to the altar and approach the throne of grace with boldness; we can ask for favor and for accelerated development through the hours of offered effort (Hebrews 4:6). We aim to portray God's nature through our works; the scope is wide and there are very few limitations to creativity. Our boundaries will not seek to push into the nebulous or depraved through boredom, because we have access to the limitless One for our inspiration – the One who hung the stars in space.

Akiane is an artist who has, at times, demonstrated a journey of holy, supernatural art with a talent beyond normal human ability for her age, ever since she was a young child.[8] She has painted heavenly places shown to her in visions and depicted them for a world that stands in awe and inhales the breath of God. Through such works, she has found great acclaim in the mountain of the arts and entertainment. I am praying for more skill in many areas, in painting, writing, sculpting and more, because I know I need it. When we truly seek to immerse our skills in the hallowed waters of Kingdom goals, then I believe there is a timely offering of acceleration for the artisans who are ready to run this race. There is promotion of favor, gifting, wisdom, influence and purpose.

BUSINESS

I had another dream that carried a warning. Its message was that artisans who want to produce art forms with Kingdom-progression as the primary object must be beware of having wrong motives for business. God will not bring us electrifying blueprints so we can make a success for ourselves in business through money or applause. Even though we may not believe that to be our aim, we need to check our motives very carefully and regularly, even the ones deeply embedded in our heart. This is not to say that God will not bring business success and financial provision through creativity, but if self-seeking motives begin to bleed into our underlying purpose, then the gauge will tip into the red.

As the new heavenly innovation starts to fall in drops of wisdom and ingenuity, then we need to learn how to steward it. Purity is a custodian of glory. Purity will steer us through the many options vying for our attention; peace signposts the paths of purpose. Business acumen can work in victorious tandem with creative DNA. This arena is wide open for fresh solution; purity turns the earth ready for us to propagate new life. Stewarding well the day of small beginnings leads to more (Luke 16:10).

But seek first the kingdom of God and His righteousness, and all these things shall be added to you. Matthew 6:33

YOUTH

It is not hard to see many of the effects of this mountain on human nature and the world we live in.

The drama of disaster and chaotic lives is not only found in the movies. However, one area that needs consideration is the younger generation. The Church frequently laments this age group's diminishing interest. As the congregations in some churches get older and older, there is minimal influx of teens and twenty-somethings. There seems to be little insight into the mass exodus of this generation away from the Christian faith, particularly in the west, and the distractions of the world are duly blamed. However, let's consider which mountain the youth love the most. Their passion often lies in the mountain of the arts and entertainment, but because we do not see the value of creativity, we think they are simply distracted by worldly pleasures. Granted, this may be true in some cases, but it is undeniable that this age group adores all things creative.

At this stage in life they have time on their hands and few responsibilities, and the residing interests of their agendas are to be found in sports, fashion, film, music, TV, dance and many other areas of this mountain. They spend much time and effort on their appearance, and up-to-date fashion codes are often an essential part of the social order of acceptance. They form social attachments through what they experience together, and that frequently focuses on something creative like music. Media and technology have become the main forms of communication. Notes passed across the classroom have been replaced by photos and messages sent all over the world, and a huge web of social networking has formed through media like Facebook and Twitter, particularly within this age bracket.

There are so many creative ways to connect with others that go beyond a few words on a blank sheet of paper. Yet in all the creative expression available in the world, how much do they find within the church experience? How often do we ask them to bring their creativity into the body of the Church and celebrate it? Creativity is about personal expression as well as the creation of new forms or new combinations. However, if there is little room to express within a church structure, then they may quickly tire, bursting with desire for exploration, imagination and expression. We mainly assume they tire of God, or have become distracted by worldly pursuits, but let's consider another option in the mix. If God is the most incredibly creative being in the universe, how can they tire of His lack of creativity?

When we have offered the spiritual gifts in creative format in venues such as festivals, where youth throng, we find that they form the largest age statistic seeking appointments. They may find creativity and some freedom for self-expression in the world, but at times this can also come with weighty shadows that entrench young lives in the sinking sand of dark forces. Over time the enemy's subtly hewn channels have drained creativity away from the church to irrigate the world, and with it the attention of many young people. It screams the ethics of his agenda in very graphic terms, yet many do not see the door of toxic darkness standing open behind the dazzling artistry of vast budgets.

world that offers neither. Powerlessness makes us search for empowerment, but again the world offers no power with any life at its kernel. The explosive fascination for the otherworldly, for supernatural power and supernatural heroes reflects the need to feel powerful, even if it is through the temporary fantasy of another's imagination. This generation is left desperate for a sense of purpose.

The antidote is for them to be drenched with the sense of destiny in God. More than any other age group, this one asks to know what we see for their life ahead; then we find that God's main agenda, having gained their attention, is to download destiny into their precious lives. They light up like Christmas trees, filling with the hope they never find out there in the world. The chasm to bridge now is that, although many feel comfortable accepting God in this setting, they will not cross the ravine into our churches. They feed back to us the memories or rigid perceptions of confining church experience, and they cannot equate it to the person of God that just touched them powerfully.

This is obviously not the experience in every church community. There are churches bursting with youth, but there are many more where God's people would love their churches to be filling with the younger generation; but they feel stuck for ideas on how to achieve this and lose hope. I have met Christians who announce with acceptant resignation that the Church is diminishing – older congregations will just fade out and the Church will disappear – as if it is a done deal. But there are more Christians on the face of the earth than ever, more miracles, healings and people being raised from the dead, right across the globe. It is not time to resign ourselves to the demise of God's Church. This would completely contradict the Bible. It is time to stand as Joseph did, to rise with new wisdom in our wings and see solutions instead of problems, creative strategy instead of passive failure.

Asking God to show us how to bring new creativity and allow increasing freedom for the Holy Spirit to move and breathe into our churches will help to turn the younger generation back to God. But let's be prepared that this may not look like a throng coming into our existing church buildings alone; creativity means something new, the space of reception needs expansion. In some churches, where creative life is bubbling up and erupting, where the expectation to dive is becoming normal and where passion abounds, there seems to be an increased interest from the younger generation. We must let the DNA emerge through them and learn from their fresh freedom.

EYES FORWARD

As we forge ahead with these discoveries in Scotland and in other nations, I believe it is very important to reach out across the geographical boundaries where God shows us to link forces.

Scotland has some part to play in helping to activate prophetic creativity in other nations; and other nations, in turn, will carry specific pieces of the jigsaw that need to be shared.

New combinations of the arts and creativity, throughout many spheres, will become important, not only for breaking individualism, but also for bringing something from heaven's store-house that will completely surprise us. These combinations will bring new considerations and give us the capacity to see solution where we could not see it before. We can release the Kingdom arts and artisans like firelighters in our communities, to inflame the creative forces of heaven that bring us ability and answer. Confronting performance and individualism will make a way for extraordinary new teams where each part holds purpose and power. And the combinations of different people working in unity will release something completely different from what we have previously experienced. The majesty and supremacy of God will be evident through such blends, taking us into deep places of prayer and petition, worship and seeking.

New art works will emerge that will rise above visual stimulation as the focus, above the message as the focus, and their ethereal form will reveal

God in blatant wonder. Even the world will struggle to deny His hand. Some works will be formed to release the power of purity right into the heart of places where there is none, and darkness will fall from the eyes of slaves. Consider that art works can go where people cannot, and then remember the power of impartation. Art forms naturally hold the power of enigma, so they can carry the heavily anointed language of God; and, like a provoking dream, they can be used to challenge the heart and stir the quest for answers. We have much to explore; the possibilities are limitless with God.

There is a season of opening deep wells of the Spirit. This will take application, intention and time, but once they are open they are to remain open. We are not to move on in hasty neglect, but seek to draw regularly for progressive wisdom, strength and strategy. In the season of opening and plunging wells, we must allow God to make us ready for what is coming, to deepen our dependence on Him. From the wells, I see the firepower of the Lord coming through His church; I see warriors rising with new resolve, bravery, grit and guts. This is an awakening from some milky patterns of faith to make the choice to rise through grace. Believers will be armed with the weapons and wisdom they found in the wells. As the creativity of God breaks through in a multitude of different ways, God's people will spark to life with their creative DNA; and an infusion of new solutions and ideas will follow, for mission, for life situations, for workplaces and for the mountains of culture.

Along with others, I believe the 'Sound of Scotland' will break out, a sound that summons the warriors opposing the shackles of man's religion on the church. But this will also be the case in other nations, as their spiritual heritage is restored and we seek the Spirit for creative reformation.

Chuck Pierce prophesied in Scotland in January 2013:
'The strength of this nation in warfare worship comes alive again. In worship you do not just sing everyone else's songs, you create the sound that begins to move because it is already here and people all over the world know it is

here. People know the sound that is in this land, and I am here to say tonight that the worship gatherings all over Scotland will become so powerful that others will say 'we must cross the border and go worship with Scotland'.[9]

"Do not fear, for those who are with us are more than those who are with them." And Elisha prayed, and said, "Lord, I pray, open his eyes that he may see." Then the Lord opened the eyes of the young man, and he saw. And behold, the mountain was full of horses and chariots of fire all around Elisha. 2 Kings 6: 16-17

The forces of heaven are poised to help us become part of the changes that must take place. The return of the creative DNA to God's people provides firepower to excel. The creative power of God will prophesy what lies ahead, as the world systems shake and the gospel message magnifies in the earth, heading towards the end of days. We must grasp that the Lord is coming to change His church into a warrior bride: formidable, phenomenal, creative ... limitless.

POETRY

COMMISSIONED
EL GRUER, 2012

Together we create the art of the heart.
Whether you come with a crayon, a child's bold step-
which is a delicate pitter-patter to your Papa
or come with the paint palette of your heart splattering
enter his gates.

We are all artists
commissioned to draw one thing-
draw close to him.
This is colour-filled art of the heart.

As we draw close to him
we will hear the shattering of glass
revealing- there is no ceiling.
Our nation's faith lungs are now receiving
new capacity for the Spirit's breathing-
breathe in, see a new perspective,

smash your rose-tinted spectacles and see
only through the colours of truth-
for there is no roof.

We are all artists
commissioned to draw one thing-
draw close to him.
This is colour-filled art of the heart.
With our Holy child crayons
and paint palette of the heart we see
them collide with his light that rainbows
through the shattered shafts of ceiling glass-
his throne room is a master class of colour.

We are all artists
commissioned to draw one thing-
draw close to him.
This is colour-filled art of the heart.

Enter through his gates, life in Trinitarian colour awaits.
Let's worship, raise praise to the beautiful
symphony of shattering glass.
This is the art of the Bride's heart, set apart for
his throne-room is a master class of colour.

PORTAL
FRANCES BRADY

fronds ripple in the wind
glass gleams in the sun
water falls and falls
our dam is broke
His grace is pouring
down on us

through the portal

healing pours
dreams flow
spiritual comfort
spiritual challenge
strength
no fear

under the portal

do not be afraid
I have redeemed you
I have called you by your name
you are mine -
you who sit now

beneath the portal

REFERENCES

Chapter 1 - VITAL

1. Website: larryrandolph.com, accessed August 2013

2. Website: Dictionary definition, Dictionary.com, accessed May 15 2013

3. Website: youtube.com, ref Transformingculture.org, accessed August 2013.
Website: wikipedia.org, iTunes Store, iPod, accessed August 2013.
Website: media.ofcom.org.uk, accessed August 2013

4. Website: Willmington's Guide to the Bible, www.swartzentrover.com, accessed June 5 2013

5. Book: Mark and Patti Virkler, How to Hear God's Voice, Destiny Image Publishers 2004

6. Audio Teaching: Eric Johnson, Ask for Wisdom, released 14 April 2013 from Bethel Church, Redding, California USA

7. Website: Dictionary definition, www.merriam-webster.com, accessed May 2013

8. Website: article 'A Present Salvation', www.flumc.org, accessed May 26 2013

Chapter 2 - DNA

1. Audio Teaching: Eric Johnson, Ask for Wisdom, released 14 April 2013 from Bethel Church, Redding, California USA

2. Photo: by Alfred Eisenstaedt, V-J Day in Times Square, en.wikipedia.org/wiki/V-J_Day_in_Times_Square

3. Website: tekton, www.ewtn.com, accessed June 5 2013

4. Strong's Expanded Exhaustive Concordance of the Bible, James Strong, published by Thomas Nelson, edition published in 2010

5. Art Piece: Damien Hirst, I Am Become Death, Shatterer of Worlds 2006, www.damienhirst.com

6. Audio Teaching: John Paul Jackson, Prophets and Psychics, Streams Ministries International

7. Prophetic Training Resources: Course: John E. Thomas Course, Practical Prophetic Training and John Paul Jackson, The Art of Hearing God, both available at www.streamsministries.com

8. Audio Teaching: Kris Vallotton, Spiritual Intelligence, from Bethel Church, Redding California USA

9 Audio Teaching: Bill Johnson, The City on a Hill, May 2013 from Bethel Church, Redding, California USA

Chapter 4 - PROTOTYPES

1. Website: ref Egypt, Nebuchadnezzar, Babylon, en.wikipedia.org, accessed June 2013

2. Film Documentary: City of Babylon and the King Nebuchadnezzar II, Discovery Civilisation Channel, accessed June 2013

3. Film Documentary: Ancient Egypt's Greatest Pharaohs, youtube.com, accessed June 2013

4. Website: Twelve Famous Dreams, www.brilliantdreams.com, accessed June 2013

5. Website: Amazing Dreams and Visions coming out of the Middle East, www.breakingchristiannews.com, accessed May 2013

6. Dream interpretation training: Streams Ministries International, Courses: 'Understanding Dreams and Visions' and 'Advanced Workshop in Dreams and Visions'. www. streamsministries.com

7. CLAN: Christians Linked Across the Nation, www.clangathering.org.uk

Chapter 5 - PURPOSE

1. St Pastors: www.streetpastors.co.uk

2. CLAN Gathering: www.clangathering.org.uk

3. Website: New Age, en.wikipedia.org/wiki/New_Age, accessed June 2013

4. Healing on the Streets: www.healingonthestreets.com

5. Quote: Dr Kent M. Keith, The Paradoxical Commandments, 1968

6. Book: Dr Barbara Jenkinson, Sharing God's love through Prophecy and the Revelatory Gifts, published by Light and Life Ministres 2011

7. Website: The Engle Scale of Evangelism, en.wikipedia.org/wiki/Engel_Scale 6

8: Streams Ministries International: www.streamsministries.com

Audio Teaching: Dawna De Silva and Teresa Liebscher, Sozo basic Saved, Healed and Delivered, from Bethel Church, Redding, California USA

9. Book: Heather Sutherland, Speaking Their Language, published by CreateSpace Independent Publishing Jan 2013

10. Book: Tommi Femrite, Invading the Seven Mountains with Intercession, published by Kingsway Communications March 2012

11. Teaching Series: Dr Lance Wallnau, The Seven Mountain Mandate, Website: www.lancelearning.com

12. Book: Johnny Enlow, The Seven Mountain Prophecy, published by Creation House 2008

Other Recommended Resources

Book: Dr Barbara Jenkinson, Reaching Spiritually Hungry People, published by Light and Life Ministres 2013.

Chapter 6 - RELEASE

1. Website: German Traits, www.dererstezug.com, accessed July 2013

2. Course: John Paul Jackson, The Art of Hearing God, www.streamsministries. com

3. Quote: Shawn Bolz, Kingdom Creativity Conference 2011, Bethel Church, Redding, California USA

4. Website: the Hubble telescope, en.wikipedia.org, accessed July 2013

5. Website: Movie Green Lantern, greenlanternmovie.warnerbros.com/dvd/ accessed July 2013

6. CLAN Gathering, www.clangathering.org.uk, accessed July 2013

7. Website: The Passion of the Christ, www.thepassionofchrist.com

8. Teaching Series: Dawna de Silva, Spiritual atmospheres, ibethel.org, store

Chapter 7 - POSITIONING

1. Exerts from the Morning Star Bulletin by Rick Joyner with Andrei and Amanda Prychodko November 17 2007, www.elijahlist.com

2. Teaching Series: Dr Lance Wallnau, The Seven Mountain Mandate, Website: www.lancelearning.com

3. Website: The Passion of the Christ, www.thepassionofchrist.com, accessed Aug 2013

4. Website: Les Miserables, www.lesmis.com, accessed July 2013

5. Website: www.clinicalkey.com, accessed Aug 2013

6. Website: The X Factor, xfactor.itv.com

7. Website: Sagrada Familia by Antoni Gaudi, www.sagradafamilia.cat, accessed June 2013

Website: The fighting Temeraire by J M W Turner, en.wikipedia.org/wiki/The_Fighting_Temeraire, accessed June 2013

8. Akiane Kramarik, www.artakiane.com, accessed June 2013

9. Chuck Pierce Prophecy January 2013, www.prayforscotland.org.uk, accessed July 2013

Chapter 7 - POETRY

1. Poet: El Gruer; Poem: 'Commissioned'; copyright El Gruer, www.elgruer.com; Written at the CLAN Women conference, Edinburgh Scotland 2011
Poetry Reference

2. Poet: Frances Brady; Poem: 'Portal'; copyright Frances Brady, www.franbrady.com; Written at the CLAN Women conference, Edinburgh Scotland 2011

ABOUT THE AUTHOR

Charity Bowman Webb

Charity is passionate about the prophetic and creativity. She loves being part of igniting new and creative ways of releasing God's Spirit in the church and on the mission field, through the arts and spiritual gifts.

She is the director of Blue Flame - a ministry which seeks to equip Christians with training for spiritual gifts so they can be used in a diversity of ways. Blue Flame also facilitates a variety of conferences and mission events. Charity has worked closely with Streams Ministries International for most of her Christian life, and loves being part of seeing it enable people, all over the world, to find life and destiny. Through her role as Creative Team leader for Scotland's New Wine network, she worked with a pioneering team to help restore creativity in the church at national events.

Throughout her involvement in these roles, she works with amazing people and together they seek to help Christians deepen their relationship with God, passionately exploring many areas of their faith.

Charity is qualified as a professional fashion and interior design and worked in the design industry for many years. She now lives in Inverness, in the Highlands of Scotland, and is married to Alan with two daughters, Sasha and Rhianna.

To find out more about Blue Flame and the development of the Creative Movement visit www.hisblueflame.org

To contact the author: hello@hisblueflame.org

LIMITLESS

A COURSE IN RELEASING CREATIVE INTELLIGENCE

WRITTEN BY

CHARITY BOWMAN WEBB

LIMITLESS: THE COURSE

THIS COURSE IS DESIGNED TO HELP YOU:
- To understand what the creativity of God is with biblical evidence of its importance and characteristics.
- Find your God given creative DNA, then stir and release this within you
- Connect with God more deeply by exploring parts of His creative character
- Understand the expansive and varied language of God more fully
- Identify the role and purpose of God's creativity for the Church and mission

THE COURSE CONTAINS:
- Teaching sessions
- Interactive exercises
- Suggested homework assignments
- Extra reading notes

To invite Charity to teach this course please contact her on: hello@hisblueflame.org

LIMITLESS ONLINE COURSE

Limitless was filmed in Dallas USA through Streams International. It is now available to purchase as an online course with a manual.

For more details please go to the online course section at www.streamsministries.com

BLUE FLAME EQUIPPING WEBSITE
www.hisblueflame.org

Full of visuals, information, ideas and connections. This website has been developed as a follow on to the Limitless message. It is packed with many examples of what our teams have been developing over the years pioneering a restoration of the arts and creativity in the church. There are many examples of what this looks like for a church setting and a mission setting.

Come and explore....

29947519R00160

Printed in Great Britain
by Amazon